RECIPES, TIPS & STRATEGIES

Short Cuts to Great Cuisine

by
Carol Foster

The Crossing Press, Freedom, CA 95019

Acknowledgments

To my sister, Anne Thomas, a belated but heartfelt thanks.
Without her support, there would be no books.

To my mother, Wynnis Perkerson, for her constant ear and unwavering
enthusiasm.

To agents Anthony Schneider and Peter Miller of PMA,
for patience beyond belief.

To Dennis Hayes, Karen Narita, Brigid Fuller, and those behind the scenes
at The Crossing Press, for making the painstaking process of producing
this book a pleasure.

To my retrievers, Riesling and Kirby, my tireless taste-testers who dash to
devour whatever's dropped on the kitchen floor. The maze of skid marks
remains an ongoing memorial to their dedication.

Copyright © 1994 by Carol Foster
Cover photograph and design by Amy Sibiga
Text design by Sheryl Karas
    Printed in the U.S.A.

Library of Congress Cataloging-in-Publication Data

Foster, Carol, 1950-
        Short cuts to great cuisine : recipes, tips & strategies / by Carol Foster.
            p. cm.
        Includes index.
        ISBN 0-89594-665-3 (cloth). —ISBN 0-89594-664-5 (paper)
        1. Quick and easy cookery.   2. Cookery, International.   I. Title.
TX833.5.F67 1994
641.5'55—dc20
                                                                93-41398
                                                                CIP

Dedication

To my wonderful husband, Warren,
who lives to eat.

Contents

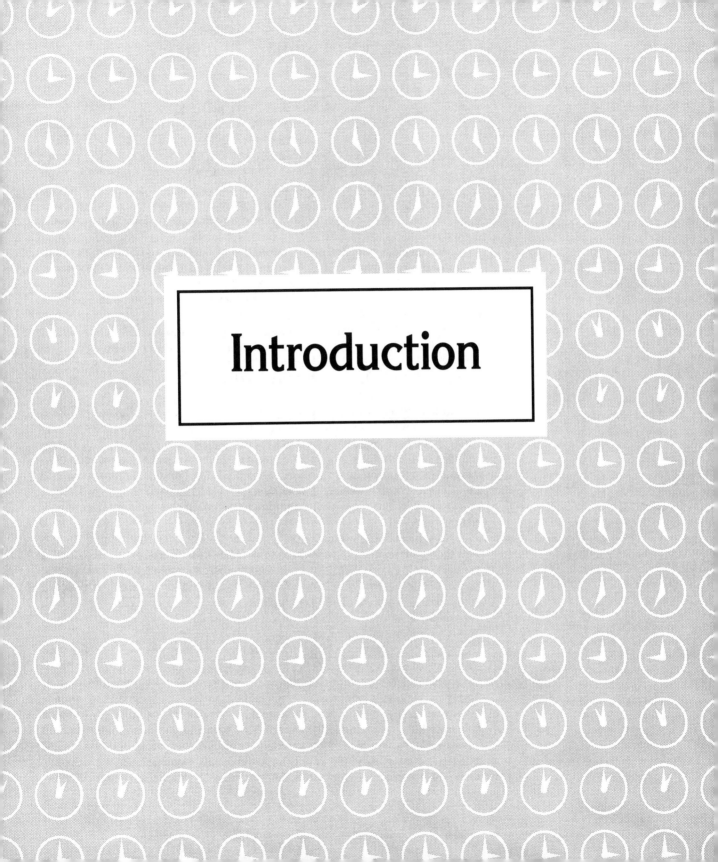

Introduction

The most fabulous dish I ever prepared took five days solid. I boned a goose and a chicken through the neck without breaking the skin and marinated them in herbs and spirits. I soaked and parboiled a beef tongue for hours, stripped its skin, and cut out the gristle and bone. Next I made a forcemeat mixture of fresh spinach, herbs, and veal. The tongue was stuffed into the chicken, which went into the goose. The whole extravaganza was filled with the forcemeat, enclosed in a pastry crust, and baked for what seemed like a day. Then it cooled. Another day.

Meanwhile, I made an aspic mixture that I poured into a hole in the crust to fill in the spaces between the birds, forcemeat, and crust. It sliced beautifully with no bones to battle, and it looked like a picture.

The Honey and Ginger-Glazed Roast Chicken on page 140 takes 7 minutes of prep time, looks gorgeous, and tastes better.

This book is filled with scrumptious foods made simply in a flash. It's written for people in a hurry who love great food. Ironically, as I became busy pursuing professional endeavors in food, I had little time to cook. No more boned birds. On the other hand, the flavor and quality of the foods I prepare quickly now are wonderful.

Instead of lengthy marinating, I duplicate those tastes with flavorings added at the last minute. I carefully choose the types of meats and vegetables to buy, knowing they are well-suited to quick cooking. Instead of preparing a dish conventionally in a number of pans or bowls, I combine steps to cut down on cooking and cleanup. My pantry is filled with prepared condiments and powerful flavorings to ensure interesting, healthy meals, and I've streamlined my kitchen to include only the most useful equipment and arranged it for maximum efficiency.

No doubt, this is a most exciting time to be cooking. Many more diverse ingredients are readily available than ever before: fresh pastas, exotic rices, bread bases, many-flavored vinegars and oils, fresh herbs, condiments, and exotic sauces. Staples of cuisines that were not so long ago considered foreign are now available at the local grocery. A stunning example is prepared salsa. A decade ago finding salsa required a trip to a specialty market—now its sales have surpassed the ubiquitous American condiment, ketchup.

Instead of measuring chefs' virtues by how well they precisely execute classic dishes, as was common practice only two decades ago, today we praise them for creativity and innovation, which was once considered heresy. Since chefs have become public personalities, this attitude impacts the home cook. Improvising and innovating may be the most important skill for the quick cook. To be able to gather a few meager pickings from the pantry and refrigerator and pull off a great meal rescues us from the mundane choices of the frozen food counter. All it takes is a bit of experience and know-how. My proudest culinary moments were not presenting a Grand Marnier soufflé on a rocking boat or a dramatic ballotine of suckling pig to a crowd, but pulling off a scrumptious meal in a kitchen without even a wire whisk or a spice less than ten years old.

I've borrowed ideas from cuisines around the world that use quick-cooking techniques and ingredients. The Chinese stir-fry and the French sauté are the quintessential fast-cooking techniques, but this book reduces the time spent preparing these dishes even further by trimming the lists of necessary ingredients and incorporating them in batches when possible. Prepared ingredients, such as coconut milk and curry pastes, salsas and tortillas, pesto and sun-dried tomatoes, offer the quick cook depth of flavor as well as convenience.

Cuisines, such as Indian, that typically require long lists of ingredients, I've pared down to those crucial to the final taste of a dish. There are some long-cooking recipes that my family loves, such as German Sauerbraten. It takes a whopping 5-6 days to marinate and a full 3 hours to cook. In such cases, I've developed recipes that mimic the flavor of the classic dish, but that require the briefest of cooking time.

Testing these recipes has been a joy. With an occasional exception, I purposely arrived in the kitchen no more than 30 minutes before serving a salad, an entreé, and a vegetable. In all cases, ingredients and procedures have been shaved to a minimum. On the other hand, if you happen to be cooking in a more relaxed mode or for a special occasion, I've included optional ideas that can transform a simple dish into a splashy centerpiece.

Many classic dishes and expensive restaurant offerings are last-minute, quickly cooked foods. Luckily for the cook in a hurry, the simplest, fastest treatment of food often yields the most refined, sophisticated, finished dish. It offers the essence of food, without changing its essential character with extraneous ingredients and long cooking. A chicken will taste like a chicken, not like a mishmash of spices or a sauce made with a heavy hand. There's a place for complicated cooking, involving long lists of ingredients and advanced processes that I still love and respect. It just doesn't fit into many of our lifestyles today.

Preparing food efficiently takes some re-thinking. *Short Cuts to Great Cuisine* does it for you, and it will also teach you to start thinking in terms of efficiency when you shop, prep, cook, serve, and clean. When you can cook and serve in the same dish, it's done. When you can prep and cook simultaneously, the recipes are written to give you that direction. In fact, cooking and prep times become muddled as one is incorporated into the other for prime efficiency. When three ingredients can be stirred into a dish at once instead of at 2-minute intervals, it's simpler. Cleanup time is shaved by cooking dishes in one pan, and, when possible, recipes are prepared in their serving dishes. Shopping trips become less frequent and more relaxed as organization pays off. Learning what to stock and what perishables to buy to last five days instead of two trims time-consuming shopping trips to a minimum.

There are advantages to quick cooking beyond saving time. The methods used to cook entreés, in particular, are based on techniques that use high heat for flavor and efficiency and very little fat. High heat brings out the flavor of meats like nothing else—even when slow-cooking a roast for hours, it benefits from searing ahead of time to bring out its flavor.

Quick cooking works best with the most tender cuts of poultry, fish, and meat that have little waste and, therefore, take up little storage space and eliminate the nuisance of leftovers. Space-efficient condiments that are packed with flavor, such as capers and sun-dried tomatoes, need the briefest of cooking time. Fruits, vegetables, and herbs retain their fresh flavors, colors, and nutrients when cooked quickly. Even dried herbs and fresh garlic deliver more pronounced flavor with fast cooking.

Expect the unorthodox. You'll find unconventional techniques and combinations of ingredients. Classic cooks will find their treasured standards shortened at every opportunity. You'll find everything that works in the shortest time possible, so that the cook can work the shortest time possible.

Short Cuts to Great Cuisine invites you to enjoy the whole process of providing food. You'll learn to simplify chores and relish the creativity that a little knowledge and a well-stocked kitchen can provide. However, it won't tell you how to cook a beef tongue stuffed in a boned chicken stuffed in a boned goose enclosed in pastry with aspic. Thank goodness.

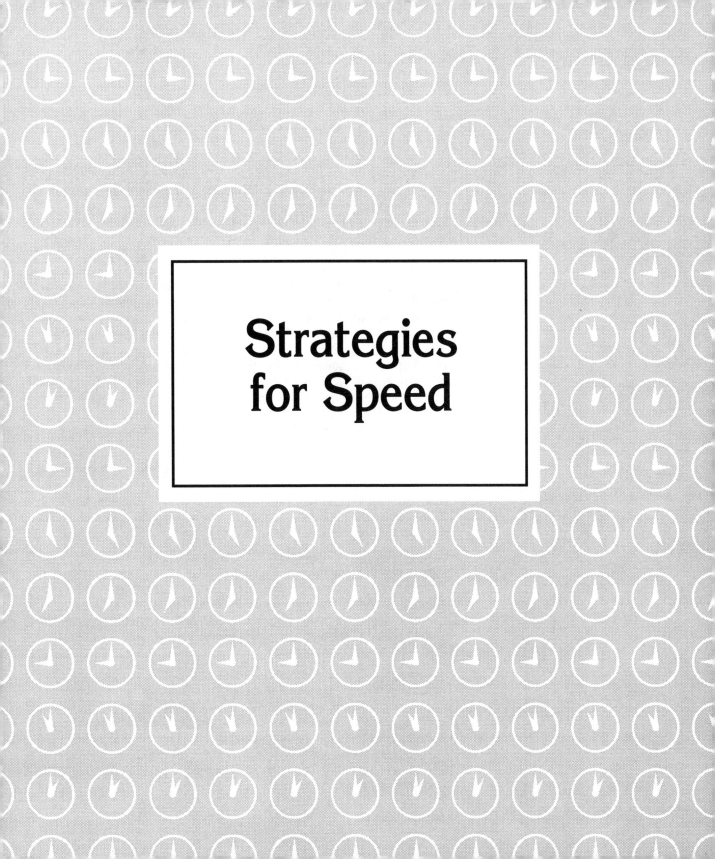

Strategies
for Speed

Time, these days, is the essential ingredient in cooking. It precludes attempting many dishes that a decade ago I would've labored over happily. Individually molded, hand-dipped, slowly simmered, and deep-fried foods have been dropped from my culinary vocabulary. Timers that measure one hour now look immensely overequipped. I decided long ago there was nothing fast about phyllo, and anything that had to proof and rise twice became laughable.

In *Short Cuts to Great Cuisine*, I've sifted through classic dishes and created innovative ones, saving only those that cook quickly and adapting only those that lend themselves to quick-cooking strategies.

These strategies include not only cooking techniques, but also shopping, preparing, serving, and cleaning. Deep-frying prawns is fast, but cleanup is messy, usually smelly, and time-consuming. Stir-frying Strange-Flavor Beef with Tree Ears and Minced Dried Shrimp takes eight minutes, but you will spend hours shopping at a number of specialty shops searching for the precise, never-to-be-used-again ingredients. Orange and Serrano-Broiled Duck cooks practically by itself, but not unless you've squirreled away the serrano-flavored oil and wild duck stock critical to its final taste. Preparing the ingredients for a New England Boiled Dinner may take ten minutes, but if you're just home from work with a roaring stomach, a three-hour wait for a slowly simmered stew won't do.

Some valuable ideas that will cut down on unnecessary hours in the kitchen follow.

- Become familiar with a favorite market or two. You'll waste less time hunting for foods and shop efficiently. If possible, avoid peak hours when shoppers are elbow-to-elbow. Shop when the store is not crowded, but avoid times when stock is low. Stores on Monday mornings may be free of traffic, but they may be free of food as well.

- Keeping the pantry, refrigerator, and freezer well stocked minimizes emergency trips to round up a key ingredient or two. Much depends upon how much space you have available. Keep a running shopping list near your work area. As soon as you're aware you're running low on something, write it down. I can count on about 30 seconds of retention, especially while cooking. If I haven't jotted it down by then, it's lost. Shopping trips eat time, so keep careful lists.

- Buying partially prepared fresh ingredients at groceries and specialty stores shaves preparation time and in no way compromises the quality of finished dishes. We're accustomed to buying boned, trimmed meat. Why not use cleaned, sliced mushrooms and peeled, shredded carrots? Salad bars have cropped up in groceries across the country, providing fruits and vegetables not only ready to eat raw, but also ready to cook. The washing and trimming, and in some cases, even the chopping and dicing, have been done for you. Some items, such as fresh spinach, that are particularly time-consuming to clean, are well worth the bit of extra expense. Buying prepared produce also allows you to purchase the right amount of a particular food, which, in turn, saves time dealing with leftovers.

Whenever possible, buy boned and skinned poultry, precut portions of meat, filleted fish, shucked shellfish, and shelled and deveined shrimp. Buy pre-grated cheeses, if you plan on using them within a few days.

Clever combinations of frozen, canned, and fresh ingredients often produce creative, healthy, tasty finished dishes. The word "homemade" makes us assume that food is tastier and better for us than store-bought. In many instances, this is far from the truth. Most fruits and vegetables that are commercially prepared are picked at the peak of their harvest when they are most flavorful and nutritious. Imagine making an appealing to-mato sauce with January tomatoes or a peach chutney in April. Frozen fruits and vegetables, in particular, are a boon to the quick cook. They have been cleaned, trimmed, and blanched before freezing. In most cases, they retain their color, texture, and nutrients far better than canned, since they require less precooking to make them safe to store.

Utilize prepared pizza bases, tortillas, and pita breads, just as we're accustomed to taking advantage of professionally baked French and Ital-ian breads. Use prepared ingredients to please your palate and benefit your time constraints.

- Keep often-used tools in an open canister within easy reach of your work area. Wire whisks, wooden and metal spoons, spatulas, hand strainers, and vegetable peelers are prime candidates. I keep two canisters full—one is for small utensils, the other for large ones. At a glance I know what's available, and I avoid fumbling around in drawers for the perfect tool. In general, tools should be arranged in accordance with how often they're needed, rarely used gadgets being relegated to the backs of drawers.

- Keep knives in a wooden block within easy reach. Drawers inflict certain injury to their blades and can injure the cook scrambling for the perfect paring knife. Keeping knives sharp takes little effort and shaves prepara-tion time. Keep a sharpening steel next to the knives. Run blades down the steel at a 20-degree angle 8-10 times each side daily, when possible, to maintain a sharp edge. If your knives are dull from abuse, get them professionally sharpened and then maintain them. A bit of daily mainte-nance takes less time than a special trip for sharpening. Electronic knife sharpeners are expensive and tend to strip knives of too much of their blades, although they do transform them to razor-sharpness.

- Most of us avoid leftovers, but planned ones may provide parts of a meal, or even an entire meal, on a rushed evening. For instance, double what you'll consume at one meal, cool half, and freeze and label it for later use. Freeze dinners in just the quantity you'll use at one time. Toast lots of nuts at the same time in the oven, freeze them in zip-lock freezer bags, and use only what you need at a time. Cook twice as much chicken breast as you'll eat for dinner, then use the rest for sandwich or salad material within a few days. When roasting a chicken, throw in some garlic cloves to have roasted garlic on hand (see page 39). Prepare lots more salad dressing than you'll use at one meal, cover it, and chill. It will keep almost indefinitely. Heat more French or Italian bread than you plan to accompany a meal and use what's left for croutons in tomorrow's salad.

⦾ Prepare for cleanup while prepping and cooking, using as few dishes as possible and avoiding difficult-to-clean situations. Line pans with aluminum foil and use vegetable sprays to avoid scrubbing baked-on food that clings stubbornly to metal, ceramic, and even glass. Whenever possible, prepare food in the same dish you'll serve it in. Blend salad dressings, for example, in the salad bowl before adding the main ingredients. When removing meat or fish from a pan to make a pan sauce, place the meat on the same plate that you'll be serving it on in a few minutes. Use paper towels or wax paper, instead of dishes, to hold grated cheese or minced garlic in reserve until ready to use in cooking. Reuse pots and pans not only for the same dish, but also for different dishes, where appropriate. Make quick pasta sauces in the pot you boiled the pasta in while the noodles drain.

⦾ Use the same cutting board for different ingredients, particularly those included in the same recipe, without even a quick rinse. Foods that will be combined in a recipe simultaneously can be chopped together. Foods that need to be drained and will be used in a recipe simultaneously can be drained together. Measure dry ingredients in the same spoon or cup first, then liquid ones, so you can use the same utensil without washing.

⦾ Prepare food in a logical sequence. Novice cooks may need to follow a recipe for one dish from start to finish without interruption, but the quick cook armed with a little experience can grab ingredients from the fridge for three dishes at once, chop scallions for a salad and a side dish simultaneously, or blend a vinaigrette while sautéing a chicken breast. Always start water to boil for pasta as soon as possible, and remove salad dressings that you've stashed in the refrigerator, so they can warm while you prepare other ingredients. Remove meats and vegetables from the refrigerator as soon as you start a meal, since room temperature food cooks faster than chilled.

⦾ Using a food processor can slice preparation time into fractions, but it must be accessible and you must learn how to use it. If you have to search for the instruction book to decide which blade to use to shred a carrot or grate some cheese, you will lose time trying to use it. Spend an hour with your processor learning its amazing capabilities, and you'll save that much time in preparing meals in the first week alone. If using a food processor for a number of chores in one meal, use it to process dry ingredients first. Plan so that all the mincing, chopping, and puréeing can be done without even a rinse of the workbowl. The more you use your processor, the faster you'll learn exactly what it can do and how to make the most of it.

- Eye-ball ingredients. Instead of wasting time measuring precisely, approximate intelligently. Once you've measured a tablespoon of butter or oil a few times, it's easy to make a near-hit. Inherently, ingredients will vary. Fresh herbs will change with the season, the soil they're grown in, and the conditions they were transported by. A clove of garlic will be large or small, mild in spring and pungent in winter. Fresh ginger will vary with age. In fact, you should vary amounts according to your taste. I usually measure fiery ingredients, such as ground red pepper (cayenne), Tabasco, chili oil, and chili sauce with precision. After trying a recipe including these ingredients once, I might add more or less heat the next time. Never measure ingredients over what you're cooking. You may suddenly taste an unwelcome extra teaspoon of chili oil, which will make any dish incendiary. Never measure over an open drawer.

- Substitute ingredients with imagination to save on shopping trips. Recipes are meant to be guidelines, not gospel. The more you cook, the more confidently and creatively you'll replace ingredients. A lot of fun in the kitchen—and some of the tastiest dishes—come from improvising and creating. Often my recipes develop due to what's available and what's missing: I forgot to buy basil but we're hungry for pesto tonight (Fettucine with Poblano Pesto, page 167), or the red grapes are threatening to grow green fuzz if not used immediately (Red Grape and Curly Endive Salad, page 85).

- Not every single item has to be put away immediately. I let foods wait next to the refrigerator and garbage lurk near the compactor until a pile accrues. Or leave a receptacle for garbage open while you're preparing a meal. This saves having to open a cabinet door or a trash compactor to dispose of every bit of garbage. Let dishes pile up or, better yet, soak in a sink full of warm water, before opening the dishwasher to dispose of every dirty dish.

- Assemble all the ingredients for a dish before you begin to cook. Many dishes in this book cook faster than you may expect. Also, you may discover you don't have a critical ingredient or suitable substitute available for a particular recipe, so you may want to try something different.

- If undertaking a complicated or attention-demanding recipe, be kind to yourself and accompany it with something simple, keeping the kitchen frenzy-level down to tolerable. Start cooking the dish that takes the longest first. For instance, if serving Bronzed Red Snapper (page 123) with Saffron and Cinnamon-Scented Basmati Rice (page 177), start the rice first. It needs to cook 20 minutes without any attention, freeing you to prepare a salad and keep a close eye on the fish, which suffers if under- or overcooked.

* If foods are not labeled effectively, do so. For instance, I keep my spices and dried herbs below eye level in a large drawer. Manufacturers place their labels on the side of the jars, which is no use to me, so I stick a small tag on the tops of the jars and alphabetize them. I can pinpoint a jar out of more than 6 dozen in seconds. Every food that goes in the freezer should bear a label. You may think you'll remember that fabulous extra portion of Pasta Puttanesca (page 169) which now graces the aqua Tupperware, but in three months, you may not.

* The more you shop and cook, the more you will learn about the characteristics of particular ingredients, the techniques that cook food quickly, and some ingenious shortcuts to great cuisine. You'll learn which perishable ingredients to use first, saving longer-lasting ones to consume later, just before another shopping trip. You'll learn to prepare a number of things simultaneously. This takes a bit of experience to learn what involves mindless time and what demands constant attention for 10 minutes. Preparing an entire meal becomes a pleasure instead of a chore.

* Consider presentation as you cook. Pouring Raspberry Chocolate Fondue (page 251) into stemmed wine glasses looks far more fetching than serving it in a cereal bowl. Surrounding it with strawberries with the stems intact is more attractive, easier for the cook, and functional for diners, since they can use the stems as handles. Vary color and texture throughout a meal. It's no more time-consuming than preparing an unappealing one. Sole with Pine Nuts and Capers (page 127) transforms plain white fish into an eye-catching, mouth-watering entrée, but preparing it is no more trouble than fixing a homely one. Serve it with Tomato Gruyère Gratin (page 197) and you have a feast for the eyes and palate in as little time as you can cook a hamburger with trimmings.

Relishing food is one of life's greatest pleasures, and its preparation, as well as dining, should be enjoyed to the fullest. *Short Cuts to Great Cuisine* invites you to appreciate the delights of quick cooking. You'll be amazed at the fabulous foods you will prepare in a flash.

Equipping the Efficient Kitchen

I cook in a kitchen that's immense. Anybody who sees it, unfortunately, assumes fabulous food will be forthcoming at a moment's notice. It has double-digit yards of counterspace, commercial appliances, a 6-foot double pot rack, fresh herbs growing on the windowsills, and enough cabinets to store a small grocery's inventory. On a boat, however, I cook in a galley that has just enough standing room for two big dogs and one pair of adult legs. There are advantages to both.

In a small kitchen, everything is within arm's reach. I can run the microwave, conventional oven, disposal, toaster, coffee maker, stove, and open the refrigerator and freezer without taking one step. There are only a few feet of counterspace to clean, and best of all, no guest dares to expect great food from it.

In a large kitchen, there's room for every imaginable appliance and gadget, stocking up on shopping trips never presents a storage problem, and, if the dishwasher breaks down, we can eat for a week without cleaning a dish.

One cook's essential equipment is another one's clutter. Setting up a kitchen is a very personal thing, depending upon how many people you typically feed and what types of food you like to prepare. Whatever you use frequently, place closest to your center of work. Whatever you use least, tuck out of the way of everyday traffic. Every kitchen has a work triangle, including a refrigerator, stove, and sink. The well-planned ones space these workhorses to ensure efficiency. Since you'll be doing most of your work within this area, consider carefully what encroaches on its valuable space.

Don't be overwhelmed by this list of equipment. These are the building blocks of the kitchen, to be added to at your discretion and over time. Without knives, a cutting board, and a few pots and pans, you should head for the nearest restaurant. Beyond that, consider these listings choices. Only you know what equipment you will use and enjoy.

The better quality kitchen equipment you invest in, the longer it will last, the faster you will be able to cook, and the better your food will taste. An inexpensive, thin pan will scorch food, one with hot spots will cook unevenly, and one without a tight-fitting lid will dry out food and lengthen cooking time. Top quality kitchen equipment will last a lifetime. It's truly an investment, but one that pays off meal after meal, year after year.

Knives may be the most important tool you buy for the kitchen. Forged knives with blades of carbon steel mixed with stainless steel are best, and a basic collection should include a paring knife, a French chef's knife with an 8-inch blade, a slicing knife with a 10-inch blade, and a knife sharpener. Wooden knife holders are ideal for preserving sharp blades and providing accessibility. Magnetic bars mounted on a kitchen wall also provide visibility and safety for knives and other steel utensils, but take care not to knick blades when attaching them. Chinese cleavers can be too heavy for some bars to hold safely.

Cutting boards are essential to every kitchen. They're my security blanket, whether at home or teaching. I don't feel quite right without one in front of me. Even if I'm using a food processor throughout dinner, a knob of ginger will need cutting or a clove of garlic must be smashed. When it's not in use as a cutting board, it doubles as counterspace. I prefer the feel of wood, but plastic ones have their advantages, including being dishwasher safe. If you have space for more than one, indulge in various sizes for different-size jobs. If I could only have one board, it would be a large one, probably 8 x 16 inches. I store mine upright in a vertical shelf underneath the sink, which gives me ideal access before using and after cleaning.

Pots and pans that are consistent, fast heat conductors in varying sizes with tight-fitting lids are critical to quick cooking. Those made of hard anodized aluminum, enameled cast iron, and heavy stainless steel with a copper or aluminum-reinforced bottom will distribute heat fast and evenly.

Size is important since crowding food prevents it from cooking properly. Pans that are too small will steam food when you want it seared. Pans that are too large will burn around the edges while food cooks in the center. A basic collection includes a 1 1/2- to 2-quart, a 3- to 4-quart, and a 6-quart saucepan, and a 5- to 7-inch and a 9- to 12-inch skillet.

Tight-fitting lids will prevent steam from escaping, thereby cooking food faster and retaining its moisture. They also eliminate constantly having to replenish cooking liquids and also unexpected burned pans. Pans with metal handles can go in the oven and under the broiler, eliminating transferring hot food that's been sautéed to an extra pan to finish with dry heat.

In order to use as little fat as possible in cooking, buy pots and pans that are nonstick or season porous ones thoroughly. Nonstick pans are easy to clean, but food does not brown adequately on a nonstick surface for some purposes, such as deglazing a pan (see page 149). I keep one nonstick pan and use it exclusively for fried eggs and omelets.

Different manufacturers recommend specific instructions for seasoning their particular line of pans. In general, pour a small amount of vegetable oil into the pan and swirl it to coat the bottom. Place over low heat for 5 minutes. Let the pan cool, wipe dry with a paper towel, and it's ready to use. Do not use soap on a seasoned pan and do not put it in the dishwasher. Clean it with hot water and a stiff brush. If using a cast-iron pan, dry it thoroughly after each use, or it will rust.

Top quality pots and pans are a substantial investment, but they should last a lifetime. I would prefer to have two or three various sizes of good quality pans than a huge set that heats unevenly and treats food poorly. Many of the better lines offer sets at discount, but choosing individual sizes that you're certain to use may be the soundest investment. Many top lines carry lifetime guarantees.

Ovenproof baking dishes are essential if your pots and pans are not ovenproof. Glass ones double for microwave use, and stainless steel and enamel-lined ones with reinforced bottoms can also be used on the stove. Consider buying those that are attractive enough to bring to the table, thereby saving on serving dishes.

Food processors, which I consider second only to my right hand for quick cooking, must be accessible. If they're stored in a cupboard behind the pots and pans or you have to dust one off each time to use, you may as well not own one. I keep mine in the center of my work area, half-way between the stove and the sink. I keep a double set of workbowls and blades, so that one is available if the other is in the dishwasher. I find it indispensable for making fresh bread crumbs, puréed soups, salad dressings, condiments such as chutney and pesto, and preparing fruits and vegetables for further cooking. I use it for dozens of foods beyond the scope of this book, and there are many dishes I wouldn't bother to prepare without a processor.

Mini-processors are small versions of standard size food processors. They are superior at mincing small quantities of ingredients, such as garlic, ginger, and fresh herbs and spices that get lost in larger-size workbowls. They make reduced quantities of bread crumbs, compound butters, and salad dressings in seconds.

Blenders make smoother soups, sauces, and purées, but they can't handle large quantities of food. They don't consume much space, they can go in the dishwasher, and they last for decades.

Immersion blenders, which are known in France as mini-pimers, are hand-held blenders that can be immersed directly in a pot of soup or sauce to purée it. They save transferring food to another container, thereby shaving cleanup time and trouble. They consume very little space and can be mounted on a wall for easy accessibility. A quick rinse under hot water is typically all the cleaning these blenders need.

Food mills look like the dinosaurs of the kitchen. If you need a soup or sauce perfectly strained, even after it's been puréed in a food processor, an old-fashioned food mill, with variously graded disks, is the answer.

Electric mixers are an arm-saver any time you whip cream or egg whites. Hand-held mixers consume much less space, but they have less power than stationary ones, and battery-operated, hand-held mixers make clumsy cords a relic from the past. Stationary mixers free the cook to pursue other chores since they don't need to be held while operating.

Microwave ovens, even if used for preparing just parts of a dish, should be placed near your work area. Most uses of the microwave are quick, and so need constant attention. Running ten feet to turn a dish every two minutes four times is annoying, at best. If possible, build it into an upper cabinet or mount it underneath one, so that you don't lose valuable counterspace. To reheat food, the microwave is ideal. It retains the texture, color, and flavor of most prepared dishes better than other reheating methods and it does it faster, to boot. Reheat food directly on the dishes you will use on the table, saving on cleanup and warming up the dishes simultaneously.

Toaster ovens are ideal for toasting nuts, heating sandwiches, browning the tops of dishes, and baking and reheating small portions of food that need dry heat. They take up little space and heat quickly, but they cannot generate as much heat as an oven broiler.

Pot racks make ideal storage for heavy pots and pans. They eliminate lifting a stack of odd sizes to get to one on the bottom. Its visibility lets you know instantly what's available, and some racks double as storage for colanders, pot lids, and large whisks and gadgets. Similarly, vertical shelves make ideal storage for cutting boards, pot lids, and baking sheets and pans. Instead of lifting and sifting through a number of them, all of these items are instantly available to you.

Stove-top grills are a relative newcomer to the kitchen, and they're treasured by many cooks in a hurry. They are inexpensive, dishwasher-proof, and a boon to healthy, fast cooking. They're comprised of two parts: an open tubular ring that holds water to catch dripping fat and a nonstick cover with slots which the fat drips through. The grill fits over a gas or electric burner and the high temperatures give the food a distinctive grilled aroma and charred surface. It requires no fat, so it's as healthy as grilling outdoors. Often I put a chicken breast, fish fillet, or hamburger on the grill and serve it plain or with a compound butter (see pages 220-224). I spend the time saved concocting an interesting side dish, sauce, or salad.

Salad spinners use centrifugal force to make quick work of drying a variety of greens so they won't dilute dressings. They're available in a range of sizes, the smallest handling just enough salad for one. If you buy one with tough enough plastic, the outer shell can double as a bowl, and the insert as a colander.

Bowls, colanders, and strainers in graduated sizes, preferably made of stainless steel, are a worthwhile investment. You'll use them constantly, and for a lifetime. A salad bowl isn't essential, especially in a crowded kitchen, but it may function as an attractive serving bowl as well. One 3- to 5-quart colander and a strainer or two, preferably of different sizes and mesh, are important.

Measuring cups and spoons. A 2-cup and a 1-cup glass measure are essential, as well as 2 sets of measuring spoons. The types of glass measures that stack are ideal for the crowded kitchen. They usually come in a set of 4-, 2-, and 1-cup measures. Deeper measuring spoons measure more precisely than shallow ones, and those made of stainless steel are sturdy and will not rust. For bakers, a graduated set of dry measures is critical.

Utensils, such as wire whisks, wooden spoons, metal and rubber spatulas, a vegetable peeler, a hand grater, a can opener, a pepper mill, a bottle opener, a corkscrew, and pot holders are bare-bones essentials.

Chef's one-handed pepper mills, which also hold salt, free one hand for stirring, a help for quickly cooked dishes. Tongs to turn meat and to retrieve asparagus or large vegetables, a reamer or juicer to remove the juice from citrus, a fruit wedger and corer, and instant-read thermometers are helpful.

Instant-read thermometers take only about 20 seconds to register, and although most of the recipes in this book use small cuts of meat, I wouldn't be without one for roasts. The thermometer does not stay in the meat, but is inserted just prior to reading.

Timers are essential if you're cooking lots of different dishes at once or if you're cooking something that takes more than 20 minutes. Most of the recipes in this book are cooked on top of the stove, where the look and smell of food make the most reliable timers.

A small rotary, single, or four-sided grater is important if you grate a lot of cheese and do not want to use a food processor. There are many times I need so little grated cheese that I opt for a simple grater.

Zesters and shrimp peelers are pet tools of mine. Zesters separate the zest from citrus in tiny shreds without any trace of pith. The shreds give you a jump-start to mincing, and often further cutting can be eliminated entirely. Shrimp peelers peel and devein all but the tiniest sizes of shrimp in seconds, they take up less space than a medium knife, and they may qualify as the least expensive kitchen gadget available.

Stocking the Kitchen for Speed

Hundreds of ready-to-use condiments, sauces, and spice blends that are a boon to the quick cook with a sophisticated palate are available today, even at general supermarkets. Experienced cook or not, a trip to a specialty store can be daunting due to its bewildering array of exotic products. I've sifted through the vast offerings and chosen basic ones that are most beneficial to the cook in a hurry. Don't be overwhelmed by the list. A basic pantry can be built on a few items and added to as you delve into more adventurous cooking. Build your pantry accordingly and to suit your own taste. Some of these entries and many of the recipes are a way of introducing you to the possibilities. Once you've experienced oyster sauce or curry paste, you'll get a feel for many other ways it can be relished.

The fewer ingredients that go into a recipe, the more critical the quality of each, since each contributes significantly to the final flavor of a dish. A few tablespoons of off-tasting butter may be lost in a stuffing that requires a dozen other ingredients, but in a compound butter that contains only a few delicate herbs, the quality of the butter is supreme.

Most of the recipes in this book contain few ingredients. Assuming that we all care about the pleasure and nourishment that food provides, it pays to buy the best, store it properly, and cook it to its greatest potential within time constraints.

Learning to shop wisely is critical to the cook in a hurry. It's better to spend an extra 10 minutes selecting top-quality meats and produce than mindlessly grabbing a package of shrink-wrapped, tasteless tomatoes or fish fillets that should have been discarded yesterday. If you get home with unsatisfactory raw materials, no matter how much time you spend doctoring them, your time will be wasted. Both your palate and nutrition will suffer.

This chapter is filled with information on what to stock in order to cook the recipes in this book. It does not include household basics, such as cereal, soda, paper towels, or tea.

The Pantry

Broths, Juices, Milk, and Coffee

Coffee, a matter of personal taste as a beverage, should be dark-roasted when used in cooking, since its heady aroma will be diluted by other ingredients. Either brew dark-roasted coffee double-strength or espresso for robust coffee flavor.

Coconut milk is the liquid strained from blending the meat of the coconut with hot water, not the liquid inside a coconut. After cracking a coconut or two, much less scraping out and infusing its meat, you'll truly appreciate this can of convenience. Combined with curry paste over heat, it's practically instant sauce. Coconut milk is available in 8- and 14-ounce cans.

Evaporated skim milk is fresh homogenized milk from which 60% of the moisture has been removed. Use it as a substitute for heavy cream in desserts and sauces.

Lemon and lime juice in a bottle make a convenient substitute for fresh. Although I always have fresh citrus on hand, more often than not, I reach for the bottled juice to save a few minutes squeezing and seeding. Always shake the bottle before using. Sometimes a bit of the pulpy solids settle to the bottom.

Stocks and broths are critical to the quality of the finished dishes we eat, and yet few of us have time to ensure that quality by making our own. Cooking with full-flavored stock won't guarantee a delicious dish, but cooking with a bad one will ensure poor results. Stock is intrinsic to the success of so many recipes that the French term for it, *fond de cuisine*, means "the foundation of the kitchen." Most prepared broth is overly salty and can ruin an otherwise wonderful meal, especially when the stock is reduced to intensify its flavor. As its water content evaporates, the salt becomes more concentrated. When using canned broth, don't forget to dilute it with water at least half-and-half.

Although stock (made from bones) and broth (made from meat) are actually two different things, industry standards interchange them. To further the confusion, bouillon refers to either stock or broth, and consommé refers to broth clarified with egg whites. No-salt and low-salt versions, such as College Inn, Hain's, or Swanson's are acceptable, as is Knorr's chicken and beef bouillon cubes. In some parts of the country, frozen stocks with no salt added are available.

Use bottled or canned *clam juice* or Knorr's fish bouillon cubes in lieu of homemade fish stock. The cubes are ideal for tiny kitchens and for cooks who'd rather not transport heavy cans.

Sweetened condensed milk is thick, with 60% of its moisture removed, and sweet, containing 40-45% sugar. Its paste-like consistency makes some desserts practically instantaneous (Key Lime Fool, page 259).

Tomato juice can be used as a soup base (see Tex-Mex Gazpacho with Avocado Purée, page 69), and can be substituted for stock or broth for a change of pace.

Oils and Vinegars

Oils are classified in one of two categories, cooking oils or flavoring oils. Those intended for cooking have high smoke points, so they do not burn under high cooking temperatures, and they have mild flavors, so their aroma doesn't overwhelm the food being cooked. Those developed to impart flavor typically have strong flavors and low smoke points; consequently they are added toward the end of cooking. Most oils are clearly defined for cooking or flavoring, olive oil being the exception.

Asian sesame seed oil is made from toasted sesame seeds; therefore, it's dark brown in color and deeply rich in flavor. It's used only as a flavoring oil, and a little goes a long way.

Chili oil is a clear infusion of oil and hot red chilies that have been strained out. Hotter than Tabasco, but used in a similar way, a few shakes over a dish will do. Some contain sesame seed oil as well. I prefer brands made with vegetable oil, since sesame flavor isn't always desirable in a particular dish. Chili oil keeps indefinitely at room temperature and is used exclusively for flavoring.

Corn, safflower, canola, peanut, and *pure olive oil* are all acceptable cooking oils. They have varying degrees of light flavors, so their aroma doesn't overpower the food being cooked, and they have high smoke points, so they don't burn over high heat.

Mayonnaise that is commercially prepared is a far cry from homemade, but it's acceptable. Stir in a little lemon juice or vinegar to give it a lift. Add fresh herbs, capers, green peppercorns, curry, jarred pimientos, sesame oil, horseradish, or mustard to vary and enliven it.

Nonstick vegetable sprays, made with vegetable and olive oil in aerosol cans, assure the easy release of cooked foods without messy buttering and greasing of pans. They're practically no-calorie and quick to use.

Nut oils, particularly walnut and hazelnut, are very strong flavoring oils, so they're often mixed with olive or vegetable oil in a salad dressing. Any salad enhanced with nuts, particularly those containing fruit or cheese, will benefit from the addition of one of these aromatic oils.

Olive oils differ in color from deep green to yellow, in flavor from bland to overpoweringly fruity, and in their smoke points and levels of acid. Virgin olive oil is taken from hand-picked olives in the first cold-pressing, that is, without the use of heat or chemicals, so it delivers unadulterated olive flavor. "Pure" olive oil is taken from subsequent pressings, making them less flavorful, higher in acid, and having a higher smoke point, which makes them suitable for cooking.

Vinegars come in such an array of brands and flavors that it's staggering, even to an experienced shopper. Their intense flavors contribute so significantly to food and the amounts called for are usually so small, that it pays to splurge on good quality brands.

Balsamic vinegar, dark, mellow, and sweet, is made in Italy from white Trebbiano grape juice that's aged in a succession of wooden barrels over a period of as long as 50 years. Most of what is sold in the United States is made from a quick process of caramelizing grape juice and adding vinegar and oak extract. It's adequate, but not the same as real *aceto balsamico*, which can be very costly.

Fruit vinegars, such as blueberry and raspberry, are usually wine vinegars infused with and carrying the distinct aroma of particular fruits. *Herbed vinegars* are wine vinegars infused with mint, tarragon, dill, or other fresh herbs.

Red and white wine vinegars are fermented twice. The first fermentation is to turn the sugar of grapes into alcohol, the second, to turn the alcohol into acetic acid, the main component of vinegar. The slower the process and the less heat applied during the process account for the best wine vinegars. They must contain at least 4% acidity, but higher levels, made by a more expensive process, are more desirable as long as the character of the wine is still evident.

Rice vinegar, made from fermented rice, is white to pale golden in color, delicate in character, low in acidity, and full-flavored compared to white vinegar.

Salt, Spices, and Herbs

Kosher salt is far superior to sea salt or table salt for cooking, and all the recipes in this book were tested with it. It contains no additives, so it enhances the flavor of food without adding extraneous flavors. Since table salt contains aluminum derivatives, it leaves a tinny taste in the mouth. Sea and table salts are actually twice as salty as kosher, and some brands of sea salt have sugar added, as well. It's easy to taste the differences in salt at home, and you'll be amazed at their various qualities.

Freshly ground black, white, green, or pink *whole peppercorns* are the only ones worth using. Pre-ground pepper resembles dust in flavor and texture, so it has no place in the kitchen. *Green peppercorns* packed in brine are soft, fresh-tasting, and less pungent. Don't get them confused, as I have more than once, with capers. The jars and their contents look similar, and they're often sold in close proximity to each other.

Buy herbs and spices as close to their whole form as possible to retain their flavor over time. For instance, buy whole nutmegs and grate them as needed. Buy leaf oregano, never ground, and crumble or rub it to release its oils just before adding to a dish.

A list of spices and dried herbs used in this book follows. Those that are most commonly used are starred.

allspice, ground	lemon peel
basil*	mustard, dry
cardamom	nutmeg, whole or ground*
cinnamon, ground*	orange peel
cinnamon sticks (3 inches)	oregano*
cloves	red pepper, ground (cayenne)*
coriander, ground	rosemary
crushed red pepper flakes	saffron threads
cumin, ground*	sesame seeds
curry powder*	tarragon
five-spice powder	thyme
ginger, ground*	turmeric, ground
	vanilla bean

Condiments

Capers are piquant, pickled, unopened buds of a bush native to the Mediterranean. They vary significantly in size and price. The very small, "fancy" varieties sell for a premium price, although they taste no different from larger ones.

Chili pastes are semiliquid blends of red chilies, vinegar, salt, sugar, and sometimes garlic and/or soybeans. They will keep indefinitely chilled or at room temperature. The Thai and Vietnamese chili pastes give nicely rounded flavor, but too much heat for most Western palates.

Chutneys are cooked mixtures of fruit, vinegar, sugar, and spices. They vary from mild to hot, but all are on the sweet side. Traditionally served with Indian curries, they are delicious with cheeses, fruit, and as an alternative to cranberry and mint sauces. Most are available in jars, and they keep indefinitely refrigerated.

Curry pastes, which deliver far more rounded tastes than curry powder, are oil-based mixtures of chilies and dozens of spices. They keep indefinitely. The red ones are generally milder than green.

Fish sauce, known as *nuoc mam*, *nam pla*, and *tuk trey*, depending on the country of origin, is Southeast Asia's answer to soy sauce. It is a rotted fish extract whose taste, thankfully, outshines its initial aroma. It's used variously as a condiment, dipping sauce, and cooking ingredient.

Hoisin sauce, made from fermented soybeans or wheat, can be thick or thin and sweet or salty, depending upon the brand you buy. Typically, American brands have a fruity sweetness and a jam-like consistency. It keeps indefinitely refrigerated.

Horseradish, prepared and bottled, comes in white, which is preserved with vinegar, and red, which is bottled with beet juice. The white is all-purpose, since its color won't distort others. It gets its heat from its large, pungent root.

Indian Pickle in Oil is, admittedly, a little-used condiment, but it duplicates time-consuming Indian spices with amazing convenience. It contains lime, mango, green chili, karonda, ginger, mustard oil, fenugreek, turmeric, and asafoetida—a blend I would never bother to concoct myself.

Mustards are available in a bewildering array, but for simplicity and cooking purposes in this book, I've used only Dijon mustard. Dijon is smooth, complex, and consistent. It packs a lot of rich flavor into small amounts. Mustard acts as a thickener in sauces and salad dressings as well as a potent flavoring.

Olives are available pitted and unpitted, sliced and chopped, canned, bottled, and in bulk, in a wide range of flavors and sizes. Greek Kalamatas, French Niçoise, and Italian Gaetas are favorites of mine. Imported, oil-cured olives contain the most flavor, and common domestic brands tend to be very bland. *Olivada*, available in jars, is a convenient mixture of olives, olive oil, lemon juice, vinegar, and herbs.

Oyster sauce is a dark-brown, thick, and savory sauce made from oysters, salt, and caramel coloring. It's commonly used in southern Chinese cooking. A little goes a long way, and it will keep indefinitely in the refrigerator.

Peppers of many types are available jarred or canned. Pickled cherry peppers, round and mild, are perfect for eating straight or minced in a sauce. Pepperoncini are pale green, elongated, and hotter in flavor. Both make flavor-packed additions to an antipasto platter. Jalapeños are available in jars, but fresh ones are just as easily incorporated into sauces.

Pesto is an uncooked Italian paste of fresh basil, pine nuts, Parmesan cheese, olive oil, and garlic, that's easily made at home with a food processor. For those of us seeking convenience, however, it's available in shelf-stable jars and cans, and plastic containers in the refrigerator section of most groceries. For those who use very little at a time, it's also available in tubes. Restaurant and homemade versions of pesto can be made from a variety of herbs and vegetables (see Poblano Pesto, page 167).

Plum sauce, a combination of plums, sugar, ginger, sweet potato, and chilies, is thick and sweet. It's practically ready to use as a dipping sauce or glaze, but it benefits from some savory additions (see Butterflied Quail in Plum Sauce, page 142).

Salsa is an uncooked, typically tomato, sauce ranging from mildly hot to blazing. Homemade (see Searing Salsa, page 47, Horseradish Salsa, page 53) and restaurant versions may be based on a range of fruits, vegetables, and even legumes. Blend commercially made salsa with sour cream or yogurt for a zesty dressing, use over eggs, with tortilla chips, nachos, and most things Mexican.

Salted black beans, Chinese black beans, salted beans, fermented black beans, and ginger black beans are all the same beast. I've wasted many hours rummaging through packages with foreign scribble searching for fermented black beans when a container labeled Chinese black beans was 6 inches from my nose. Black soybeans are simmered, inoculated with a mold, and left to ferment in a brining solution for about 6 months. Salted black beans seasoned with ginger are far preferable to those infused with five-spice powder, which tends to overwhelm their aroma. They need no washing before using, and they'll keep indefinitely at room temperature.

Soy sauces vary dramatically in flavor and intensity. They are a blend of cooked soybeans and wheat that has been injected with a mold and left to ferment in a briny solution for 6-24 months. Then the liquid is drained off. Both the Japanese and Chinese use light and dark soy sauces for different purposes. In order to simplify the pantry for this book, and since many other products that are used as a convenience in quick cooking contain salt, I've used Kikkoman low-sodium soy sauce throughout these recipes.

Tabasco Sauce is a thin, incendiary, red sauce made from fermented tabasco peppers, vinegar, and salt. It's used as a condiment as well as a cooking ingredient.

Tahini, a Middle Eastern staple, is a smooth paste of ground raw, hulled sesame seeds. It's available in white and gray versions, the white giving a creamier flavor.

Tomato paste is available in tubes for those of us who don't need whole 6-ounce cans. Sun-dried tomato paste is also available in tubes. Tomato and spaghetti sauces are available in a variety of flavors and sizes, canned and jarred, and they can easily be perked up with extra garlic, herbs, and wine.

Worcestershire sauce is a thin, dark sauce originated by the English. Its savory, piquant flavor and deep color make valuable additions to quick sauces.

Pastas, Grains, and Legumes

Barley, or pearl barley commonly available today, is a hardy grain with its bran removed that has been steamed and polished. It has a subtle, nutty flavor and mildly chewy texture.

Beans, or the seed pods of legumes, are variously available fresh, dried, and canned. Beans are regaining popularity since they're a welcome, inexpensive source of protein. The availability of canned black beans, cannellini, and chickpeas places them within the realm of quick cooking.

Bulgur is made of steamed, dried, and crushed wheat kernels. A staple in Middle Eastern cuisines, it comes in fine, medium, and coarse grinds.

Cornmeal, or polenta, consists of ground corn kernels that are slightly sweet. Available in yellow and white, they can be used interchangeably in cooking. Water- or stone-ground cornmeal has a fuller flavor and contains the germ of the corn, but it doesn't keep as well as regular cornmeal.

Kasha, or buckwheat kernels, is one of the best plant sources of protein. It's available in most supermarkets in boxes of fine, medium, or coarse grains. The finer the grain, the more quickly it will cook. It can be cooked in the microwave or on the stove as a breakfast cereal, a side dish, and a base for an entrée. Its earthy aroma makes it an acquired taste.

Lentils are lens-shaped pulses available in two varieties, the brown lentil containing a seed coat and creamy exterior, and the red lentil, requiring no pre-soaking and only short cooking time. Red lentils, the only choice for quick cooking, can be found in specialty shops and some supermarkets.

Pasta is readily available dry and fresh in most supermarkets. Imported dry pasta is made from hard semolina flour and maintains its bite when properly cooked. American versions may be made with softer wheat, but both last indefinitely at room temperature. Fresh pasta, typically made with egg and soft flour, is perishable and cooks quickly relative to dry. Thinner or smaller sizes of pasta also cook more quickly. Pasta shapes vary from long to short, and some, such as ravioli and tortellini, are available filled. Dry pastas are available in amusing shapes, such as bow-ties, hats, shells, tubes, and spirals. Asian noodles are typically made from a variety of flours, such as buckwheat, cornstarch, mung-bean, rice, and soy, resulting in a soft cooked noodle.

Quinoa is a tiny, ivory-colored grain that cooks like rice. It contains all 8 amino acids, so it's considered a complete protein. Use it as a breakfast cereal, a side dish, or a salad or entrée base.

Rices can all be categorized as white or brown and as long-, medium-, or short-grain. In general, the shorter the grain of rice, the stickier it will be when cooked. Long grains make ideal pilafs and salads, since they separate when fluffed. Medium-grain rices make a reasonable substitute for long-grain, but use short-grain rice only when specified. I love the nuttiness of *brown* and *wild rice* (which is actually the seed of a grass), but, unfortunately, both need a full forty minutes to cook. You can soak either in plenty of water, allowing for them to swell for 24 hours, and then cook them for twenty minutes. *Aromatic rices* make flavorful, easy side dishes for cooks in a hurry. Since we value them for their nuances in aroma, they need little adornment to enjoy their fragrant subtleties. Try wild pecan rice for a popcorn-like nuttiness or basmati or Texmati for a delicately nutty, milky flavor. Wehani tastes like a combination of wild, brown, and white rices, and jasmine gives off a delicately sweet aroma. *Arborio rice*, grown in the Po Valley of Northern Italy, has a distinct opaque white spot on one side which contrasts with the rest of the grain. It maintains a bite even after simmering 20 minutes. This quality, similar to dried pasta made with semolina flour, makes it invaluable for risottos, where a slight resistance to the bite is desired.

Vegetables and Fruits

Artichokes, cooked, trimmed, and ready to use, are available in water-packed cans and marinated in various size jars.

Baby corn, a favorite in Thai and Chinese cuisines, is available water-packed in cans and jars. The ears, eaten whole, lack strong corn flavor, but are colorful and amusing additions to salads and stir-fries. They range in length from 2 to 4 inches.

Bamboo shoots are the young, tender shoots of an edible species of bamboo. They can sometimes be found fresh in Asian markets, but canned ones are readily available in most supermarkets.

Beets are available pickled or plain, whole, sliced, diced, and shredded in cans and jars. Canning doesn't affect their flavor badly, but they lose a bit of texture.

Dried fruits are concentrations of intense sweetness and flavor. Aside from eating out of hand, they can be reconstituted quickly in warm liquids (see page 87). Since their moisture content has been reduced to 15-25%, they can be stored at room temperature, tightly wrapped, up to a year. Raisins, pitted prunes, pitted dates, currants, and apricots are most valuable in cooking.

Green chilies are roasted, peeled, and canned. They have a mild chili flavor and are available whole and chopped in 4- and 7-ounce cans.

Lychees, a cherished fruit of China for centuries, have creamy white flesh that is juicy and delicately sweet. Canned ones are a real time-saver, since the rough brown exterior of each 1 to 2" fruit must be peeled and the flesh removed from a tenacious pit.

Mandarin oranges are loose-skinned satsumas that are small, practically seedless, and packed in water with no added sugar. They're available in convenient 11-ounce cans.

Nuts are dried fruits containing an edible kernel encased in a hard shell. Peanuts, although treated as nuts, are actually legumes. For convenience, buy shelled hazelnuts, pecans, pine nuts, almonds, and cashews, and, if not using quickly, freeze them to prevent them from turning rancid. Jarred whole chestnuts and chestnut purées place these starchy, delicately flavored nuts within the quick cook's reach. Chestnuts require two stages of cooking, a softening of the shells to make peeling possible and another softening of the meat to make it palatable. The first stage is particularly tedious, since not only does the shell need removing, but also the bitter skin that encases the nut.

Pimientos (see Roasted red peppers).

Refried beans are red or pinto beans that have been cooked, mashed, and fried. They're available in 8-, 15 to 16-, and 30-ounce cans.

Roasted red peppers in a jar provide considerable, if costly, convenience to the cook. Instead of roasting, steaming, peeling, seeding, and chopping the peppers, all you have to do is open a jar. Imported brands have more texture than soft domestic ones.

Straw mushrooms, readily available canned, provide mild taste and a slippery texture to soups, salads, and stir-fries. They are small, brown, and phallic-shaped.

Tomatoes are available whole, stewed, crushed, puréed, sauced, and in paste form. Most have more flavor than fresh, with the exception of the month or so vine-ripened tomatoes are available in season. *Sun-dried tomatoes*, which are dried as their name implies or by artificial means, are chewy, concentrated, and intensely flavored. They are available dry or packed in oil in jars. Since the dried ones need to be reconstituted, it's more expedient to buy those already packed in oil.

Water chestnuts, available in 5-ounce cans, are smaller than fresh and they have lost some of their sweetness; however, their convenience is worth a slight bit of lost flavor.

Fish

Anchovies are tiny fish that are filleted, salt-cured, and canned in oil. They're sold either flat or rolled, and since they're very salty, anchovies are typically used sparingly. Anchovy paste is also available in tubes, for those who use very little at a time.

Caviar, sieved and lightly salted fish roe, should be bought from a reputable dealer with substantial turnover, since it's highly perishable. The three main types are beluga, osetra, and sevruga. Malossol does not refer to a type, but means the eggs were preserved with little salt.

Baby clams are available in cans and jars. The cans sometimes contain tough, large clams that have been minced. Jars give you a clear look at what you're buying—the clams should be whole and no larger than your little finger nail.

Smoked mussels, *clams*, or *oysters* are available in cans and make convenient, tasty tidbits for hors d'oeuvre, pastas, and salads.

Smoked salmon and *trout* have undergone a smoking process, either by hot-smoking or cold, but they vary in flavor and texture. Some are malleable and soft in texture, while others are hard and dry, but packed with flavor.

Tuna is available in cans packed in oil or water. The lightest, least oily, and mildest domestic tuna flavor in a can is albacore, or white-meat tuna. Yellowfin, bigeye, and skipjack are also mild, and bluefin is the oiliest, darkest, most fishy-flavored. Tuna imported from France or Italy packed in 4-ounce cans in olive oil is sweeter and moister than American versions. If you can find it, stock up.

Spirits

Wines and liqueurs contribute a sophisticated, wide range of flavors to food. They can be simmered down or reduced to intensify these flavors. They can be added early in cooking to meld their aroma with others or at the last minute for a stronger wininess. Dry wines, whether red or white, are best for cooking savory dishes. Never, never buy cooking wines. They contain salt and other additives, making them unpalatable to drink, so consequently, they can be sold as food on grocery shelves where alcoholic beverages are not allowed. Ironically, buying a decent quality drinking wine is typically a better buy and definitely a better choice for cooking. Never cook with a wine you wouldn't drink. You'll be eating a concentration of poor flavor.

Fortified wines—sherry, port, Marsala, Madeira, and vermouth—are shelf-stable, needing no refrigeration after opening. If you don't use wine often or you keep a crowded refrigerator, these make long-lasting alternatives to non-fortified wines. Substitute dry vermouth for one-half the amount of dry white wine called for in savory recipes, diluting it with an equal amount of water. Dry sherry makes an ideal substitute for rice wine often called for in Asian dishes.

Liqueurs are also shelf-stable and deliver intense flavors. Orange-flavored liqueurs, such as Grand Marnier, Cointreau, curaçao, and Triple Sec, may be used interchangeably, but they differ in their particular characteristics. Almond-flavored amaretto, cherry-scented kirsch, and mint-scented crème de menthe are two other liqueurs used in this book.

Sweeteners

Chocolate varies in quality and flavor. Bittersweet and semisweet, containing cocoa butter, sugar, and vanilla, may be interchanged, but unsweetened contains no sugar, so recipes must be altered to accommodate it. Milk chocolate is used primarily for eating, and white chocolate is a misnomer, since it contains no chocolate liquor. Cocoa powder is dried and pulverized chocolate liquor with no cocoa butter, so it's ideal for a low-fat alternative to chocolate. Like powdered sugar, it can be dusted decoratively over desserts.

Corn syrup is valuable as a sweetener and for inhibiting crystallization. It's available in light and dark, and, unless otherwise stated, light corn syrup should be used.

Extracts are intense concentrations of flavor, so they don't dramatically change the liquid volume of a recipe. Since they're alcohol-based, they'll keep indefinitely at room temperature in a cool, dark place.

Honey should be mild in flavor for cooking purposes. Some honeys, such as those made from buckwheat, are especially strong and can overpower a dish.

Jams and *jellies* make convenient bases or additions to savory and sweet sauces and glazes, since they deliver intense flavors and need only be melted to be incorporated (see Spicy Apricot Glaze, page 219, and Jalapeño Glazed Plantains, page 203).

Lemon curd, a refreshingly tart and sweet paste made from lemon juice, egg yolks, sugar, and butter, is convenience-in-a-jar. With equal parts of whipped cream, it's transformed into a marvelous dessert or sauce in minutes (see page 241). It's shelf-stable, but should be chilled after opening.

Maple Syrup imitations abound, but pure maple syrup can't be beaten for intensely sweet flavor and consistency.

Molasses, a by-product of refining sugar, is a dark, thick, sweet liquid. As a general rule, the darker the molasses, the thicker, less sweet, and more bitter it will be. Unless otherwise specified, use light or dark, never blackstrap, molasses.

Sugar refers to granulated, unless otherwise specified. *Brown sugar* is granulated sugar with molasses added, the darker containing greater amounts of molasses. Unless otherwise specified, brown sugar refers to light brown sugar. *Powdered or confectioners' sugar* is granulated sugar that has been crushed to a powder, and cornstarch has been added to prevent clumping. It dissolves easily and can be dusted decoratively on desserts.

See also: sweetened condensed milk (see page 17).

Fresh and Frozen Foods

Dairy

Butter, or cream churned into a semisolid state, varies in the amount of salt it contains. Since the convenience-oriented cook uses other ingredients that contain varying amounts of salt, such as canned broths, it pays to use unsalted butter. You can always season a dish further just before serving it. Also, salt masks off-odors in low-quality butters and keeps it tasting fresh, even when it is not. Practically all professional cooks use unsalted butter, and are assured of quality and freshness. Since butter may burn at relatively low temperatures, especially when pan-frying or sautéeing, use half butter and half pure olive oil or vegetable oil to raise its burning point but retain the taste of butter.

Cheeses, especially hard cheeses, such as Parmesan, last a long time when bought in a block. When buying cheeses pre-grated, consider that they will not last as long as chunks of cheese. Check the code date on them to verify their freshness, be sure they're free of beads of moisture or mold, and try to buy in the quantity you'll use within a few days or that you're willing to freeze. Read the labels. Some pre-grated products are artificial.

Blue-veined cheeses, such as Roquefort, Stilton, and Cambozola, are inoculated or sprayed with the spores of molds and aged. They contain pockets of strong flavor and are variously crumbly and creamy.

Chèvre, or goat cheese, comes in a multitude of flavors, shapes, and textures. Some are velvety, creamy, and spreadable, especially those mixed with cow's milk. Others are aged and hard enough to grate. They vary in flavor from tangy and zesty to mild. Montrachet is particularly versatile since it's mild, creamy, meltable, spreadable, and readily available.

Cream, heavy cream, or whipping cream that's commonly available in supermarkets contains 30-36% butterfat. Heavier cream can be found in specialty stores. Most of the cream we buy has been pasteurized; ultra-pasteurized will not whip.

Cream cheese, spreadable and slightly tangy, is soft and unripened. At least a third of its content is butterfat, and some contain additives to contribute to firmness and shelf life. Low-fat versions are available and make fine substitutes.

Double- and triple-cream cheeses, varying between 60 and 75% fat, are luxuriously rich. Their flavors vary from mild to full-bodied, and they should be ripened to their peak of flavor to enjoy them at their best. L'Explorateur, St. André, and Saga Blue are favorites, usually saved for the beginning or ending of a special dinner.

Hard cheeses, such as Parmesan, Asiago, and Romano, are carefully aged, some up to over 7 years. They're grainy in texture, nutty in flavor, and intended primarily for grating.

Ricotta is a fresh, rich cheese that's moist and slightly grainy in texture. It's popular in Italian savory and sweet dishes.

Semifirm and semisoft cheeses, such as Cheddar, Jarlsberg, Gouda, and Monterey Jack, are firm but not crumbly. They can be grated, they melt nicely in cooking, but they do not keep as well as hard or blue cheeses.

Soft-ripening cheeses, such as Brie and Camembert, contain 50% fat, have a creamy consistency, and a white, edible rind. They need to ripen before they are eaten.

Eggs, unless specified otherwise, refers to large eggs.

Half-and-half contains equal parts of cream and milk. I find it easier to stock its components, since I often use them separately.

Ice cream prepared commercially provides a convenient base for desserts which can be easily personalized with fresh fruits, liqueurs, nuts, and crumbled cookie toppings.

Milk, unless specified otherwise, refers to whole, homogenized fresh milk.

Sour cream, cream treated with lactic acid to lend its characteristic tang to foods, contains 18-20% fat. It lends tart creaminess to foods hot and cold.

Yogurt also contains lactic acid that provides tart creaminess. It cannot be heated, or it will separate, but in uncooked sauces, substitute plain low- or non-fat yogurt in equal parts for sour cream for a low-fat alternative. Frozen yogurt makes a reasonable, low-fat substitute for ice cream.

Fruits

Whenever possible, handpick fresh fruits. Check them for bruises, discolored patches, and signs of mold. They should feel heavy for their size, but they don't have to look picture-perfect. Citrus can bear skin-deep scars or rough patches, and apples show rough, tan patches without lessening the quality within. Fruits such as pineapples, melons, and tomatoes should give off a faint aroma when ripe.

Grocers have tried to indulge shoppers with a year-round supply of fresh fruits, most of it imported. The quality of many of the fruits is questionable, as are their price tags. The smartest way to buy fruit is by the season—fruit will be of the best quality and the cheapest, to boot.

Frozen fruits, especially berries and melons, are a buy in winter, when the prices of fresh ones skyrocket. Stick to fruits that are quick-frozen, since those packed in sugar syrup lose their texture and are overwhelmed with sugar. A few fruits, such as raspberries that are packed in syrup, make a convenient dessert ingredient.

Canned fruits are usually lacking altogether in texture. I usually keep a can of mandarin oranges on hand for an easy salad ingredient and a can of lychees, since their season is so short and they're a nuisance to prepare fresh.

Some fresh fruits that appear in this book that you may not be familiar with follow:

Cranberries, available fresh in the fall in 12-ounce plastic bags, are valued for their intense tart flavor and vibrant scarlet color. Since they freeze well, it's easy to keep a year-round supply.

Key limes are rounder, more yellow in color, and more decided in flavor than the common Persian lime. They are native to southern Florida.

Kiwi, or the Chinese gooseberry, resembles a furry brown egg. The sweet and tart flesh is a beautiful green flecked with many delicate, crunchy black seeds.

Mangoes, most frequently available in summer, are oblong in shape with thin, tough, mottled green to yellow to red skin. They contain large, tenacious pits, so their smooth, sweet flesh must be carefully carved away.

Papayas, pear-shaped but decidedly larger, contain flesh that is silky smooth and sweet and tart. Their thin skin is golden-orange in color, and they have a center section of round black seeds that some people eat for their peppery flavor.

Plantains are actually used like vegetables, due to their starchy, barely sweet flavor. They are bananas, however, which they resemble except for their green color and skin that's difficult to pull from their flesh.

Starfruit, or carambola, is 3-5 inches long with 5 deep ribs. It's bright yellow in color, citrusy in flavor, and when sliced crosswise, the ribs define a clear star shape. The larger the ribs and those speckled with brown spots will be the sweetest.

Vegetables

Whenever possible, handpick fresh vegetables. They should look bright in color and feel heavy for their size and firm in texture. Check them for bruising, cracks, discolored patches, or mold. Smaller, younger vegetables will be the most tender with quick-cooking.

Canned and frozen vegetables are picked at their peak and processed almost immediately after picking. In general, frozen vegetables are superior in texture and flavor to canned because canning requires processing under high temperatures to make them safe for storage. They are also usually processed with added salt. Canned beets, chilies, baby corn, straw mushrooms, water chestnuts, roasted red peppers, tomatoes, and legumes such as beans and chickpeas are acceptable substitutes for fresh. Canned tomatoes are a particular standout, not only for convenience, but for the quality they supply us that's unavailable fresh for most of the year.

Frozen artichokes, corn, green beans, green peas, brussels sprouts, pearl onions, and lima beans are superior to fresh except during their short seasons. For the quick cook, they provide tremendous convenience, since they are ready to use with no time-consuming cleaning, shelling, peeling, or trimming. Frozen spinach provides a ready-to-cook alternative to the painstaking process of picking through each leaf and cleaning carefully for grit.

Some fresh vegetables that appear in this book that you may not be familiar with follow:

Arugula, also called rugula, rocket, and rucola, is an assertive salad green that has leaves that resemble elongated radish leaves. It's valued for its strong, peppery mustard flavor and can be found in small bundles with its roots intact.

Belgian endive has whitish, tightly packed, spear-like leaves about 6 inches long. It's best between September and May, and its taste is slightly bitter. It can be cooked or eaten raw.

Bok choy is a Chinese cabbage with crunchy white stalks and dark green leaves. It's available year-round in many different varieties, and all are interchangeable.

Curly endive has loosely packed, lacy leaves ranging from white near its center to yellow to dark green on its tips. It has a firm texture and a bitter edge.

Escarole is mild in flavor and has medium-green, broad, slightly curved leaves. It's eaten both raw and cooked.

Ginger, a staple ingredient in Asian and Indian cooking, is a slightly sweet, peppery rhizome, not a root as is often thought. Mature ginger is most commonly available with its thin, tan skin and stringy texture. Young, or spring ginger, is only available in spring. It offers a milder flavor and a thin, pale skin that requires no peeling. The easiest way to store fresh ginger, if you don't use lots of it regularly, is to place it, as is, in the freezer. Slice off as much as you need, trimming off any ends that may have shriveled. *Preserved ginger* or stem ginger is available in specialty markets. It's used as a dessert ingredient or as a confection (Gingered Lychees, page 263). *Crystallized ginger* has been candied in a sugar syrup and coated with coarse sugar. It's usually available in small boxes.

Japanese eggplant is slender and varies from solid purple to purple with striations of white. Its skin and flesh is tender and less bitter compared to bulbous types, making it the best eggplant for quick-cooking.

Lemon grass resembles straw-colored, stiff scallions and is used widely in Southeast Asian cooking. Since it is now being grown in California, it's turning up in more and more produce markets. Strip the grass of the outermost tough stalks and use only the lower 6 inches, which is fragrant and relatively soft.

Parsnips are creamy-colored root vegetables similar to carrots in shape, except the parsnip is usually broader at its stem end. Its flavor is slightly sweet.

Radicchio, or red-leaf chicory, has burgundy-colored leaves striated with white. It grows in a small, tight head, and is usually served raw. Its flavor is slightly bitter.

Scallions, or green onions, are long, thin, grass-like onions. All parts except the fragile root tendrils are edible. They are mild in flavor and available year-round.

Shallots, a member of the onion family, are composed of a head with multiple cloves encased in a brown papery covering. The flesh is white, tinged with purple or green, and has a mild onion flavor.

Watercress has bright green, delicate leaves that deliver peppery, slightly bitter pungency.

Wild mushrooms, such as chanterelles, morels, and shitakes, have diverse shapes, colors, and flavors. They're available more frequently now in supermarkets. Mushrooms continue to breathe after picking and need air circulation to stay fresh, so place them in paper bags instead of plastic when purchasing and storing. Dried mushrooms deliver the most intense mushroom flavor, but they need a full 30 minutes to soak in hot water to reconstitute.

Fresh Herbs

Basil, an annual member of the mint family, has a pungent aroma reminiscent of anise and clove. It's essential to Mediterranean cooking and a key ingredient in pesto (see page 20).

Cilantro, a staple in Latin American, Mediterranean, and many Asian cuisines, has more delicate and paler leaves than parsley and a slightly sweet taste. Due to its burgeoning popularity, it can be found in most supermarkets today alongside other popular fresh herbs.

Oregano, a member of the mint family, is valued for its pungent aroma.

Parsley, both the common curly and stronger-flavored Italian flat-leaf parsley, are valued for fresh, grassy flavors and bright green color. Dried parsley is useless and should never be substituted for fresh.

Rosemary is a woody member of the mint family with stiff needle-like leaves. It's valued for its piney, lemony aroma.

Sage, strong and musky with overtones of mint, is only of value when fresh. It has narrow, gray-green leaves that are 1-3 inches long and fuzzy in texture. Commercially prepared dried sage is dust-like in appearance and taste.

Tarragon is aniselike in flavor with pointed, narrow green leaves. It's a classic in French cooking and often flavors commercially prepared wine vinegars.

Thyme has small, roundish, gray-green leaves that give off a minty, lemony aroma. It's native to Southern Europe and the Mediterranean, where it's used extensively.

Baked Goods

Amaretti are crisp Italian macaroons with a bitter almond flavor. They're delicious by themselves, but they also make a ready-to-use flavor enhancer for desserts and savories that lend themselves to a sweet touch. They can be pulverized in a food processor or crushed between sheets of wax paper with a rolling pin, mallet, or meat pounder.

Breads of all sorts are serious time-savers for the cook. Aside from the special breads below, finding a good source for French and Italian breads is important.

Bread crumbs can be purchased in some bakeries, or they can be made in seconds in a food processor with a dry workbowl. One slice of sandwich bread will yield 3/4 cup fresh bread crumbs.

Croutons, crunchy bits of bread for salads and soups, are available plain, herbed, or seasoned with garlic or cheese. Many bakeries make their own, and shelf-stable packaged brands are available.

Pita breads or *pocket breads* are a Middle Eastern staple, round and hollow inside, making them suitable for stuffing. They are usually found in bakery sections of groceries or Middle Eastern specialty stores. If not you do not intend to use the pitas quickly, freeze them.

Pizza bases are yeast-based flat breads and are suitable for topping. They are variously found shelf-stable and refrigerated.

Prepared cakes and *pastries* will save the cook in a hurry from multi-stage dessert preparations. They can be personalized with dessert sauces (see pages 230-233), fresh fruits, purchased or homemade ice creams or sorbets (see pages 255-257, 261), or a drizzling of wines or liqueurs. Pound cakes and angel food cakes can be used as dips for dessert fondues.

Prepared cookies, such as biscotti and cigarette cookies, make valuable accompaniments to assorted desserts.

Tortillas are unleavened, round, and flat breads made either with flour or corn. The base for many Mexican dishes, tortillas can also be eaten plain or as a sandwich or hors d'oeuvre base. They come in various sizes, usually found refrigerated, and they also freeze well.

Wonton wrappers or skins are paper-thin, 3 x 3-inch pieces of prepared dough found in the refrigerated section of groceries. They're traditionally used to make Chinese dumplings, but they can be cooked to make crisp bite-size breads and hors d'oeuvre. They freeze well, if not using within a few days.

Fish, Poultry, and Meats

Fish must be fresh. Save time by checking at the market to be certain that your purchase will be acceptable to cook when you get home. Buy it unwrapped, if at all possible, so you can check it for freshness, and buy it cut and cleaned, so it's ready to cook. The first clue to freshness is a lack of fishy odor. The flesh should feel firm to the touch, and there should be no slime or bruising. If buying whole fish, look for bright red gills and clear eyes. Don't hesitate to refuse a questionable choice or to ask a sales clerk to unwrap a packaged fish, so you can check it. It can always be rewrapped.

Buy fish and shellfish in their most prepared form, when possible. Fish should be cleaned and, unless using whole, steaked or filleted. Buy mussels and clams with clean shells, shrimp peeled and deveined, and oysters shucked, unless serving on the half-shell.

Meat should be young so it will be tender when cooked. Younger cuts will be lighter in color, a phenomenon that's particularly dramatic with *veal*. Pale pink, almost white veal with no marbling indicates milk-fed veal from 2- to 3-month old calves. Deeper pink or reddish veal is grass-fed, tougher, and lacks the mild flavor of young veal.

Beef should be well-marbled, containing striations of fat throughout the meat, which bastes it as it cooks. Steaks one inch thick or less and ground beef formed into 1-inch patties are ideal for quick-cooking. Well-trimmed cuts with little fat and no bone are the most convenient and most expensive; however, they also contain little waste.

"*Lamb*," "spring lamb," and "genuine lamb," should be 5-7 months old, and should have pinkish-red meat of a fine-grained texture. Some specialty shops carry milk-fed 6- to 10-week old lamb variously labeled "baby lamb," "hothouse lamb," or "milk-fed lamb." The meat is pale and soft with a delicate flavor. Yearling lamb and mutton are both older, tough, and have very strong, undesirable flavors. Steaks, chops, and noisettes up to one inch of thickness are ideal for quick cooking, and leg of lamb is also tender enough to be cut up and used in stir-fries.

Pork comes primarily from young animals, since older pigs are usually cured, smoked, or otherwise processed. This explains the fewer choices of cuts available compared to beef or lamb. Pork should have a gray-pink, fine-grained flesh, and the fat, which typically surrounds the meat instead of marbling it, should be firm and creamy white. Cuts from the center loin or sirloin, including chops, cutlets, and the tenderloin, will be tender enough for quick cooking.

Poultry that's fit for quick cooking should be young and tender, reserving older birds for the slow stew pot. Chickens labeled "broilers" or "fryers," ducks labeled "duckling," and turkeys sometimes labeled "yearling" are the youngest whole birds. Breasts from all three birds are the mainstay of quickly cooked, poultry-based meals, since they cook quickly and are readily available. Poultry is always best fresh, and if you can buy free-range chicken that hasn't been confined before butchering, it will be more flavorful. Ground poultry provides a low-fat alternative to ground beef, and many specialty shops carry turkey processed into flavorful sausages. Quail that are partially boned and split, usually found frozen, can be cooked as quickly as chicken breasts.

Using This Book

Since we are striving to eat healthier, lighter, and often on the run, food delineations have become blurred. Eating the traditional meat, starch, and vegetable is too much food for most of us, especially if accompanied by a salad and bread. Consequently, many hors d'oeuvre in this book double as lunches and late-night dinners; many salads, soups, and pastas may be served as a complete dinner with bread.

Most of us are cooking for fewer people than in the past, so every recipe is written to serve four people. Almost all can be halved, and most can be doubled.

Most of the recipes in this book are cooked so quickly that it pays to assemble the ingredients first. If you're deglazing a pan with wine until it reduces to a glaze in about 30 seconds, you don't want to be fumbling for a can of broth to dilute the glaze.

I've included the volume and weight of many fresh ingredients, so that if you want to buy them prepared, you'll have a measurement to follow. For instance, if you can buy Parmesan pre-grated, you'll know to use one-quarter cup.

If you cannot buy it grated, or if you prefer to store it in a chunk, you'll know that you should grate one ounce.

These recipes are written for prime efficiency. When the ingredients should be completely prepared before starting a recipe, the instructions are written accordingly. When you can save time by preparing ingredients while cooking, the recipe will show you how. Prepping is often accomplished while water comes to a boil for pasta, a chicken breast sautés, or butter melts, *so, if you're not devoting your total attention to a dish or if you're a novice cook, prepare the ingredients first*. Read through the recipe and peel, chop, dice, and assemble before cooking.

Finger Foods

Recipes

The term *hors d'oeuvre* conveys an image of fussy, time-consuming little morsels made painstakingly, one at a time. The quick cook's challenge is to provide appetizers that deliver pleasure and amusement with ease. It's also critical that the food can be eaten with ease, so no hostess hovers over a dish to be sure it remains at an acceptable temperature and no guest agonizes over spills on the carpet.

Almost any savory food can serve as an hors d'oeuvre, but the sandwich is the paradigm, since it is designed for snacking *sans* knife and fork. Use prepared bases such as tortillas, pita bread, wontons, pizza, and French and Italian bread, to provide portable food, easy to eat out-of-hand.

Preparing pots and slabs of food is more efficient than fidgeting over individual bitefuls, and often it's just as tantalizing. The robust aroma of Bagna Cauda (page 45), for instance, lures us to indulge in colorful, crisp raw vegetables and breads that tempt our eyes as well. Brook Trout Mousse (page 41) is equally tantalizing packed into a single decorative dish, surrounded by crostini, as it is spread onto individual canapés. And a whole wheel of Brie Baked with Chutney (page 56) is more dazzling to the eye than single bites that have been fussed over.

Malaysian-Spiced Shrimp Sauté

These shrimp make instant eye-catchers with bright yellow color and flecks of green. Their stunning appearance, however, takes a back burner to the fiery Malaysian blend of flavors. For a picture-perfect presentation, slice the scallions very thin on an angle by hand. If you have an hour to spare for marinating, blend all the ingredients together with the shrimp. Then they can be grilled instead of sautéed. If you like, use this recipe for an entrée, serve the shrimp warm over cold greens, or cool and chop them to use in a cold shrimp and egg salad.

4 scallions
2 cloves garlic
2 teaspoons ground turmeric
2 teaspoon ground coriander
1 teaspoon ground cumin
1/2 teaspoon crushed red pepper flakes
1 pound medium shelled and deveined shrimp (about 24)
2 tablespoons corn or vegetable oil
2 tablespoons fresh or bottled lemon juice
1 tablespoon fish sauce
4 leaves of leaf lettuce

Trim the scallions, cut them into quarters crosswise, and drop them with the garlic through the feed tube of a food processor with the motor running. Add the turmeric, coriander, cumin, and red pepper. Mince until finely chopped and blended, scraping down the sides of the bowl, as needed. Remove the spice mixture to a medium bowl and reserve.

If the shrimp have not been cleaned, peel and devein them. Toss the shrimp thoroughly with the spice mixture, preferably using your hands to coat the shrimp evenly.

Heat the oil in a heavy medium sauté pan or wok over medium-high heat. Add the shrimp, tossing frequently, until opaque and barely cooked, about 4-5 minutes. Pour in the lemon juice and fish sauce, and stir to coat the shrimp evenly. Spear each with a toothpick and serve immediately or at room temperature on a platter lined with lettuce leaves.

Yield: 24 hors d'oeuvre

Buy shrimp already peeled and deveined. Although they are sometimes a bit more expensive than those in the shell, often the savings in time is worth the price. Shelled Florida rock shrimp are available seasonally at a reasonable price. If using shrimp in the shell, a shrimp peeler removes the shells and intestinal veins in one quick move. The peelers take up little space, clean easily in the dishwasher, and cost only a very few dollars.

Turmeric, the brilliant orange ingredient dominant in most commercially prepared curry powders, will stain countertops and other surfaces. In fact, it's been used for centuries in Eastern cultures as a dye. To save time cleaning, be sure turmeric only touches glass, ceramic, stainless steel, and other non-porous surfaces.

Honey-Glazed Garlic with Cambozola

As garlic cooks, it becomes spreadable, mellow, and nutty in flavor. Roasted garlic is a staple in trendy Italian restaurants as an accompaniment to bread, but it takes an hour to attain its smoothness. For those who love the taste but don't have an hour to wait, garlic can be poached to tenderness in 15 minutes and sautéed with a bit of butter and honey to glaze it with a golden sheen. Paired with a rich, ripe cheese, it provides a deliciously smooth contrast to crusty French or Italian bread. I especially like thin baguettes for this hors d'oeuvre, since they deliver a lot of crust.

This is easy for entertaining, because it can sit out of the refrigerator for a couple of hours and, in fact, tastes better at room temperature. Also, the garlic gives guests a healthy alternative accompaniment for bread than heavier ingredients.

> **2 heads of garlic**
> **1 French baguette**
> **4 ounces ripe Cambozola, Brie, or Camembert,**
> **room temperature, if possible**
> **1 tablespoon unsalted butter**
> **1 tablespoon mild honey**

Bring 2 cups of water to boil in a heavy small saucepan. With a sharp knife, cut the papery tips off each head of garlic and discard. Separate the cloves, cut off the tips of any cloves remaining encased in paper, and simmer covered about 15 minutes, or until tender when pierced with a sharp knife.

While the garlic is cooking, slice the bread. Place it on a serving plate with the cheese. When the garlic is tender, drain it well and slip the skins off each clove. Melt the butter in the same saucepan over medium-low heat and sauté the cloves about 1 minute. Drizzle in the honey and sauté until golden and glazed. Arrange the garlic alongside the cheese, and serve warm or at room temperature.

Yield: 4 servings

Anytime you have the oven on at a moderate temperature for an hour, roast a head or two of garlic at the same time, so you'll have some on hand. When roasting in an oven, there's no need to separate the head into cloves, but cutting off the papery tip of each clove will make it easy to slip the cooked cloves out of their jackets. Brush the head with olive oil, cover, and roast one hour. Let the garlic cool, cover it, and keep refrigerated for up to a week. You can use it as a spread for bread or crackers, as an accompaniment to meat, or to thicken and flavor a sauce.

Many hors d'oeuvre that are rolled or wrapped need to be secured with toothpicks or bamboo skewers. If securing them prior to cooking in an oven, broiler, or grill, soak the picks in water at least 10 minutes before exposing to heat to prevent them from burning. If you have time, a one-hour soaking is best.

Sea Scallops with Basil and Prosciutto

The slightly anise aroma of fresh green basil, like the traditional accompaniment, Pernod, complements sweet sea scallops in flavor and color. Wrapped with paper-thin prosciutto, these bite-size morsels need no adornment but a light brushing of olive oil, which protects the prosciutto from drying out and preserves the basil's bright color. The prosciutto tightens around the scallop as it cooks, making a secure, flavor-packed appetizer.

6 paper-thin slices prosciutto
18 medium sea scallops (about 20 ounces total)
18 fresh basil leaves
olive oil

Preheat the oven to 425 degrees. Line a baking sheet with foil and reserve.

Cut each slice of prosciutto into thirds lengthwise. Top each scallop with a basil leaf and wrap it with a length of prosciutto. Place seam side down on the baking sheet and brush each hors d'oeuvre with olive oil. Bake until the scallops are barely cooked, about 5-10 minutes, depending upon their size. Serve immediately with or without toothpicks.

Yield: 18 hors d'oeuvre

Brook Trout Mousse on Crostini

Crostini, Italian bread bases that can be toasted or not, are typically made from rustic breads that keep well. Toasting them lends them a crispness that provides an appealing contrast to a creamy, smoky mousse and makes the topping easily transportable. Make them ahead and store airtight, if not using right away. If you don't have time to make crostini, serve the mousse on chunks of fresh celery, spears of Belgian endive, or purchased miniature bagels or crackers. Garnish with chives or tiny slices of scallion, if you like. Leftovers make a tasty sandwich spread for lunch or a bagel topping for breakfast.

> 8 1/4-inch slices Italian bread
> olive oil
> 2 scallions
> 4 ounces skinned, boned smoked trout
> 3 ounces cream cheese, room temperature, if possible
> 1 tablespoon fresh or bottled lemon juice

Preheat the oven to 350 degrees. Brush the bread slices with olive oil and place on a large baking sheet lined with foil. Bake until the centers are crisp, about 10 minutes.

Meanwhile, cut the scallions into quarters crosswise and mince in a food processor. Add the trout, cream cheese, and lemon juice, and purée until completely blended. Spread on the crostini and serve immediately. Alternatively, pack the mixture into a small crock or individual soufflé dish, cover, and chill until ready to serve. Surround the mousse with the crostini on a serving plate.

Yield: 8 hors d'oeuvre, about 1 cup of mousse

Food processors eliminate the need to bring cream cheese to room temperature, since they cut through it quickly to make it smooth. If not using a food processor, microwave the cheese to soften it, then whip it with a mixer.

Hot and Sweet Pecans

Hot, sweet, and addictive, these pecans can be served warm or at room temperature, and they'll keep for a month, if stored airtight. This recipe was inspired by Barbara Tropp's Fire-Dried Pecans that require 30 minutes of soaking in hot water, 30 minutes or more of drying in a low oven, and then 3-4 minutes of caramelizing on the stove. From start to finish, this adaptation won't require more than 15 minutes. Double the amount, if you like, and after making them once, adjust the heat, sugar, and salt to suit your own taste.

2 tablespoons sugar
1/2 teaspoon salt
2 tablespoons vegetable or corn oil
1/2 teaspoon hot sauce, such as Tabasco
1/2 pound (about 2 cups) pecan halves

Preheat the oven to 425 degrees. Line a baking sheet with foil and reserve. Blend the sugar, salt, oil, and hot sauce directly on the foil. Add the pecans and toss, preferably with your fingers, to coat them evenly.

Spread the pecans on the foil in a single layer and bake 8-10 minutes, or until the nuts are toasted. Check them occasionally to be sure they don't burn. Carefully grasp the foil with both hands, remove the foil to a wooden cutting board or heat-resistant counter top, and let the nuts cool at least 10 minutes. Serve warm or at room temperature. If not using immediately, let the nuts cool and store them airtight.

Yield: 2 cups

Tortellini in Basil Vinaigrette

Serve these bite-size, fresh-scented hors d'oeuvre immediately after cooking, if you like, or let them sit at room temperature for a couple of hours. If you'd rather not spend time making a vinaigrette on the spot, use 1 cup Caper Vinaigrette (page 226) or a store-bought favorite. Let the tortellini steep in the dressing warm, so they'll absorb some of the flavoring. Double this recipe for an entrée for four, if you like.

> 1/4 cup freshly grated Parmesan (about 1 ounce)
> 1/2 cup packed fresh basil leaves
> 2 tablespoons balsamic vinegar
> 1/4 cup olive oil
> salt and freshly ground pepper, to taste
> 9 ounces fresh tortellini, preferably stuffed with
>   Italian sausage

Bring a large pot of lightly salted water to boil. Meanwhile, if not using pre-grated Parmesan, grate it in a small food processor. Add the basil and mince together. Pour in the vinegar and drizzle in the olive oil in a stream. Adjust the seasoning with salt and pepper, if needed, and remove to a medium glass or ceramic serving bowl.

When the water comes to a boil, stir in the pasta and cook according to the package directions, about 6-7 minutes. Drain thoroughly and toss while hot with the vinaigrette. Serve with toothpicks or bamboo skewers, warm or at room temperature.

Yield: About 30 hors d'oeuvre

Always be careful not to overcook tortellini. Simmer them gently, since boiling vigorously can cause them to fall apart. Be especially cautious when using tortellini for finger food, since they must travel from service plate to mouth, suspended by only a toothpick.

Skewer individual hors d'oeuvre yourself or, for ease in preparation, offer a tiny glass of toothpicks or a tall glass with long skewers for guests to help themselves.

If not already pitted, lightly crush olives with the flat side of a knife or cleaver and discard the pits.

Kalamata Olive and Pimiento Bruschetta

In this recipe, robustly flavored olives, capers, and roasted red peppers embellish the traditional Italian bruschetta, made simply by rubbing garlic over toasted bread and drizzling it with olive oil. The intense flavors are matched by vibrant bright red, purple, and green colors, and pleasing contrasts in texture. The bruschetta is crisp outside and soft inside. Without a food processor, mince the garlic by hand, top with the drained ingredients, and continue to mince until fine-textured. You can buy commercially prepared olivada, typically made with olives, olive oil, lemon juice, vinegar, and herbs to spread on bread and broil, but the blend of flavors made here quickly is superior. Substitute Niçoise olives for the Kalamata, if you prefer.

> **4 cloves garlic**
> **1 4.5-ounce jar Kalamata olives (about 1 cup)**
> **1/2 cup bottled roasted red peppers (about 3 1/2 ounces)**
> **1 tablespoon capers**
> **8 large slices rustic Italian bread, 3/4" thick**
> **olive oil (about 2 tablespoons)**

Preheat the broiler. Drop the garlic through the feed tube of a food processor with the motor running. Drain the olives, peppers, and capers together, and mince them in the processor with the garlic to a fine, even texture.

Place the bread on a baking sheet and broil until golden. Turn and repeat. Spread the mixture evenly over the slices of bread, drizzle lightly with olive oil, and broil until heated through. Slice each piece into thirds, if desired, and serve immediately.

Yield: 8 large or 24 small hors d'oeuvre

Bagna Cauda with Crudités

Bagna cauda is a lusty, earthy dish traditional in the northwestern Piedmont region of Italy. It's packed with the flavors of anchovy and garlic, and Italians often shave bits of precious white truffle into the dish. In the Piedmont it's almost always served with sweet red bell peppers and cardoons, an edible thistle found in the Mediterranean. Make it a feast for the eyes with a colorful array of vegetables surrounding a warm decorative pot.

Slice a baguette and serve with the vegetables, if you like, to catch any flavorful drippings. Then guests can enjoy the bread, as well. This recipe allows for large portions, but it's delicious reheated. Also, it doubles and triples easily for a large gathering.

1 cup unsalted butter
1/4 cup olive oil
4 2-ounce cans anchovies
6 cloves garlic
crisp raw vegetables
grissini (long Italian breadsticks) or
    a French baguette, sliced

Place the butter and olive oil in decorative heatproof saucepan or fondue pot over low heat. While the butter melts, drain the anchovies and mince them together with the garlic. Blend the anchovies and garlic with the butter.

Whisk occasionally over low heat until the anchovies melt and the sauce becomes thick and smooth. Serve it at room temperature or over very low heat.

Surround with crisp raw vegetables and bread for dipping.

Yield: 4 servings

If you use an attractive saucepan or fondue pot to make the bagna cauda, you can cook and serve it in the same pan. Although it's traditionally kept warm over a low flame, the dish remains tantalizing at room temperature for an hour or so.

Buy prepared vegetables from the supermarket, if hurried. Broccoli and cauliflower florets and peeled baby carrots are often available in plastic bags in the vegetable section, and salad bars offer a variety of cleaned, trimmed vegetables.

If not using watercress right away, immerse the stems in water, cover loosely, and refrigerate. Slightly over-the-hill watercress, unappealing in salads, still makes tasty soups, sandwiches, and compound butters (see pages 220-224).

Watercress Triangles

Watercress stems, which contain all of the characteristic pepperiness we relish in the leaves, used to be relegated to the soup pot or worse, the garbage. The food processor makes quick use of the stems, mincing them in seconds. Since it also eliminates the need to bring cream cheese to room temperature, it ensures that this colorful spread can be ready in seconds. For special occasions, remove 16 of the leaves before mincing them. Dot each hors d'oeuvre with a leaf before serving.

To make watercress sandwiches, use twice the amount of bread. Sandwich the spread between two slices and then trim the crusts, if desired.

> **3 ounces watercress leaves and stems (1/2 medium bunch)**
> **5 ounces cream cheese**
> **1/4 teaspoon freshly ground pepper, or more, to taste**
> **4 slices firm, thin sandwich bread (8 slices, for sandwiches)**

Place the watercress in the bowl of a food processor and mince. Add the cream cheese and pepper, and blend until smooth, scraping down the sides of the bowl, as needed. Do not overprocess.

Spread on the bread and, if desired, trim the crusts. Slice each piece of bread from corner to corner, turn the two halves together ninety degrees, and repeat, creating 4 triangles. Serve immediately, or cover and chill.

Yield: 4 luncheon sandwiches or 16 hors d'oeuvre

Quesadillas with Searing Salsa

Quesadillas, flour tortillas that are filled with combinations of refried beans, cheese, or cooked meat and folded before cooking individually, are made quickly by cooking a number at once in the oven, open-faced. Baking quesadillas in an oven makes it possible to cook 4 at a time, instead of in single file in a hot pan on the stove, and using a wire rack in the oven allows both sides of the tortilla to crisp at once.

In the summer when you're inclined to crank up the grill, place the tortillas 4-6 inches above a solid bed of low coals and cook until the cheese melts. Not only do they make great finger food, but they also serve as a quick hot lunch. Top with a shredding of iceberg lettuce, chopped tomatoes and scallions, if you like.

For a special-occasion alternative, top the tortillas with thinly sliced smoked salmon. Spread with a mixture of 4 ounces of goat cheese blended with 2 tablespoons sour cream, 1 tablespoon prepared horseradish, and 2 teaspoons minced fresh dill. Grill or bake as below.

Use commercially prepared salsa, if you prefer.

1 8-ounce can refried beans
4 8-inch flour tortillas
1 4-ounce can diced green chilies
 (or jarred chopped pimientos)
4 ounces Monterey Jack cheese (or Cheddar)
1 jalapeño chili
1 1/4-inch thick slice medium red onion (about 2 ounces)
1/4 cup lightly packed cilantro leaves and tender stems
2 plum tomatoes
1 teaspoon fresh or bottled lime juice
1/2 cup sour cream (optional)

Preheat the oven to 400 degrees. Spread the beans evenly over the tortillas and arrange them on a large wire rack. Drain the chilies or pimientos, sprinkle them over the beans, and grate the cheese directly over the tortillas.

Bake until bubbling, about 8 minutes. Meanwhile, make the salsa. Remove the stem of the jalapeño and mince it together with the red onion and cilantro. Mince the tomatoes and blend in a bowl with the jalapeño mixture and lime juice.

Spread a heaping tablespoon of sour cream around the center of each tortilla, if desired. Cut each into sixths and serve immediately with the salsa on the side.

Yield: 4 luncheon servings or 24 hors d'oeuvre

Much of the heat of a chili resides in the seeds and membranes, so you can tame their fire by removing them. Anytime you're handling chilies, be sure to wear gloves or wash your hands thoroughly before touching sensitive areas, such as your eyes and nose.

Anytime ingredients need to be minced and added to a recipe simultaneously, mince them together to save time.

Chutney Roll with Apples

Curry, chutney, dried fruits, and nuts are a favorite hot and sweet combination of mine. Instead of reserving it only for a classic curry dinner (see Indian Curry Sauce, page 213), the flavors meld here into a versatile appetizer. Roll the log shape into chopped nuts or coconut, if desired, or pack it into a small crock or soufflé dish instead. Serve with carrots, celery, or rolled in prosciutto (see Pinwheel Smoked Salmon, page 51), if you prefer. Leftovers softened with mayonnaise make an unusual sandwich spread with cooked meats or seafood.

> **6 ounces cream cheese**
> **2-3 teaspoons curry powder**
> **1/2 cup prepared chutney**
> **1/2 cup toasted almonds or dry roasted unsalted peanuts**
> **1/4 cup raisins or dried currants**
> **2 red or green apples**

Blend the cream cheese with the curry in a food processor or with a hand mixer until smooth. Blend in the chutney, toasted almonds, and raisins, and process or whip until thoroughly blended. Spoon the mixture in about a 6-inch length onto wax paper and, using the paper as an aid, roll the cream cheese mixture into a tube two inches in diameter. Cover and freeze while slicing the apples. If not using immediately, cover, and chill the roll up to two days.

Core the unpeeled apples and slice into thin wedges. Serve the roll surrounded with the apple slices.

Yield: 4 servings

Pesto-Stuffed Mushrooms

A softened, creamy, herb-scented filling tops warm mushrooms in this simple hors d'oeuvre. Mushrooms make bite-size, ready-to-stuff packages for a variety of flavors. Instead of pesto and cream cheese, use any compound butter (see pages 220-224), if you like, as a filling. Instead of broiling, grill them on a lightly greased grill 4-6 inches above a solid bed of medium coals. If there's time, the mushrooms will shine beautifully if brushed with olive oil or melted butter first. Serve these as a vegetable side dish as well as an hors d'oeuvre.

> **16 medium-size mushrooms**
> **2 ounces cream cheese, preferably room temperature**
> **1/4 cup prepared pesto (or Poblano Pesto, page 167)**

Preheat the oven to 400 degrees. Twist the mushroom stems off the cap and reserve them for another use (Herbed Mushroom Soup, page 76). Place the caps top down on a baking sheet.

Blend the cream cheese and pesto in a small food processor or whip them together in a small bowl. Spoon the pesto into the cap of each mushroom. Bake until the filling softens and the mushrooms are warm but still firm, about 8 minutes. Serve immediately.

Yield: 16 hors d'oeuvre, serves 4 as a vegetable

To remove mushroom stems cleanly, hold the mushroom cap in the palm of your left hand and twist the stem off with your right. Never peel mushrooms since their outermost layer contains most of their earthy flavor. Mushrooms can dry out quickly, so use them within a day or two. Handle them gently and store them in a single layer, if possible, to prevent bruising.

Jalapeño Pizza, Tex-Mex

This zesty pizza combines ingredients typical of the Southwest, but be creative. Pizzas invite innovation. Any toppings that blend well when heated, including bits and pieces of leftovers, have pizza potential. Most pizza toppings also bake nicely on 8-inch flour tortillas or pita breads sliced in half. Since these crusts are lighter and thinner, cut the cooking time to about 5 minutes. If you prefer, substitute four plum tomatoes, sliced thin, for the tomato sauce.

> 1 8-ounce can tomato sauce (or 1 cup spaghetti sauce)
> 4 prepared 6-inch pizza crusts
> 1 jalapeño chili
> 1 1/4 cup grated Monterey Jack, Cheddar, or Mozzarella cheese
>   (about 5 ounces)
> 4 teaspoons minced fresh cilantro

Preheat the oven to 475 degrees. Spread the sauce evenly over the crusts. Remove the chili stem, mince the jalapeño, and grate the cheese, if not pre-grated. Sprinkle both evenly over the sauce. Place directly on a wire rack in the oven and bake until melted and bubbling, about 8 minutes. Remove from the oven, dot with cilantro, and cut each pizza into six slices. Serve immediately.

Yield: 4 lunch-size servings or 24 hors d'oeuvre

To slice pizzas efficiently, place on a cutting board and use a long sharp knife to cut in half. Move the board so you can easily cut across both halves simultaneously to cut each into thirds.

To mince cilantro quickly, hold the stems together and mince from the top of the bunch downward. The upper stems are flavorful and tender enough to use.

When baking a food containing ingredients that are likely to drip directly on a wire rack, place a sheet of aluminum foil on the bottom of the oven to catch any drips and avoid unnecessary cleanup.

Pinwheel Smoked Salmon

These pinwheel rolls of soft-textured, pink smoked salmon and onion- and caper-packed white cream cheese appear to be painstakingly put together. In fact, ten minutes is all you'll need from start to finish. If you have time, the salmon rolls will slice more easily if well-chilled. Substitute chopped fresh dill for the capers and minced scallion for the red onion, if you prefer.

1 1/4-inch thick slice medium red onion (about 2 ounces)
6 ounces cream cheese, room temperature, if possible
1 tablespoon capers, drained
6 ounces thinly sliced smoked salmon

Mince the onion and blend it with the cream cheese and capers in a small bowl. Spread the mixture evenly over the salmon slices. Roll the salmon and cut it crosswise into 1-inch lengths. Serve immediately or cover and chill until ready to serve.

Yield: About 24 hors d'oeuvre

To drain capers quickly, dip a measuring spoon into the jar to pick up a spoonful, hold it against the side of the jar to drain, and remove. (Since I love the piquancy of capers, I always have a jar on hand that's large enough for a tablespoon.)

To peel garlic cloves quickly, place the flat side of a knife or cleaver over the clove and hit the knife hard with the heel of your hand or your fist. The peel will separate from the garlic and the clove will be lightly crushed. If mincing garlic in a food processor, drop it through the feed tube with the motor running to help prevent the garlic from sticking to the sides of the workbowl.

The food processor doesn't slice scallions well at all, but many times perfectly sliced scallions are less important than their mild onion flavor. Here, mincing the scallions provides flecks of green, as well as flavor, throughout the hummus.

Hummus, Two Ways

Sharp lemon juice tempers the pungent flavor of garlic in this recipe for hummus, the classic Middle Eastern purée of chickpeas. Traditionally, this dish is started a day ahead and pounded with a mortar and pestle. Canned chickpeas and the food processor make this healthy hors d'oeuvre materialize in minutes. For a thinner spread, add some of the chickpea liquid, but this formula makes a firm, manageable, pick-up food. Substitute well-drained black beans for the chickpeas, if you prefer. Since they are moister than chickpeas, eliminate the olive oil and reduce the lemon juice to two tablespoons.

> **2 scallions**
> **3 cloves garlic**
> **1 15-ounce can chickpeas**
> **1/4 cup fresh or bottled lemon juice**
> **3 tablespoons olive oil**
> **salt and freshly ground pepper, to taste**
> **4 pita breads (optional)**
> **4 plum tomatoes, sliced (optional)**
> **1 ripe avocado, sliced (optional)**

Cut the scallions into quarters crosswise and drop with the garlic in the workbowl of a food processor with the motor running. Drain the chickpeas thoroughly, and pat them dry with a paper towel. Add them to the processor, and purée with the lemon juice and olive oil. Adjust the seasoning, if needed, with salt and pepper.

Pack into a small crock or individual soufflé dish to serve with crackers. Or split the pita breads in half crosswise, spread the hummus evenly inside each half, and top with tomato and avocado slices. Press down lightly on the halves and cut each into 3 rounded triangles. Serve immediately.

Yield: 24 hors d'oeuvre or 4 sandwiches

Oysters with Horseradish-Tomato Salsa

Horseradish salsa is a fresh, feisty update on traditional cocktail sauce. If you prefer, serve the oysters with Processor Aïoli (page 229) or Cajun Mayonnaise (page 228), or serve all three sauces as options. A party where guests take part is fun for all, so offer a willing guest an oyster knife and a glove to shuck the oysters. Be sure to keep the deeper shell on the bottom while shucking to collect the oyster liquor. If you don't want the liquor on the spot, save it for another use (Oyster Stew, page 71).

> 2 scallions
> 1 clove garlic
> 2 tablespoons prepared white horseradish, well-drained
> 2 teaspoons fresh or bottled lemon juice
> 4 ripe plum tomatoes
> salt and freshly ground pepper, to taste
> 24 small oysters in the shell

To make the salsa, cut the scallions into quarters crosswise and drop them with the garlic through the feed tube of a food processor with the motor running. Blend in the horseradish and lemon juice. Quarter the tomatoes and process until coarsely chopped.

Alternatively, mince the garlic and scallions together. Place in a small bowl and blend in the horseradish and lemon juice. Coarsely chop the tomatoes and blend with the horseradish.

Adjust the seasoning with salt and pepper, if needed. Cover and chill while opening the oysters. Shuck the oysters and arrange on a serving plate. Place the sauce alongside the oysters and serve immediately.

Yield: 24 hors d'oeuvre

An unorthodox trick to shucking oysters is to microwave them just until they begin to open. Then you can get an oyster knife or your fingers between the shells and separate them easily. The oysters will remain uncooked, for the most part. Place the oysters in a single layer, deeper shell down, on a microwave-proof serving dish. Cover, and microwave on full power 4 minutes, or until they just begin to open. Pry off the top oyster shells and discard. An easy cooked alternative is to place the oysters, deeper shell down, on a preheated outdoor grill. Cover and heat just until the shells begin to open, or cook thoroughly for those who prefer cooked shellfish.

Classic Cheese Fondue

Inherited as a tradition from my husband's family, this fondue has been a staple in our house for Sunday lunch for years. Since it works as a help-yourself hors d'oeuvre, there's very little fussing to be done by the cook. Once when I was out of the hallowed ingredients, I followed the same formula, substituting beer for the wine and Cheddar for the cheeses. With the addition of some dry mustard, we had a close resemblance to Welsh Rarebit. I prefer it now to Rarebit, since the dry French bread cubes stand up better than the toast traditional for the British dish. Don't hesitate to experiment with different cheeses. At times, I've married whatever bits of cheeses looked like they wouldn't last another day with fine results.

> **1 long baguette, preferably a day or two old**
> **1/2 bottle dry white wine (about 1 2/3 cups)**
> **3-4 tablespoons cornstarch**
> **14 ounces Gruyère, grated**
> **7 ounces Emmenthaler, grated**
> **splash of Kirsch (optional)**

Cut the baguette lengthwise in half. Roll a quarter-turn, and repeat. Holding the quarters together, slice across them, forming 3/4" cubes. Place on a serving dish and reserve.

Pour the wine into a fondue or a decorative heat-proof pot. Blend in the cornstarch and place it over medium heat. Bring to a simmer, stirring. Blend in the cheeses, stirring occasionally, until melted and smooth. Stir in the Kirsch, if using, and maintain the fondue over very low heat. Stir the cheese occasionally to prevent it from sticking to the bottom of the pot.

Provide long forks or bamboo skewers for guests to dip the bread into the cheese.

Yield: 4 luncheon servings, 30-40 hors d'oeuvre

Many specialty shops will grate cheese on request for no extra charge, and some groceries carry pre-grated cheeses. Keep in mind that pre-grated cheese, due to its greater exposure to air, will go bad quickly compared to solid blocks. Buy just what you'll use within a few days. Using a food processor or hand grater allows you to grate precisely the amount you need.

Cumin-Scented Wontons

Wontons make versatile vehicles for imaginative blends of herbs, spices, and butter. They bake quickly into thin, crunchy, 3 x 3 inch bites to use for hors d'oeuvre, snacks, and crisp breads to accompany soups and salads. The raw pastries are sold refrigerated, but they freeze well, if they are not to be used within a few days. If you prefer, use them plain, baked with just oil to brown them, or spread them very thin with a room temperature or melted herbed butter (see pages 220-224). Add your favorite dried herbs to the oil in this recipe, if you like. Since wontons are coated lightly with cornstarch, they won't stick to baking pans. If you don't intend to use them within a few hours, store them airtight. Serve these with Spicy Apricot Glaze (page 219), if you like, as a dipping sauce.

> **4 teaspoons olive oil**
> **1 1/2 teaspoons ground cumin**
> **16 3-inch square wonton wrappers**
> **kosher salt, for sprinkling**

Preheat the oven to 400 degrees. In a small bowl, blend the oil and cumin. Brush onto the wontons and place them in a single layer on a large baking sheet. Sprinkle evenly with the salt.

Bake 7-8 minutes, until golden and crisp. Serve warm or at room temperature.

Yield: 16 hors d'oeuvre

Not only does kosher salt have a superior flavor to table salt (see page 18), but it's easier to pick up with your fingers and sprinkle evenly on food. Reserve the table salt for eliminating garden slugs.

Brie Baked with Chutney

The sweetness and acidity of chutney provide a pleasant foil for creamy Brie. Often the small wheels lack the characteristic flavor of Brie, and they take a long time to ripen. Use this recipe with a wedge from a larger wheel, if you like, and heat it just until the cheese begins to ooze. At Thanksgiving and Christmas, I like to serve this with cranberry chutney, which lends it a festive touch and flavor.

1 4 1/2-ounce wheel of ripe Brie
1/2 cup prepared chutney
1/4 cup sliced almonds, preferably toasted
sliced French bread, crackers, or wedges of fruit

Preheat the oven to 250 degrees. Line a baking sheet with foil and spray it with nonstick vegetable spray. Place the Brie on its side and slice off the top rind. Place skinned side up on the foil and spread the chutney over it evenly. Sprinkle the almonds over the chutney.

Bake until the cheese is just soft, but not runny. Using a wide spatula, move the cheese to a serving plate. Serve immediately with sliced French bread, crackers, or fruit.

Yield: 4 servings

New Potatoes with Caviar

These festive bite-size hors d'oeuvre can be served warm, room temperature, or cold, and as a first course or finger food. Sprinkle the sour cream with finely minced chives instead of caviar, if you prefer, or substitute Brook Trout Mousse (page 41) for the sour cream topping.

Shop for caviar at a reputable store with rapid turnover, to ensure freshness and quality. The eggs should separate easily from each other, and should crunch, yet still be tender, when bitten. They should give a slightly salty, nutty flavor without a distinctly fishy aroma.

> **8 baby new potatoes**
> **1/2 cup sour cream**
> **2-3 tablespoons caviar**

Place the potatoes, unpeeled, in a saucepan that will hold them in a single layer. Cover them with one inch lightly salted cold water and bring it to a boil (see page 88). Reduce the heat and simmer until tender when pierced with a sharp knife, about 12-15 minutes, depending upon their size. Place in a colander and run cold water over the potatoes to cool them. Drain thoroughly.

Slice each potato in half and place on a serving plate. Top each with a small spoonful of sour cream and sprinkle with caviar. Serve immediately.

Yield: 16 hors d'oeuvre

If a fruit or vegetable needs to sit level, whether to serve or to cook it, slice a tiny sliver off the bottom and it will sit without rocking. Particularly when cooking by broiling, making a food sit perfectly level will prevent over- and undercooking, since all of the food will be the same distance from the source of heat.

Pita breads, available in most supermarkets, make versatile bases for sandwiches and spreads. They freeze well and defrost in minutes at room temperature. If frozen, let them sit at room temperature while making a filling or spread. Split them in half vertically to form an open pocket for sandwich fillings (Hummus, Two Ways, page 52) or in half horizontally to form two thin flat breads to accept a topping. Use a sharp knife or scissors to slice them horizontally.

Sun-Dried Tomato Pita Toasts

Powerful Mediterranean flavors highlight these crisp pita bites. Deep red sun-dried tomatoes, white goat cheese, fresh green oregano leaves, and pungent garlic make a colorful, full-flavored spread. If you don't have time to bake the pitas, pack the spread into a small crock or individual soufflé dish and surround with crackers or crudités. Mince the garlic, tomatoes, and oregano in small food processor, if you like, and then blend in the cheese and oil, but mincing the first three ingredients together by hand is just as easy.

> **2 pita breads (about 5 ounces total)**
> **2 cloves garlic**
> **4 sun-dried tomatoes packed in oil, drained**
> **1 tablespoon fresh oregano or 1 teaspoon dried**
> **1/4 cup goat cheese, such as Montrachet (about 2 ounces)**
> **2 tablespoons olive oil (or oil from the sun-dried tomatoes)**

Preheat the oven to 375 degrees. Open the pita breads to form two thin horizontal halves. Mince the garlic, sun-dried tomatoes, and oregano together and blend with the goat cheese and olive oil in a small bowl. Spread the inside of the breads evenly with the cheese mixture and place on an ungreased baking sheet. Bake 10-12 minutes, watching carefully, so the toasts do not burn.

Remove from the oven and slice or break each round into 6 pieces. Serve immediately or at room temperature.

Yield: 24 hors d'oeuvre

Quick Hors d'Oeuvre Ideas

- Wrap quartered kiwi, halved fresh figs, whole strawberries, or chunks of honeydew or cantaloupe with prosciutto and secure with a toothpick.

- Make an antipasto platter mostly from the pantry of marinated artichoke hearts, olives, pickled cherry peppers, peperoncini, cherry tomatoes, marinated mushrooms, and sliced meats and cheeses from the deli.

- Arrange sliced smoked salmon with thin sliced red onion and capers on a platter and serve with crackers or purchased mini-bagels.

- Serve smoked oysters, clams, or mussels with Cajun Mayonnaise (page 228) on crackers.

- Grill shrimp or thin strips of chicken breast or flank steak threaded on bamboo skewers and serve with Satay Sauce (page 214) for dipping.

- Spread any compound butter (see pages 220-224) or Poblano Pesto (page 167) on sliced French bread and heat; spread very thin on tortillas, pita halves, or wontons and bake until the butter is melted and the base is crisp.

- Spread prepared olivada or pesto on crostini.

- Blend small cooked shrimp with Cajun Mayonnaise (page 228) or Processor Aïoli (page 229) and serve on cucumber rounds, Belgian endive spears, or crackers.

- Cover room temperature Brie or cream cheese with jalapeño jelly and serve with crackers.

- Skewer chunks of fresh pineapple with cocktail sausages and broil just prior to serving.

- Serve Hot Sesame-Ginger Broccoli (page 186), Carrot Coins with Orange and Ginger (page 187), or Brown Sugar-Glazed Chestnuts (page 200) warm or at room temperature with toothpicks.

- Offer leftover pan-fried risotto (see page 175) warm or at room temperature.

- Skewer Sweet and Spicy Shrimp (page 132) or Scampi (page 134).

- Serve chicken wings and drumettes roasted with honey and ginger glaze (see page 140).

Soups,
Hot and Cold

Recipes

Some of the best soups I've ever made, unfortunately, cannot be repeated. Containers of "Purée of Leftover Soup" are always in my freezer, but I'm never sure of precisely what's in them. The star of the unrepeatables occurred when my freezer accidentally defrosted. The veal roast, frozen vegetables, and leftover lasagna were transformed into seven gallons of "Mystery Minestrone." Even after repeated servings throughout a year, I wish I could duplicate it.

Soups, unfortunately, have earned a reputation for slow-cooking. Seductive and soothing as they are, most in this chapter can be made in about 15 minutes. Cold Hot-Pink Borscht (page 65) and Tex-Mex Gazpacho with Avocado Purée (page 69) require no cooking at all, just a quick-fix in the food processor. Black Bean with Italian Sausage Soup (page 77) and Mussel Soup with Saffron and Cannellini (page 80), among others, make complete meals with a simple salad and some crusty bread.

Most soups freeze easily with little loss in texture or flavor. Freeze them in the quantity you will use and label them clearly. If I'm expecting company, I always make a few soups ahead and freeze them. If you crave soups that are based on seasonal ingredients, freezing provides a way to relish them all year round. If you're strapped for space, freeze soups with less stock than called for and entirely without cream. You can add these just before serving.

Soups are ideal for using up odds and ends hiding in the refrigerator. Old but still edible vegetables that you wouldn't permit raw in a salad make flavorful additions to soup. In fact, older vegetables, just like older cuts of meat, deliver more flavor than young ones. If you want to add vegetables that are frozen, add them directly to the soup pot. They'll defrost quickly in the hot stock.

Keep in mind that many cream soups are delicious without the cream. If following a recipe that calls for it, I usually taste it first, and then add it only if necessary or if feeling indulgent.

A 3-quart saucepan is ample for all the soup recipes in this chapter, a relief for those with small kitchens and weak biceps. I often use a wok to create soups. Their curve is ideal for sautéeing soup starters, such as onion, garlic, celery, and carrots, yet they'll hold ample liquid.

The mini-pimer or hand blender, blender, food mill, and food processor can all be used to purée soups. Hand blenders can be immersed in the soup itself, saving the transference of food from the pot to a processor or food mill. It not only saves dishes, but also the inevitable mess from moving the soup from one vessel to another. Blenders give soups the smoothest texture, but may require puréeing in batches, since they have a small capacity. Standard-size food processors can usually handle soup for four with ease, and most often they purée adequately. The surest way to achieve a smooth purée from a food processor is to place the solids with a little liquid in the workbowl. Process this mixture, adding just enough liquid to get a silky texture. Return the purée to the pot with the remaining liquid. Purée soups to any degree you want, leaving them a partly chunky texture or continuing to achieve a perfectly smooth soup.

Thai Peanut Soup

Coconut milk and peanut butter tame and enrich feisty spices in this bright yellow soup. It's stunning with a dried red chili floating in it, and an extra garnish of fresh cilantro leaves would be in order, as well. It takes all of 10 minutes to prepare. If you don't keep unsalted, smooth peanut butter on hand, regular and even crunchy will do. Peanut butter is a much more versatile ingredient than most people realize. Practically worldwide, it goes into soups, sauces, curries, and desserts, not to mention the ubiquitous American sandwich with jelly.

2 tablespoons corn or peanut oil
4 dried red chilies or 1 1/2 teaspoons crushed red pepper flakes
2 cloves garlic
1 small onion
1 tablespoon all-purpose flour
1/2 teaspoon ground coriander
1/4 teaspoon ground turmeric
1/4 teaspoon ground cumin
1/4 teaspoon freshly ground black pepper
4 cups chicken stock or broth
1 cup unsalted smooth peanut butter
1 cup canned coconut milk
salt and freshly ground pepper, to taste

Heat the oil in a heavy 3-quart saucepan over low heat. Stir in the chilies and cook 3 minutes. While the chilies are flavoring the oil, mince the garlic and onion. Increase the heat to medium-low, add the garlic and onion to the pan, and cook over medium heat until softened, about 5 minutes.

Add the flour, coriander, turmeric, cumin, and black pepper and cook, stirring, for 1 minute. Blend in the stock and bring the mixture to a boil over high heat. Whisk in the peanut butter and coconut milk, warm through, and season with salt and pepper, if needed. Serve immediately, including one red chili pod per bowl.

Yield: 4 servings

Cold Hot-Pink Borscht

Aside from its subtle blend of slightly sweet beets and tangy buttermilk and yogurt, this borscht is one of the most beautiful soups I've ever seen. It's truly hot-pink, and the optional garnishes make it a picture. Since fresh beets require slow cooking and messy peeling of their skins, take advantage of canned ones. Due to the high temperatures required to can vegetables, most of them lose texture and flavor, but beets are one of the best vegetables available canned. Since this soup is best served cold, it's practically instant soup.

When puréeing soup in a food processor, it's best to start with the solids and add just enough liquid to make a smooth mixture. If you add too much liquid all at once, the blades won't reach the solids as efficiently.

2 1-pound cans diced beets
1/4 small onion or 1 large shallot
2 cups buttermilk
1/2 cup plain low-fat or nonfat yogurt
2 tablespoons fresh or bottled lemon juice
1 teaspoon dried dill or 1 tablespoon minced fresh dill
salt and freshly ground pepper, to taste
sour cream (optional garnish)
4 sprigs fresh dill (optional garnish)

Drain one can of beets, discarding the liquid. Place the juice from 1 can and the solids from both in a food processor. Peel and quarter the onion. Add the onion to the beets and purée, scraping down the sides of the bowl as needed.

Pour in the buttermilk, yogurt, lemon juice, and dill, and purée completely. Season with salt and pepper, if needed.

If not serving immediately, cover the borscht tightly and refrigerate. When ready to serve, stir, pour into bowls, and garnish with a tablespoon of sour cream topped with a sprig of dill, if desired.

Yield: 4 servings

Most cheeses straight from the refrigerator grate more easily than at room temperature. Hard cheeses, such as Parmesan and Romano, have such a dense texture that they grate most easily at room temperature. A rotary drum grater is ideal for grating small amounts of hard ingredients, such as Parmesan or chocolate. Many restaurants use them to offer patrons an extra topping of Parmesan.

Stracciatella

This simple, delicate, Roman soup reminds me of Chinese egg drop soup, and it's equally easy to make. Its name means "little rags," referring to the streaks of egg that cook in the broth. Since there are so few ingredients in stracciatella, the quality of each is critical. Save your best-quality chicken stock for this soup.

> **4 cups chicken stock or broth**
> **4 sprigs fresh parsley, Italian flat-leaf, if possible**
> **2 eggs**
> **1/4 cup freshly grated Parmesan (about 1 ounce)**
> **pinch of freshly grated or ground nutmeg**
> **salt and freshly ground pepper, to taste**

Heat the stock in a medium saucepan. Meanwhile, remove the tough stems of parsley and mince the leaves. Whisk the eggs in a small bowl. If you haven't bought pre-grated Parmesan, grate it and reserve.

When the stock comes to a simmer, stir the eggs into the hot liquid. Stir constantly until the egg cooks, about 30 seconds. Stir in the parsley, Parmesan, and nutmeg. Season with salt and pepper, if needed, and serve immediately.

Yield: 4 servings

Roasted Red Pepper Soup

One of my favorite aromas is that of roasted red bell peppers. They enhance omelets, risottos, and pastas, and, with the help of a blender or food processor, they provide practically instant sauces and soups. If you're not inclined to roast and store your own, this recipe lets you enjoy that aroma effortlessly, by using jarred roasted peppers. Large jars of peppers are available in specialty stores. They're often less expensive and better in quality than the small jars commonly available in supermarkets. Garnish this soup, if you like, by floating croutons or cilantro leaves on the surface.

> **3 1/2 cups roasted red bell peppers (24 ounces jarred)**
> **3 cups chicken stock or broth**
> **3/4 cup cream**
> **salt and freshly ground pepper, to taste**

Purée the peppers with their liquid in a food processor or blender with just enough stock to make a smooth paste. Pour into a heavy medium saucepan along with the remaining stock and cream. Heat through, adjust the seasoning with salt and pepper, if needed, and serve immediately.

Yield: 4 servings

If you enjoy stashing food at its best, buy red bell peppers in late summer when they're a bargain. Roast them under the broiler or over a gas flame until completely charred and blackened. Peel and freeze them in usable quantities to enjoy all year. While roasting, bell peppers exude liquid that's packed with flavor. Be sure to save it. When roasting your own peppers, pack the liquid with the vegetable to use in soups and sauces. If using peppers from a jar, use all the liquid included in it. For a perfectly smooth Roasted Red Pepper Soup made with jarred peppers, strain them before pouring the smooth mixture into the saucepan, since some manufacturers leave a bit of the pepper skin in their product.

When slicing scallions or any long, thin vegetable or fruit, align them side by side, slice them in half crosswise, align the ends, and repeat. Your chopping time will be chopped into fractions.

Velvet Crab and Corn Soup

This soup is a delightful mishmash of colors and textures with bright green scallion slices, shreds of egg, lumps of pink crabmeat, and golden kernels of corn. It's a Chinese classic that's simple and rich. The soup cooks so quickly that it's critical to have all the ingredients prepared and within reach. There's no extra time to mince a scallion or peel fresh ginger. Cooked, shelled crabmeat is expensive, but since picking through it for fragments of shell is dreadfully time-consuming, I consider it worth the extra expense.

> 1 tablespoon corn or peanut oil
> 2 teaspoons minced fresh ginger
> 2 scallions, sliced thin
> 1 tablespoon sherry or rice wine
> 8 ounces cooked, picked-over crabmeat
> 1 quart chicken stock or broth
> 1 17-ounce can cream-style corn
> 1 tablespoon cornstarch
> 1 egg
> salt and freshly ground pepper, to taste

In a heavy medium saucepan or wok, heat the oil over medium heat. Stir in the ginger and scallion and stir-fry briefly, about 30 seconds. Pour in the sherry and crab and cook quickly to coat the crab with the seasonings.

Blend in the stock and corn. Bring to a simmer, stirring occasionally, over high heat. Meanwhile, blend the cornstarch with 2 tablespoons water in a small bowl and beat the egg lightly in another bowl. When the stock simmers, pour the cornstarch into the soup, stirring constantly. Simmer one minute. Blend the egg into the soup, stirring constantly so that the egg cooks in threads, about 30 seconds.

Adjust the seasoning with salt and pepper, if needed, and serve immediately.

Yield: 4 servings

Tex-Mex Gazpacho with Avocado Purée

The grassy aroma of cumin and soothing avocado highlight this Southwest version of the traditional uncooked Spanish gazpacho. Like the original, it's crammed with colorful chunks of fresh tomato, cucumber, and bell pepper floating in a tomato base. Omit the purée, if time doesn't allow, but it adds a cooling touch to an otherwise peppery soup. A dollop of sour cream or yogurt will make a fast substitute for the avocado. Add a dash or two of Tabasco to start, and add more to taste, if you like. This makes an ideal soup for entertaining, since you can make it a day or two ahead (except for the avocado), and it can remain at room temperature, if necessary, for an hour. Just before serving, shake or stir it well and pour into bowls.

Use your food processor to achieve whatever texture appeals to you. With on-off turns, you can control how finely vegetables become diced, minced, or puréed.

2 scallions
1 clove garlic
1 small green bell pepper
1/2 medium cucumber
3 plum tomatoes or 1 beefsteak tomato
3 tablespoons fresh or bottled lemon juice, divided
1 teaspoon ground cumin
3 cups tomato juice
1/4 teaspoon Tabasco Sauce, or more, to taste
salt and freshly ground pepper, to taste
1 ripe avocado, preferably Haas

Cut the scallions into quarters crosswise and drop with the garlic through the feed tube of a food processor with the motor running.

Cut the pepper in half and remove the seeds and stem. Cut it into 1-inch pieces. Peel the cucumber, cut in half lengthwise, and slice in 1-inch pieces across. Quarter the tomatoes. Add the bell pepper, cucumber, and tomatoes to the processor, and chop with on-off turns just until chunky.

Remove about half the vegetables to a large bowl. Purée the remaining vegetables with 2 tablespoons lemon juice and the cumin. Stir them into the bowl with the tomato juice and Tabasco. Adjust the seasoning with salt and pepper, if needed.

Without washing out the workbowl of the processor, purée the avocado with the remaining 1 tablespoon lemon juice, scraping down the sides of the bowl as needed. Ladle the soup into bowls and top each with 1/4 of the avocado.

Yield: 4 servings

Lemon Grass and Coconut Soup

Redolent with coconut and lemon, this Thai soup gets its heat from fresh green chilies and its richness from coconut milk. Lemon grass flavors Southeast Asian soups, curries, and condiments, lending a sweet, citrusy perfume. It's available from July until November and will keep a week or two in the refrigerator. Oriental and specialty food outlets carry lemon grass regularly, and, since the demand for it is increasing, it's becoming available at more and more groceries. If you can't get lemon grass fresh, use the juice and peel of 2 lemons for the soup. Both lemon zest and lemon grass contain citral, an oil that gives both their lively sour taste and fragrance.

Control the amount of sting from chilies according to your heat tolerance. Thai chilies, traditional in this soup, can be incendiary, a culinary favor to some and punishment to others. Serranos make a reasonable substitute when fresh Thai chilies aren't available. If you prefer less fire, either choose a less potent chili or use less of it. In this particular recipe, gauging heat is easy. Mince a bit of chili, add it to the stock, simmer a minute, and taste. Stop there if you need to, or add more, depending upon your sense of culinary adventure.

Choose lemon grass with thick bulbs, and, if the outer leaves are too dry, use only the inner, tender base. If you have any left, slice it thin and serve raw as a refreshing salad ingredient or freeze it for later use.

> 1 quart chicken stock or broth
> 2 cups unsweetened coconut milk
> 2 stalks lemon grass
> 2 fresh green chilies
> 1/2 cup fish sauce
> juice and peel of 1 lemon (or 2 tablespoons bottled
>   lemon juice and 2 teaspoons dried lemon peel)
> 1 8-ounce can straw mushrooms
> 1/2 teaspoon sugar
> salt and freshly ground pepper, to taste

In a large heavy saucepan, heat the chicken stock and coconut milk together. Meanwhile, remove and discard the tough outer stalks of the lemon grass and the stems from the chilies. Mince the lemon grass and the chilies together. Stir them into the broth with the fish sauce, and simmer 10 minutes.

While the broth simmers, peel and juice the lemon and mince the peel. Drain the mushrooms and stir them into the broth with the lemon juice, lemon peel, and sugar. Stir until the sugar dissolves and the mushrooms are heated through. Season with salt and pepper, if needed, and serve immediately.

Yield: 4 servings

Oyster Stew

Contrary to the popular notion of stew, this one is cooked in five minutes. It is as perfectly simple and straightforward as a soup can be, with just butter and milk or cream complementing plump, briny oysters and their flavor-laden liquor. The richer version with half milk, half cream (or half-and-half) is my favorite, but choose your own. Add a sprinkling of nutmeg, paprika, or freshly minced parsley, if you like. Some people stir in a tablespoon of butter or a handful of crushed crackers to each bowl as it's served.

1 quart whole milk (or 2 cups cream plus 2 cups milk)
1 quart shucked oysters, preferably extra-small, and their liquor
3 tablespoons unsalted butter
salt, freshly ground pepper and nutmeg, to taste

Bring the milk to a simmer in a heavy medium saucepan over medium-high heat. Meanwhile, place the oysters in a strainer and add the liquor to the milk.

While the milk heats, melt the butter in a heavy medium skillet. Add the oysters and cook 2-3 minutes, turning once, or until the edges fan open. Pour the oysters carefully into the milk and bring to a simmer. Do not allow to boil. Season with salt, pepper and nutmeg, and serve immediately.

Yield: 4 servings

Shucked oysters provide tremendous convenience. Look for oysters that are plump, shiny, and sweet-smelling. Keep them for up to a week, but for prime flavor, cook them right away. Placing the oysters in a strainer that fits over the pan of milk to make the stew will allow the oyster liquor to drain into the pan, thereby saving a dish.

To quickly slice a block of tofu into matchsticks, place it flat on a cutting board. With a long, sharp knife or cleaver, make horizontal slices about 1/4 inch apart throughout the block, then make vertical slices 1/4 inch apart, and it will separate into perfect *julienne*, or matchsticks.

Hot and Sour Soup

This classic soup features a balance of traditional Chinese flavors. If you prefer more heat or acidity, add more chili oil or vinegar, to taste. Use dried shitake mushrooms, if you can't find fresh ones, but allow 30 minutes for them to soak in hot water to reconstitute them. Be sure to remove their tough stems before slicing. When serving this colorful soup for a special occasion, stack the bamboo shoots and slice them into precise matchsticks to mimic the tofu. If you've never cut a block of tofu before, prepare it before starting the soup. Be sure to have all the ingredients within easy reach, since you'll only need ten to fifteen minutes from start to finish.

1 quart chicken stock or broth
4 medium shitake mushrooms
1 5-ounce can bamboo shoots
10 ounces fresh tofu
2 tablespoons white vinegar, or more, to taste
1/4 teaspoon chili oil, or more, to taste
2 tablespoons cornstarch
1 egg, lightly beaten
1 tablespoon soy sauce
1 teaspoon sesame oil
1 scallion, sliced thin
salt and freshly ground pepper, to taste

In a heavy 3-quart saucepan, bring the chicken stock to a simmer. While the broth heats, slice the mushrooms into 1/4-inch strips and drain the bamboo shoots. Add the mushrooms and bamboo to the stock and simmer about 3 minutes.

While the mixture simmers, drain the tofu and slice it into thin strips. Stir the tofu, vinegar, and chili oil into the broth and bring to a simmer again.

In a small bowl stir the cornstarch with 4 tablespoons of water and blend it with the stock, stirring. When the soup returns to a simmer, add the egg, stirring constantly until it cooks into shreds. Remove the soup from the heat and stir in the soy sauce, sesame oil, and scallion. Adjust the seasoning with salt and pepper, if needed, and serve immediately.

Yield: 4 servings

Roasted Peanut and Chili Pepper Soup

Two culinary exports from the New World that are now staples of African cuisine, chilies and peanuts, lend their intense, roasted flavors to this porridge-like soup. It's practically effortless, made almost exclusively from the pantry, so most of the work has been done for you. Its thick consistency is characteristic of African soups and stews, but thin it, if you prefer, with more milk. The blender yields a smoother soup than the processor, but both are equally tasty. Reserve a tablespoon of the diced chilies, if desired, to float on top of the soup for a garnish.

> **2 cups dry roasted unsalted peanuts (about 10 ounces)**
> **2 cups chicken stock or broth**
> **1 7-ounce can diced green chilies**
> **1 1/2 tablespoons Worcestershire sauce**
> **1 cup milk, or more, for a thinner soup**
> **salt and freshly ground pepper, to taste**

In a blender or food processor, purée the peanuts with the stock, chilies, and Worcestershire, scraping down the sides of the bowl, if needed. Remove to a medium saucepan and stir in the milk. Bring to a simmer, adjust the seasoning with salt and pepper, if needed, and serve immediately.

Yield: 4 servings

Some salted nuts have too much salt for my taste. If you have salted nuts on hand and a recipe calls for unsalted, remove as much salt as possible before using them. I often put them in a large strainer and shake them over the sink to remove most of the salt. You can get the same result by rubbing salted nuts between paper towels.

Pumpkin Soup with Curry

I have often made this slightly sweet, slightly hot soup with butternut squash and sometimes with yams. Canned pumpkin saves the cook baking time and makes it possible to make the soup all year round. The pumpkin lends subtle sweetness and enough body to make a substantial soup with no further thickening.

Curry powder, often shunned by culinary purists, is a combination of many spices that Indian cooks blend, roast, and grind at home. They choose the spices with each particular dish in mind, but the British invented a standard blend as a convenient imitation. I'm often discouraged from cooking Indian dishes after glancing at the lengthy list of ingredients, even though most are spices. So, despite its lack of authenticity, pre-blended curry is a gift to the cook in a hurry. The amount in this recipe is hefty. If you prefer less heat, cut it in half.

2 tablespoons unsalted butter
1 small onion
1 tablespoon curry powder
3 cups chicken stock or broth
1 1-pound can pumpkin purée
salt and freshly ground pepper, to taste

Melt the butter in a heavy medium saucepan over medium-low heat. Meanwhile, mince the onion. Add the onion and curry powder to the butter and cook until softened, about 5 minutes. Blend in the stock and pumpkin. Bring to a boil and simmer 5 minutes. Adjust the seasoning with salt and pepper, if needed, and serve immediately.

Yield: 4 servings

Creamy Poblano Soup with Tomatoes

This rich soup delivers very mild chili flavor that's perked up with chunks of colorful, lively, acidic tomato. Warm and soothing hot, creamy poblano soup is surprisingly tasty, if more bland, cold. Substitute 1/2 cup ricotta for half of the cream cheese in this recipe, if you like, and substitute low-fat cream cheese for regular. Substitute 5-6 fresh poblano peppers, roasted and peeled, for the canned.

2 tablespoons olive oil
1 small onion
3 cups chicken stock or broth
4 plum tomatoes or 2 large tomatoes
1 7-ounce can chopped green chilies
8 ounces cream cheese
4 ounces plain yogurt
salt and freshly ground pepper, to taste
cilantro (optional garnish)

Heat the olive oil in a heavy medium saucepan. Meanwhile, peel, quarter, and mince the onion in a food processor. Add it to the oil and cook about five minutes, stirring occasionally. Add the stock, bring to a boil, and simmer uncovered about 10 minutes.

Meanwhile, quarter the tomatoes and, without washing out the workbowl, chop them coarsely in the food processor. Remove them to a serving dish, and reserve. Blend the chilies with cream cheese in the processor. Pour in the broth mixture and purée until smooth. Return to the pan. Whisk in the yogurt and tomatoes and heat through. Do not allow to boil. Adjust the seasoning with salt and pepper, if needed, and pour into warm bowls. Top with cilantro, if using, and serve immediately.

Yield: 4 servings

Tomatoes will taste best if left unrefrigerated and used within a day or two. Use large tomatoes when in season, but plum or Roma tomatoes have more flavor consistently throughout the year. Avoid them if they feel hard. Smell the stem ends of tomatoes to detect ones that are likely to have a lot of flavor.

Herbed Mushroom Soup

Earthy, fragrant, and rich, this mushroom soup bears no resemblance to canned varieties. It's acceptable without the cream, but outstanding with it. Mushrooms with open caps, or with their gills showing, are older than those with closed caps. As long as older mushrooms aren't slimy or dark-tinged, they'll deliver more flavor than young ones. Since this soup is puréed, flavor takes precedent over looks and texture. On the occasion that I find almost-over-the-hill mushrooms on sale, I make batches of mushroom soup and freeze it.

2 tablespoons unsalted butter
1 small onion, peeled
1/2 pound mushrooms
3 tablespoons all-purpose flour
3 cups chicken stock or broth
1/4 teaspoon dried thyme
1 cup cream
1/4 cup sherry (optional)
salt and freshly ground pepper, to taste

Melt the butter in a large heavy saucepan over medium-low heat. Mince the onion in a food processor, add to the pan, and stir occasionally until softened, about 4 minutes. While the onion is cooking, mince the mushrooms in the processor. Add them to the onions and cook, stirring, 5 minutes.

Sprinkle the flour over the vegetables and cook 1 minute. Increase the heat and blend in the stock and thyme. Bring to a simmer while stirring, until slightly thickened. If you have time, let the soup cool slightly.

Purée in the processor. Return the soup to the saucepan, stir in the cream and sherry, and adjust the seasoning with salt and pepper, if needed. If the soup has cooled, reheat it and serve immediately.

Yield: 4 servings

To save time, buy clean mushrooms. Until recently, cooks assumed that mushrooms shouldn't be washed because they absorbed water. We were told either to wipe them clean with a paper towel or a gentle mushroom brush. Thanks to food science guru Harold McGee, whose straightforward experiments have dispelled many culinary myths, we can wash mushrooms again without worry. If you have many to wash, swish them in a large bowl of water and drain.

Black Bean with Italian Sausage Soup

Black bean soup has been a staple at our house for years. The beans soak over-night and then stew with ham hocks and vegetables for hours. Then I purée the mixture in the food processor in batches. As many times as I've made it, I can't seem to avoid messing up the entire kitchen. It's such an ordeal that I make a year's supply at once, freezing it in carefully portioned sizes that I'll serve later. This recipe is quick enough to make on the spot.

Lots of trendy black bean soup recipes are highly spiced with Caribbean or Southwestern flavors; they have their place, but I'm happy to enjoy the subtlety of the beans, enhanced with a bit of smokiness and, perhaps, some sherry. The Italian sausage provides lots of flavor and seasonings without overwhelming the beans, and sherry is a traditional enhancer.

> *If you intend to use a food processor to purée a soup, save time by preparing the ingredients for it in the processor and returning the workbowl to the machine without washing. Most processors are made of such heavy plastic that they can handle hot liquid straight off the stove. If you have time, however, it's safer to let it cool a bit before pouring into the workbowl. Puréeing mostly the solids first (see page 65) makes the temperature change gently compared to pouring in its full capacity of liquid.*

- 8 ounces bulk Italian sausage
- 2 cloves garlic
- 1 onion
- 2 cups chicken or beef stock or broth
- 2 15-ounce cans black beans
- 1/4 cup dry sherry (optional)
- salt and freshly ground pepper, to taste

In a heavy medium saucepan, cook the sausage on medium-low heat until it exudes some of its fat. Meanwhile, mince the garlic, coarsely chop the onion, and stir them into the sausage. Increase the heat to medium-high as the sausage releases its fat, and break it into small pieces as it cooks. When the onion is tender, in about 5 minutes, pour off any excess fat.

Increase the heat to high and pour in the stock and beans with their liquid. Simmer 5 minutes and purée, if desired. If necessary, reheat, stir in the sherry, if using, and adjust the seasoning with salt and pepper. Serve immediately.

Yield: 4 servings

To chill a soup quickly, heat only the ingredients that must be cooked. Pour them in a metal bowl (metal transfers heat more quickly than glass or ceramic) and place the bowl directly over and touching ice contained in a larger bowl. Whisk occasionally. Alternatively, place the bowl in the coldest part of the freezer. Stir occasionally, until the mixture is as cool as you like, but do not allow it to freeze.

Rhubarb-Strawberry Soup with Port

Sweet soups, traditional in Scandinavia, can be served for dessert or as a refreshing first course or luncheon soup. When rhubarb and strawberries are plentiful in spring, make a triple batch to freeze without the port or cream. You can add these ingredients when defrosting and enjoy the soup all year long. Port adds depth of flavor, but if you prefer, use a dry white wine and increase the sugar to 1 1/3 cups. I enjoy it with and without the enrichment of cream, and it can be served at room temperature, or, as is traditional, cold.

1 pint fresh strawberries, trimmed and quartered, if large
2 cups fresh rhubarb, sliced (2 average stalks)
1 cup sugar
1 cup port
1 cup chicken stock or broth
1/2 cup cream
extra berries for garnish (optional)
4 sprigs of fresh mint (optional)

Place the strawberries, rhubarb, and sugar with 1/2 cup water in a heavy medium saucepan. Bring to a simmer, stirring, over medium-high heat. Cover, reduce the heat to low, and cook until the fruits are tender, about 8 minutes. Purée with the port, stock, and cream. Chill the soup over ice or in a freezer (see sidebar). Serve cold or at room temperature, garnished with an extra strawberry or a sprig of fresh mint.

Yield: 4 servings

Tortellini and Vegetable Soup

This hearty Italian soup, accompanied by a salad and bread, makes a quick, balanced meal packed with flavor. Fresh vegetables, pasta, and herbs complement well-spiced Italian sausage, typically flavored with garlic and fennel or anise. Fresh stuffed pastas, such as ravioli and tortellini, are available in the refrigerated sections of most supermarkets, and they freeze well, if not using within a few days. If you don't have a well-seasoned pan, add a bit of olive oil to the pan while cooking the sausages to prevent them from sticking.

Chop fresh basil just before adding it to a soup, salad, or sauce. Soon after cutting its fragrant leaves, they turn black and lose their pristine green appearance.

    8 ounces mild or hot Italian link sausage
    1 small red onion (about 4 ounces)
    3 cups beef stock or broth
    1 9-ounce package fresh spinach tortellini
    1 small zucchini
    1 plum tomato
    1 sprig fresh basil
    salt and freshly ground pepper, to taste

Align the sausages and slice them crosswise into 1/2-inch pieces. Place in a heavy medium saucepan and cook over medium-low heat, stirring occasionally to keep them from sticking. Meanwhile, coarsely chop the onion and add it to the sausage. Cook until the sausage is firm and no longer pink, increasing the heat as the sausage releases some of its fat. Drain off any excess fat.

    Pour in the stock over high heat and, when boiling, add the tortellini. Reduce the heat to a simmer and cook gently until the pasta is just tender, about 7-10 minutes. Meanwhile, dice the zucchini and tomato and add to the stock during the last 5 minutes of cooking. Meanwhile, chop the basil and stir it into the soup. Adjust the seasoning with salt and pepper, if needed, and serve immediately.

Yield: 4 servings

To dice tomatoes, onions, and shallots quickly, use the root ends as bases. With the root end on a cutting board, make parallel downward slices without cutting through the base. Turn the vegetable a quarter-turn and repeat, slicing downward lengthwise at 90-degree angles to the first cuts without slicing through the base. Turn the vegetable onto its side and, holding the base, slice downward across the width of the vegetable and make parallel cuts downward.

Mussel Soup with Saffron and Cannellini

This soup is meaty with mussels and white beans, and the tomatoes provide a pleasant, colorful counterpoint. Since the mussels make their own broth, the soup wafts a briny aroma complemented with saffron. The dark mussel shells, creamy meat, bright red tomatoes, and white cannellini make the soup a picture with no adornment. Serve with crusty French or Italian bread and a light salad for a complete meal.

3 dozen mussels
3 tablespoons unsalted butter
2 cloves garlic
1 1/2 cups dry white wine
1/4 teaspoon saffron threads
4 plum tomatoes
1 15-ounce can cannellini beans
salt and freshly ground pepper, to taste

Scrub and debeard the mussels (see page 130), if necessary. Melt the butter in a heavy large saucepan over medium-low heat. Meanwhile, mince the garlic, add it to the butter, and sauté until softened, about 3 minutes. Add the mussels, white wine, and saffron. Increase the heat, cover, and steam, shaking the pan occasionally, until the mussels open. With a slotted spoon, remove the mussels to four soup bowls, discarding any that did not open.

Simmer the broth about 4 minutes. Meanwhile, dice the tomatoes and add them to the broth with the beans and their liquid. Bring back to a simmer, adjust the seasoning with salt and pepper, if needed, and serve immediately over the mussels.

Yield: 4 servings

Side Dish and Main Course Salads

Recipes

It was a salad that convinced me I had joined the ranks of desperate cooks deprived of time. One evening I dashed into the kitchen with twenty minutes until dinner, started an entrée and vegetable, and realized something was missing. That was when I made good on a threat to serve my husband the quintessential cafeteria salad: a quarter-wedge of iceberg lettuce with gooey orange bottled dressing.

Salads, without a doubt, are my favorite course, but they take time to prepare. At the very least, they require the cleaning of ingredients. At their most demanding, they require cleaning, trimming, chopping, and cooking and cooling various meats and vegetables, not to mention baking croutons and toasting nuts. Instead, use salad bar ingredients, and take advantage of blends of prepared greens that are conveniently packaged in resealable plastic. Don't hesitate to take advantage of their convenience, even for salads to be made at home.

Enlist the ones you're feeding to do some of the work. You can save a lot of time by serving a salad in layers or large chunks and arming your guests with a knife and fork. Stack whole lettuce leaves instead of tearing them into bite-size pieces, serve a small bunch of watercress with only the toughest stems trimmed, quarter tomatoes and accompany with a wedge of cheese. Expensive restaurants serve dressed leafy greens stacked high and dub them lovely presentations, so serve them with confidence at home.

Salads invite innovation. They require no precise balance of ingredients, as in baking, for instance, to succeed. Even an untrained eye can pick and choose from beautiful greens, fruits, and vegetables and create a lovely salad. Nature has given us a guide, since different colors and textures of food provide us with different nutrients. Consequently, a varied, colorful array of salad ingredients is the tastiest and most interesting to eat, and also the most valuable nutritionally. Add bits of leftover cooked meats, pasta, and cheeses, or pieces of raw vegetables and fruits that would otherwise go unused.

Many of the salads in this chapter that involve cooking ingredients are served warm, so you can enjoy them immediately. Warm vegetables served with cold greens and a room temperature dressing provide interest aside from the usual texture and taste, but also in temperature. Alternatively, cooked vegetables can be cooled quickly by running cold water over them in a strainer or colander until they are chilled. A bath in ice water is ideal, but dealing with a large bowl and ice cubes isn't my idea of quick-cooking. If changing the temperature of ingredients, keep in mind that chilled ingredients need more seasoning than room temperature ones, since both heat and cold anesthetize the taste buds a bit.

All of the dressings in this chapter are made-to-order for each salad, so you don't have to turn back and forth between pages of this book. To cut down on dishes, most of the dressings are made directly in a salad bowl. Many of these dressings, however, I make in quantity, chill, and store to enjoy at a moment's notice. If you have prepared salad dressings ahead of time, take them out of the refrigerator a half hour, or as soon as possible, before serving. Olive oil congeals and becomes cloudy when chilled, but once it warms, it becomes clear and pourable again. When pressed for time, uncap the dressing, microwave it briefly, recap, and shake. Repeat, if necessary, until the dressing is blended. Often, however, the tastiest dressing is simply a quality vinegar, extra-virgin olive oil, and a bit of seasoning blended on the spot.

Double any side-dish salads, if you like, to serve as luncheon or dinner entrées, or cut main course salads in half to serve as a side dish. Reserve salad leftovers for sandwich fillings or possible soup ingredients.

Red Grape and Curly Endive Salad

This salad is a lively contrast of flavors and color. The curly endive is dark green with a slightly bitter taste, while Boston lettuce is pale and subtle in flavor. Sweet deep red grapes and white cheese dot the greens, providing welcome sweetness and saltiness. I often make this for guests, since it's especially eye-catching, but it's easy enough to prepare every night of the week. Substitute a mild goat cheese, such as Montrachet, if you prefer, for the feta. For a special dinner, slice the grapes in half.

> 1/4 cup extra virgin olive oil
> 2 tablespoons balsamic vinegar (or a fruit-based vinegar)
> 1 1/2 cups seedless red grapes
> 2/3 cup crumbled feta or blue cheese
> 2 scallions, sliced
> 1/2 small head curly endive (2 cups torn, lightly packed)
> 1/2 small head Boston lettuce (2 cups torn, lightly packed)
> salt and freshly ground pepper, to taste

Whisk the olive oil and vinegar in a large salad bowl. Add the grapes, cheese, and scallions to the bowl. Tear the endive and lettuce into bite-size pieces and toss thoroughly with the dressing. Adjust the seasoning with salt and pepper, and serve immediately.

Yield: 4 side-dish servings

Curly endive stands up well to heavy salad ingredients and dressings. Its slightly bitter flavor is a welcome counterpoint to strong and/or sweet flavors, and its firm, lasting texture withstands heavy ingredients. The darkest green part of endive is the most bitter and the white, the least. Some bitterness in food, especially when countered with sweet ingredients, is pleasant, so use the parts of endive that suit your own taste.

If keeping avocado halves intact, gently squeeze the half with the pit to remove it. Then peel the halves and brush with lemon juice, if not using immediately. Avocado skinners provide a quick, tidy alternative to peeling by hand. The skinners have a blunt, curved blade that slips between the peel and meat of an avocado half, freeing it in one neat piece. It's also handy for removing the pit.

Corn and Pepper-Stuffed Avocado

Avocados are the richest and most versatile of fruits. They can be served hot, cold, in solid halves, puréed, sliced, diced, or fanned out to make an elegant presentation (see page 109). Due to their cooling qualities, they make an ideal foil for spicy foods, such as the cumin and peppers in this colorful salad. Add diced ham or leftover cooked poultry or seafood, if you like, for a stunning entrée salad. For variety, stuff avocado halves with Warm Cajun Seafood Salad (page 110). Instead of tossing the seafood with lettuce, pile it on avocados arranged on lettuce leaves.

Substitute frozen corn, if you like. Cook it in water just until it comes to a boil. Drain, and run cold water over it until cool.

3 tablespoons olive oil
1 tablespoon fresh or bottled lemon juice
1/2 teaspoon ground cumin
1 12-ounce can water-packed corn, drained
6 pickled red and green cherry peppers, stemmed and minced
2 scallions, sliced
1 cup cilantro leaves and tender stems, minced
salt and freshly ground pepper, to taste
2 ripe avocados, preferably Haas

Blend the olive oil, lemon juice, and cumin in a medium bowl. Add the corn, peppers, scallions, and cilantro to the dressing. Adjust the seasoning, if needed, with salt and pepper.

Halve, pit, and, peel the avocados. Mound the corn mixture over them and serve immediately.

Yield: 4 side-dish servings

Sun-Dried Tomatoes
with Chèvre and Arugula

In this particular salad, the less time spent tearing greens and tossing them, the more stunning the presentation. Layer the lettuce and arugula, and top with the white chèvre and deep red sun-dried tomatoes. Keeping these colorful ingredients separated heightens their dramatic contrasts of flavor, texture, and color.

Arugula, peppery and pungent, is more widely favored in Europe than here. Occasionally it's served by itself, but its power is better diluted with milder ingredients (Arugula Butter, page 220). You may find it under the names rocket, garden rocket, rugula, or rucola, as well.

> 3 tablespoons olive oil
> 1 tablespoon balsamic vinegar
> 1 teaspoon Dijon mustard
> 4 cups lightly packed torn leaf lettuce
> 4 cups lightly packed torn arugula
> salt and freshly ground pepper, to taste
> 1/2 cup crumbled mild goat cheese, such as Montrachet
> 3/8 cup sun-dried tomatoes packed in oil, drained, sliced
> salt and freshly ground pepper, to taste

In a large salad bowl whisk the olive oil, vinegar, and mustard. Toss the dressing with the leaf lettuce and arugula. Adjust the seasoning, if needed, with salt and pepper, keeping in mind that the cheese will be salty. Divide the greens among salad plates. Sprinkle with the cheese and tomatoes, season with salt and pepper, if needed, and serve immediately.

Yield: 4 side-dish servings

When pressed for time, use the inner leaves of leaf lettuce for salad material, since they require practically no cleaning. Save the tougher outer leaves that often harbor dirt for sandwiches. You won't need to clean as much lettuce at once, and tenderness is less important in a sandwich.

Sun-dried tomatoes, much like dried fruits, are concentrated in texture and crammed with flavor. Dry ones need time to be reconstituted in a liquid or oil, so stick to those already packed in oil. As a bonus, the tomato-flavored oil can be used in salad dressings and sauces. When plum tomatoes are plentiful and inexpensive, buy them in quantity to "sun-dry" your own. Slice them in half lengthwise, and bake (dry) in a slow oven until they lose most of their moisture and turn chewy and sweet. Pack them into jars and cover with olive oil. They'll keep a year in the refrigerator, and they make useful gifts.

Placing the potatoes in cold water and then bringing the pot to boil prevents the potatoes from bursting when plunged into hot water. It also saves the cook from the unwelcome splatter of hot water. Use the same treatment to cook hard-boiled eggs to prevent the eggs from cracking.

Anchovies contain so much salt that it's a good idea to drain them of their oil, rinse them with water, and pat them dry with paper towels before using in a recipe. If you have plenty of time, let them soak in a bowl with a lot of water to leach out more of the salt.

Vegetable Salad with Mediterranean Flavors

The intense, robust flavors of anchovies, capers, olives, red onion, and olive oil, typical of the Mediterranean, dominate this colorful salad. Eat it right away or chill it for an hour. It's perfect for picnics or entertaining, since it's even tastier at room temperature than cold. To complement the salad further, serve it in a decorative bowl or on lettuce leaves.

6 baby red potatoes
2 tablespoons capers
3 anchovies, rinsed and dried
3 tablespoons fresh or bottled lemon juice
1/2 cup olive oil
salt and freshly ground pepper, to taste
6 ripe plum tomatoes
1 small red onion (about 4 ounces)
1/4 cup ripe Mediterranean oil-packed black olives

Place the potatoes in a heavy medium pot, cover with water, and bring to a boil over high heat. Cover and simmer until tender when pierced with a sharp knife, about 15 minutes. Meanwhile, purée the capers, anchovies, and lemon juice in a food processor or blender. With the motor running, drizzle in the olive oil and adjust the seasoning, if needed, with salt and pepper.

Cut the tomatoes and the onion into thin slices and place in a medium salad bowl with the olives. When the potatoes are tender, drain them and run cold water over them until they are cool to the touch. Slice the potatoes thin and toss with the tomato and olive oil mixture. Serve immediately, or chill up to 24 hours.

Yield: 4 side-dish servings

Mixed Fruit
with Strawberry-Mint Dressing

Fruit salads are a favorite of mine, especially when combined with garlic or onion and lots of leafy greens. If your family isn't one to eat fresh fruit out-of-hand, incorporating them into salads is a sure-fire way of getting them into your diet. Fruit-based vinegars, such as raspberry, with their piquancy and floral fragrance, always enhance salads containing fruit. I keep Berry Vinaigrette (page 225) as a refrigerator staple for dinners when I'm especially rushed. The sweetness and acidity in this strawberry dressing would also be the perfect foil for a spinach salad with ham or bacon.

> 1 small clove garlic
> 3/4 cup strawberries, trimmed
> 2 tablespoons raspberry vinegar
> 4 teaspoons mint jelly
> 1/3 cup olive oil
> salt and freshly ground pepper, to taste
> 1 avocado
> 1 banana
> 1 cup red seedless grapes
> 6 cups lightly packed torn red leaf lettuce

Drop the garlic through the feed tube of a food processor with the motor running. Add the berries to the workbowl with the vinegar and jelly, and purée. With the motor running, drizzle in the olive oil. Adjust the seasoning with salt and pepper, and remove the dressing to a large salad bowl.

Peel and dice the avocado, slice the banana, and add them to the bowl with the grapes and lettuce. Toss thoroughly and serve immediately.

Yield: 4 side-dish servings

Most fruits, including avocados, will ripen more quickly enclosed in a brown paper bag at room temperature. Haas avocados, those with rough black skins, have a smaller pit and less water content than other varieties, so they're more flavorful and a better buy, to boot.

Leek Bundles in Mustard Vinaigrette

Leeks typically harbor dirt in their layers of flesh. To clean them easily, trim off the root and slice the remaining vegetable crosswise. Swish in a bowl of water and drain the leeks, leaving the grit in the bowl. If using the length of the leeks, hold the base and make lengthwise slits through the vegetable. Swish and drain as above.

Cooked, cooled leeks are often served in a mustard-based vinaigrette as a first course or salad. This is a version that looks dramatic and fussy, but takes minutes. Each serving consists of a lettuce leaf topped with two small leeks fanned out and bound at their bases with a wrapping of paper-thin prosciutto. Aficionados leave the fat on prosciutto, since its moistness and sweetness maintain a delicate balance with the firm, dry, and salty characteristics of the meat. The leeks are best served warm, so they will absorb the dressing; however, if you want them cold quickly, run the cooked leeks under cold water until they are cool to the touch. Be cautious adding salt to this recipe, since both the mustard and prosciutto are high in salt.

8 small leeks
2 teaspoons sherry, orange sherry, or wine vinegar
1 teaspoon Dijon mustard
1/4 cup olive oil
salt and freshly ground pepper, to taste
4 paper-thin slices prosciutto
4 leaves red leaf lettuce

Bring 2 inches of lightly salted water to boil in a heavy medium saucepan. Meanwhile, trim off the leek root and the tops down to the palest green. Split them lengthwise to within 1 1/2" of the root ends. Make a quarter-turn and split again. Wash to remove any grit or sand. Add the leeks to the water and cook until tender when pierced with a sharp knife, about 8-10 minutes.

Blend the vinegar and mustard in a small bowl. While whisking, drizzle in the olive oil. Season with salt and pepper, if desired, and reserve.

Trim the prosciutto of any excess fat, if desired. Line 4 salad plates with lettuce leaves. When tender, drain the leeks thoroughly. Double each slice of prosciutto lengthwise, wrap it around the base of 2 leeks, and place on the lettuce. Repeat until all the leeks are wrapped. Drizzle the dressing over the leeks and serve immediately.

Yield: 4 side-dish servings

Tropical Fruit in a Curry Vinaigrette

This curry vinaigrette is very mild for my taste; however, mangoes are so expensive most of the year, I don't dare mask their delectable flavor. Taste the dressing before adding the fruit, and whisk in as much curry as you like. The amount of curry will also vary with the brand that you buy, since the powders differ in the amounts of heat they deliver. Sprinkle the salad with coarsely chopped macadamia nuts for a luxurious tropical treat.

Due to their large, tenacious pits, mangoes are easily mangled. I find it easiest to peel them first and then, with a sharp knife, make slices into the flesh, scraping each away from the pit. Their extraordinary flavor is worth every minute spent preparing them.

3/8 cup olive oil
2 tablespoons fresh or bottled lemon juice
2 teaspoons mild honey
1 teaspoon curry powder
1 avocado
1 mango, peeled and diced
1/4 small red onion, sliced (about 1 ounce)
1 small head butter lettuce, torn
salt and freshly ground pepper, to taste

Whisk the olive oil, lemon juice, honey, and curry powder in a medium-size salad bowl. Peel and dice the avocado and, if not finishing the salad right away, toss with the vinaigrette to prevent discoloring. Add the mango, red onion, and lettuce to the salad bowl. Toss thoroughly, and adjust the seasoning with salt and pepper, if needed. Serve immediately.

Yield: 4 side-dish servings

Canned black beans save huge amounts of time for hurried cooks, since dry ones require soaking overnight and cooking for hours to tenderize them. However, canned black beans contain a lot of moisture and a thick liquid surrounding them in the can. Depending upon how they're to be used, drain them thoroughly and pat them dry (Hummus, Two Ways, page 52) or use the beans and all their liquid (Black Bean with Italian Sausage Soup, page 77).

Tex-Mex Black Bean Salad

The colors and shapes in this Southwestern-flavored salad are beautiful, and since it can be served at room temperature, it's an easy dish for entertaining. In case you'd like more fire in this recipe, use more jalapeño or pass the Tabasco when serving. Serve the salad on green leaf lettuce for a dramatic backdrop, or on prewarmed flour tortillas. If you're a cilantro fan, dot the salads with a handful of delicate leaves. The food processor does an adequate job of preparing vegetables, but it will not slice scallions or bell peppers perfectly. For hurried dinners, no one cares. But for the times that the look of a dish matters, slice the scallions by hand, preferably on the diagonal. Quarter the trimmed bell pepper, stack the quarters, and cut crosswise for tidy slices.

> 2 16-ounce cans black beans
> 3 scallions
> 1/2 jalapeño pepper
> 1 clove garlic
> 1/2 teaspoon cumin seeds or 1/4 teaspoon ground
> 1 tablespoon prepared red salsa (or Searing Salsa, page 47)
> 2 tablespoons red wine vinegar
> 2 tablespoons olive oil
> 1 red bell pepper (or 1 cup trimmed, sliced)
> salt and freshly ground pepper, to taste

Rinse the black beans and drain them thoroughly. Pat them dry with paper towels and place in a medium-size salad bowl.

Slice the scallions into quarters crosswise. Drop them through the feed tube of a food processor with the motor running with the jalapeño, garlic, and cumin. Mince, scraping down the sides of the bowl, as needed. Add the salsa, vinegar, and oil, pulsing to blend. Cut the bell pepper in half, remove the stem and seeds, and slice with the thin slicing disk of the food processor. Scrape the peppers and flavorings over the black beans and toss thoroughly.

Adjust the seasoning with salt and pepper, if needed. Serve immediately, or chill, if not using right away.

Yield: 4 side-dish servings

Strawberry and Pine Nut Salad with Mint

This salad looks and tastes like spring. Bright red berries, refreshing green spearmint, and golden pine nuts dot the salad. Pine nuts lend a delicately sweet, nutty flavor. Although grocers import strawberries from long distances when unavailable locally, they rarely have the flavor or shelf life of local ones, since by the time they arrive, they're on the tail-end of their prime. Enjoy the seasonality of food. It provides change of pace and grand anticipation.

> 1/4 cup olive oil
> 1 tablespoon raspberry or mint vinegar
> 1/2 cup fresh mint, lightly packed
> 1 pint strawberries, trimmed and quartered, if large
> 1 small head red or green leaf lettuce, torn
>   (about 4 cups, lightly packed)
> 1/4 cup pine nuts, preferably lightly toasted
> salt and freshly ground pepper, to taste

Blend the olive oil and vinegar in a large salad bowl. Chop the mint coarsely and add it to the dressing. Toss the strawberries with the lettuce, pine nuts, and dressing. Taste for salt and pepper and adjust the seasoning, if needed.

Yield: 4 side-dish servings

Toasting pine nuts enhances their flavor, but they're delicious as is. If you have time, place them in a skillet over medium heat, shaking occasionally, until lightly toasted, about 4 minutes. I prefer to toast them in a 350-degree oven until golden, about 10 minutes. I toast them in quantity and freeze them, since they can turn rancid quickly. If not using soon after buying them, store them, toasted or not, in a zip-lock bag in the freezer.

Wild Mushroom Salad with Walnut Vinaigrette

Combining a variety of wild mushrooms, with their diverse shapes and colors, makes an unusual salad. Pale, delicate oyster mushrooms; dark brown, meaty shitakes; and orange, trumpet-shaped chanterelles comprise a stunning blend. Use cultivated mushrooms, if wild ones are unavailable or too pricey. This salad is packed with nutty aroma from the walnut oil, but lightly dressed. If you want more dressing, drizzle with extra olive oil.

> 3/8 cup walnut oil
> 3 tablespoons red wine vinegar
> salt and freshly ground pepper, to taste
> 1/2 pound assorted wild mushrooms, trimmed and sliced
> 1 small head leaf lettuce, torn
> 4 ounces Gorgonzola
> 3/4 cup walnuts, coarsely chopped

Whisk the oil, vinegar, and salt and pepper in a large salad bowl. Toss the mushrooms with the dressing and use immediately, or let marinate up to an hour.

Divide the lettuce among serving plates. Top with the mushrooms and crumble the Gorgonzola over them. Sprinkle with the walnuts and serve immediately.

Yield: 4 side-dish servings

Panzanella

Bring out the best ingredients for this rustic salad from central Italy. It's worthy of extra virgin olive oil, balsamic vinegar, and the most flavorful tomatoes and basil. Some recipes call for more complicated treatments, such as salting and draining the tomatoes, puréeing part of the tomatoes, soaking the bread in water and then squeezing it dry, drying the bread in the oven, or pounding anchovy fillets and capers into the dressing. This rendition is the fastest and my favorite.

Panzanella makes an ideal use for bread past its prime. If you cannot find fresh basil, however, wait until it's available, since the salad needs its pungent flavor and bright green leaves. Be sure to toss this salad quickly and thoroughly—otherwise, parts of the bread will absorb too much dressing quickly.

Often dried herbs substitute adequately for fresh, but not universally. Dried versions of basil, among others, release a pleasant aroma, although not the same as fresh. As a general rule, use three times the amount of a fresh herb when dried is called for, one-third the amount of dried when fresh is called for. Don't count on carbon-copy flavor, however. The substitution may be delicious, but it won't be the same.

1/4 cup olive oil
1/4 cup red wine vinegar, preferably balsamic
1 clove garlic, minced
1 6-ounce section crusty French or Italian bread,
   torn or sliced into bite-size pieces
2 ripe, large tomatoes or 4 plum tomatoes, diced
2 ounces red onion, sliced thin (about 1/2 cup)
16 fresh basil leaves
salt and freshly ground pepper, to taste

Whisk with the oil, vinegar and garlic in a large salad bowl. Add the bread, tomatoes, onion, and basil to the vinaigrette, tossing all together quickly and thoroughly. Adjust the seasoning with salt and pepper, if needed. Divide between serving plates and serve immediately.

Yield: 4 side-dish servings

Diced Fruits in Orange Cream

Never having been a fan of plain yogurt, I'm amazed at what creamy, pleasant tartness it lends to salad dressings, especially when combined with sweet or spicy ingredients. Since most salad dressings aren't cooked, yogurt can be substituted entirely for more fat-laden sour cream. Whisk in 1/2-1 teaspoon curry powder or ground ginger into this dressing, for variety.

Some people make salad dressings from papaya seeds, since they are peppery in flavor; however, they are toxic to others. Papain, an enzyme contained in papayas, is a natural tenderizer that will break down the fibers in meat. Although gelatin isn't included in this book due to the time it takes to set, keep in mind that papaya also breaks down gelatin salads.

> **1/2 cup sour cream or plain yogurt**
> **2 tablespoons orange or apple juice**
> **1 tablespoon honey**
> **2 ripe avocados, preferably Haas**
> **2 ripe papayas or mangoes, peeled and diced**
> **1 pint fresh ripe strawberries, trimmed and quartered, if large**
> **3 scallions, sliced**
> **4 lettuce leaves (optional)**

In a large bowl, whisk the sour cream, orange juice, and honey. Peel the avocados and dice the flesh, dropping it into the dressing. If not finishing the salad right away, toss to prevent discoloration.

Add the papayas, strawberries, and scallions, and toss with the avocados. Line 4 salad plates with the lettuce and mound the fruit on the leaves. Serve immediately.

Yield: 4 side-dish servings

It's easiest to peel papayas entirely while whole. Then slice them in half and scrape out the seeds with a medium spoon. The halves form an appealing shape with a hollow, much like avocados, and they can be used in the same way as a base for substantial salads or heated to hold an entrée. Curried Chickpeas and Shrimp (page 114) or cooked meat, poultry, or fish with Indian Curry Sauce (page 213) are delicious served in papaya halves.

Apple and Endive with Watercress

Peppery, sweet, and subtly bitter, this salad is a picture. It's bright with red apple skin, dark green delicate watercress leaves, and white spokes of endive and dots of goat cheese. If you prefer, cut out the core of the endive and slice it crosswise into thin half-moons. This makes an ideal side dish for winter, when salad pickings are slim. Apple, endive, and watercress are among the best fresh ingredients available during that time.

1 red apple, quartered, cored, and chopped coarsely
1 tablespoon fresh or bottled lemon juice
2 Belgian endives, trimmed
2 small bunches watercress (4 cups leaves and tender stems)
4 ounces mild goat cheese, such as Montrachet
1/4 cup extra virgin olive oil, or more, to taste
salt and freshly ground pepper, to taste

Toss the apple with the lemon juice and reserve.

Arrange the spears of endive in a spoke pattern on 4 salad plates. Cut and discard the tough stems from the watercress. Divide the leaves among the plates. Crumble the goat cheese over the watercress, top with the reserved apple, and drizzle lightly with olive oil. Sprinkle with salt and pepper, if desired, and serve immediately.

Yield: 4 side-dish servings

Due to its ease of preparation, Belgian endive makes a model ingredient when hurried. It needs practically no cleaning, and although expensive, there's no waste to speak of. Slice off a slender piece of its base and separate into spokes, or remove its small core with a sharp knife and slice crosswise.

Chiffonade of Radicchio and Fennel

Striking in contrasting taste and color, radicchio and fennel are both welcome, but acquired, tastes. An Italian red-leafed chicory, radicchio varies from slightly, pleasantly bitter to overwhelming. Its purple color with white ribs is a welcome contrast to green lettuces, especially in mid-winter, when it looks fresher than most salad ingredients. I love to pair it with red grapes and red onion on greens for a stunning show of color. Fennel gives the aroma of anise, although more delicate, and its white strips cut from the bulbous base make a happy contrast to the radicchio, especially atop bright green lettuce leaves. Both vegetables can be cooked, as well.

> *Stacking and slicing leaves is a quick way to shred them evenly, called chiffonade. The French term means "made of rags," and it's used for raw ingredients and cooked ones as well. Separate the leaves and stack them, matching them as perfectly as possible, and shred by making continuous parallel cuts through all the layers. For speed, sometimes I cut a stack of large leaves in half, and stack the stacks. Classically, sorrel and lettuce are cut into chiffonade, but many leaves, such as fresh basil, spinach, and escarole, are easily and attractively shredded.*

2 tablespoons olive oil
1 tablespoon balsamic vinegar
1 teaspoon Dijon mustard
1 bulb fennel
1 small head radicchio
salt and freshly ground pepper, to taste
4 leaves green leaf lettuce (optional)

In a medium bowl, whisk the olive oil, vinegar, and mustard, and reserve.

Discard the stems and the tough outer layer of the fennel bulb. Cut the bulb into quarters, remove its core, and slice it into thin strips.

Separate the radicchio leaves from its stem, stack them, and cut into thin slices. Toss the radicchio and fennel with the dressing and adjust the seasoning, if needed, with salt and pepper. Serve immediately, mounded on lettuce leaves, if using.

Yield: 4 side-dish servings

Spinach Salad with Anchovy Vinaigrette

Spinach has a strong enough flavor to handle an assertive dressing, and this vinaigrette made of robust anchovies qualifies. Unless frozen (and used for cooked dishes) or bought pre-washed, spinach doesn't qualify for quick-cooking. It's best to buy it at a salad bar, since pre-washed, packaged fresh spinach tends to be old and tough. The packaged spinach is usually so old that each leaf needs its coarse stem removed, hardly a savings in time. Use one-third or one-half Napa cabbage for a lively contrast to the spinach's flavor and color.

> 3 anchovies
> 1 clove garlic
> 3 tablespoons balsamic vinegar
> 1/2 teaspoon Dijon mustard
> 1/2 cup olive oil
> 1 1/2 quarts lightly packed fresh spinach
> 1/2 cup minced red onion (about 2 ounces)
> 2 cups prepared croutons
> salt and freshly ground pepper, to taste

Rinse the anchovies and pat them dry. In a small food processor, mince the garlic with the anchovies. Add the vinegar and mustard to the processor. With the motor running, drizzle in the olive oil. (Alternatively, mince the anchovies and garlic together by hand. In a large salad bowl, whisk them with the vinegar and mustard. Drizzle in the olive oil while whisking vigorously.)

In a large salad bowl, toss the spinach, onion, croutons, and dressing. Season with salt and pepper, if needed, and serve immediately.

Yield: 4 side-dish servings

The quickest way to clean fresh spinach, if you must, is to trim off and discard the toughest leaves and stems. Place the remaining leaves in a large bowl of cold water. Swish the spinach well and let rest a minute. Grasp the leaves and remove them. Empty the bowl of the water and grit and repeat. Dry in a salad spinner.

Since much of the time spent making a salad involves the boring chore of cleaning ingredients, buy hydroponically-grown Boston lettuce. All the treatment it needs is removing the root end. Butter lettuce leaves, torn from their base stem, form attractive, individual cups for salads in seconds. Radicchio mimics the size and curvature, if not the color, of butter lettuce, and it forms a cup strong enough to hold sauces.

Sesame-Flavored Radishes

Round, red radishes have beautiful color, but their larger cousins, the icicle and especially the large daikon, cut down on trimming time. All are peppery hot with flavor, and all slice or shred easily and cleanly in a food processor. In this particular salad, however, I prefer to use red radishes, since the white daikon takes on the brown color of soy sauce quickly. Shred the radishes with the large shredding disk of a food processor or slice thin with a vegetable slicer. Sprinkle this salad with black sesame seeds for a dramatic look.

> **2 tablespoons soy sauce**
> **1 tablespoon rice vinegar**
> **1 tablespoon sugar**
> **2 teaspoons sesame oil**
> **4 cups trimmed, sliced red radishes**
>   **(24-30, depending upon their size)**
> **3 scallions, sliced thin**
> **4 large leaves Boston lettuce**
> **black sesame seeds (optional)**

In a medium bowl, blend the soy sauce, vinegar, sugar, and sesame oil. Add the radishes and toss them with the dressing and scallions. Serve immediately on lettuce leaves. Drizzle any remaining dressing over the salads and sprinkle with black sesame seeds, if you wish.

Yield: 4 side-dish servings

Cucumbers, Japanese Style

I like to serve this delicately sweet and sour salad with curries and other spicy foods. It's refreshing and light as can be. It takes only 5 minutes to prepare the cucumber and dressing, but if you allow it to marinate for 1 hour, the salad will deliver more of its cooling flavor. Also, the cucumbers will pack more crunch, since the salt and sugar firm them by drawing out some of the cucumbers' moisture. Peeling the cucumber and cutting it into small pieces allows it to absorb more of the marinade quickly. For special occasions, seed the cucumbers with a melon baller.

1/4 cup sugar
1/4 cup vinegar
1 teaspoon salt
2 medium cucumbers, peeled
2 scallions, sliced
4 leaves butter or red leaf lettuce (optional)

In a medium bowl, stir the sugar, vinegar, and salt with 1/2 cup of water until the sugar and salt dissolve and the liquid is clear.

Cut the cucumbers into quarters lengthwise, align the ends of the slices, and slice them about 1/8" thick across. Toss them with the scallions in the reserved liquid. Cover and chill at least 10 minutes or, even better, up to an hour.

Line 4 salad plates with lettuce leaves, if desired, mound the cucumbers on the lettuce, and serve immediately.

Yield: 4 side-dish servings

Cucumber seeds can be bitter and watery. If you have time to remove them, slice the cucumber in half lengthwise and use a melon baller to scrape out the seeds. If you don't have a melon baller, a small spoon will do.

*Placing the eggs in cold wa-
ter before heating it makes
them less likely to crack,
since the eggs change temperature gradually. Plunging
cold eggs in boiling water
practically guarantees cracks
in the shell and dribbles of
white in the water.*

Asparagus, Egg, and Tomato Salad

This salad is simple and beautiful, since the contrast of colors, shapes, and textures is striking. Substitute leeks for the asparagus in this recipe, if you like, or to
avoid cooking a vegetable entirely, substitute one ripe avocado half per person.
Cutting it into a fan shape (see page 109) gives it a dramatic look, or mound the
chopped egg onto each solid half. Use a mild vinaigrette instead of the mayonnaise, if you prefer.

> **2 eggs**
> **1 pound fresh asparagus**
> **2 ripe plum tomatoes**
> **4 leaves lettuce, preferably red-leaf**
> **1/2 cup prepared mayonnaise (or Cajun Mayonnaise, page 228,
>   or Processor Aïoli, page 229)**

Place the eggs in a small saucepan and cover with water by 1 inch. Bring the
water to a boil and simmer 15 minutes.

While the eggs are cooking, bring 2" of lightly salted water to boil in a medium saucepan. Trim the asparagus (see page 184) and add to the water. Simmer
3-5 minutes, depending upon its thickness. Drain and hold under cold running
water until the asparagus feels cool. Quarter the tomatoes lengthwise and reserve.

Remove the eggs from the pan and hold under cold running water until cool
to the touch. Remove the shells and chop the eggs coarsely.

Line 4 plates with lettuce leaves. Divide the asparagus among the plates and
top with the chopped egg. Garnish with 2 quarters of tomato and a spoonful of
mayonnaise.

Yield: 4 side-dish servings

Watercress with Starfruit and Walnuts

Walnuts and walnut oil lend earthy, nutty aromas to citrusy starfruit and peppery watercress. Substitute hazelnuts and hazelnut oil for the walnut ingredients, if desired. This show-stopping salad demonstrates that starfruit is appropriately named, for more than one reason. When sliced crosswise, the flat slices resemble bright yellow star shapes, and so take center stage to other ingredients. The dark green watercress provides a dramatic backdrop in color and flavor.

> 2 tablespoons balsamic or fruit-flavored vinegar
> 1 teaspoon Dijon mustard
> 1/4 cup walnut oil
> 1 tablespoon olive oil
> salt and freshly ground pepper, to taste
> 1 large bunch watercress, tougher stems removed
> 2 ripe starfruit, sliced thin, seeded
> 1/4 cup walnuts

In a small bowl, whisk the vinegar and mustard. Whisk in the walnut and olive oils, and adjust the seasoning, if needed, with salt and pepper.

Divide the watercress between 4 salad plates. Arrange the starfruit in an overlapping pattern on the greens. Dot with the walnuts, drizzle with the vinaigrette, and serve immediately.

Yield: 4 side-dish servings

When starfruit, also known as carambola, shows brown tinges on its points, it's as sweet as it will get. (Unripe starfruit can be bitter and tart.) It needn't be peeled, only sliced across into star shapes. Don't neglect its possibilities in cooking, especially in stir-fries, salsas, and curries. For an amusing drink presentation, cut through the radius of a slice of starfruit and attach to the side of a glass.

If you have a citrus zester, before peeling oranges, run the zester over it, so the zest falls away into shreds. They'll contribute intense orange flavor to a salad with no further effort.

Since tahini goes rancid easily, refrigerate it after opening and use it within 2 months. Its oil separates, much like unhomogenized peanut butter, so it must be stirred vigorously before adding to a recipe.

Mixed Greens
with Oranges and Sesame Cream

Tahini gives this creamy salad dressing a nutty aroma, and yogurt and orange juice, a tart-sweet flavor. If you hold the oranges over the salad bowl while segmenting them, you can catch the juice that runs out of them to use in the salad. Whisk this into the dressing and reduce the amount of orange juice by half. Substitute an 11-ounce can mandarin oranges, drained, if you don't have time to segment fresh ones.

> 1/2 cup unflavored yogurt
> 3/8 cup orange juice
> 2 tablespoons tahini
> 4 oranges
> 1 large bunch watercress or spinach, toughest stems removed
>   (5 cups lightly packed)
> 1/2 head Boston lettuce, torn (3 cups lightly packed)
> 2 tablespoons toasted sesame seeds
> salt and freshly ground pepper, to taste

In a large salad bowl, whisk the yogurt, orange juice, and tahini until smooth. Remove the peel and pith from the oranges. Section the fruit by running a sharp knife between the membranes, nudging the sections out whole.

Toss the watercress and lettuce with the oranges, dressing, and sesame seeds. Adjust the seasoning, if needed, with salt and pepper, and serve immediately.

Yield: 4 side-dish servings

Year-Round Green Pea Salad

You can make this slightly sweet, minty salad with peas straight from the freezer by running cold water over them while making the dressing. Although fresh spearmint is a sure harbinger of spring, many supermarkets carry it all year round. Substitute fresh green peas, if you like. Shell and blanch them for 3-5 minutes, or until tender. Drain and run cold water over them to cool and dry thoroughly before using. If using Cajun Mayonnaise, eliminate the fresh mint, and serve in a ripe papaya half, if desired.

> **16 ounces frozen green peas**
> **1/2 cup fresh mint leaves, tightly packed**
> **1/2 cup prepared mayonnaise (or Cajun Mayonnaise, page 228)**
> **2 ounces red onion, minced (about 1/2 cup)**
> **salt and freshly ground pepper, to taste**
> **lettuce leaves (optional)**

Place the peas in a colander and run cold water over them to defrost. Drain thoroughly, patting them dry with paper towels, if needed.

Mince the mint. Blend with the mayonnaise in a medium bowl and combine with the peas and onion. Adjust the seasoning with salt and pepper, if needed, and serve immediately on lettuce leaves.

Yield: 4 side-dish servings

To save time, buy red onions already peeled. Often you can buy them peeled and minced from the salad bar section of most supermarkets. Red onions are available year-round, but their strength varies greatly. Taste a nibble and adjust the amount accordingly, if the onion is particularly potent or bland.

Use a sharp paring knife to pull off jicama skin in sheets, rather than a vegetable peeler. Jicama skin is so fibrous that it gets caught in most peelers. If the skin develops any dark spots, remove them to keep the deterioration from spreading.

Tender greens wilt when dressed for more than a few minutes, since the acid in vinegars and lemon juice "cooks" the greens. A few salad ingredients, such as dried fruits, avocado, and cheeses can be held in a dressing longer with no problem. If you have leftover dressed greens that you want to save, rinse off the dressing, dry, and refrigerate.

Dried Fruit, Radicchio, and Gorgonzola Salad

This tasty, colorful salad is full of contrasting textures and flavors, particularly good in winter when fresh fruits are limited. The sweetness of fruit and the saltiness in cheese, especially blue cheese, balance each other beautifully. Jicama also adds a subtly sweet crunchiness, belying its unattractive exterior.

> **3/8 cup olive oil**
> **1/4 cup balsamic vinegar**
> **4 dried Turkish figs or 8 dried apricots**
> **1/4 cup crumbled Gorgonzola, Roquefort, Stilton,**
>   **or Danish blue (about 2 ounces)**
> **6 ounces jicama**
> **3 ounces radicchio (1 1/2 cups torn, lightly packed)**
> **1/2 small head romaine lettuce (2 cups torn, lightly packed)**
> **salt and freshly ground pepper, to taste**

Blend the oil and vinegar in a medium salad bowl. Slice the figs or apricots thin and add them to the dressing, so that the fruit softens a bit while preparing the remaining ingredients.

If not already crumbled, break up the cheese over the salad bowl. Peel and dice the jicama and add to the bowl. Tear the radicchio and romaine over the jicama and toss thoroughly. Season with salt and pepper, and serve immediately.

Yield: 4 side-dish servings

Caesar-Style Salad

Happily, Caesar salads are enjoying a resurgence in popularity across the country. Since many of us are nervous about using uncooked eggs, a staple dressing ingredient in classic Caesar salads, this recipe eliminates the egg entirely with no loss of flavor. The anchovy and Dijon help thicken the dressing, as well as packing a wallop of flavor.

    4 anchovies
    2 cloves garlic
    2 tablespoons fresh or bottled lemon juice
    1 tablespoon Dijon mustard
    1/4 cup olive oil
    1/2 cup freshly grated Parmesan (about 2 ounces)
    1 head romaine lettuce, torn
    2 cups prepared croutons
    salt and freshly ground pepper, to taste

Mince the anchovies and garlic together and place in a large salad bowl. Whisk in the lemon juice, mustard, and drizzle in the olive oil while whisking. If not using pre-grated Parmesan, grate the cheese and toss it with the lettuce, dressing, and croutons. Adjust the seasoning with salt and pepper, and serve immediately.

Yield: 4 side-dish servings

Croutons, light and crisp and well-seasoned, can make the difference between an adequate Caesar salad and a memorable one. Unless you're willing to make your own, splurge on the best packaged croutons available. Many of the tastiest ones are available in produce sections. They may seem expensive, but they'll make a distinctive difference in salads.

Farfalle with Artichokes and Quick Aïoli

Only true garlic aficionados should try this versatile pasta salad. Since the garlic is raw, its pungency is untamed, just the way many people love it. Substitute spirelli for the farfalle, add imported black olives or sun-dried tomatoes, or use leftover cooked broccoli or green peas instead of the artichokes. Double all the amounts, if you prefer, for an entrée-size salad and serve with crusty bread. If you have time, use Processor Aïoli (page 229), eliminating the garlic, mayonnaise, and lemon juice from this recipe.

3 cloves garlic
1/2 cup prepared mayonnaise
2 tablespoons fresh or bottled lemon juice
salt and freshly ground pepper, to taste
8 ounces farfalle
1 6 1/2-ounce jar marinated artichoke hearts
4 plum tomatoes
4 leaves red leaf lettuce (optional)

Bring 2 quarts of lightly salted water to boil in a heavy large saucepan. Meanwhile, mince the garlic and blend it with the mayonnaise and lemon juice in a medium-large bowl. Adjust the seasoning with salt and pepper, if needed.

When the water reaches a rolling boil, stir in the pasta and cook according to the package directions. Meanwhile, drain the artichokes, dice the tomatoes, and add them to the dressing.

When the pasta is cooked, drain it in a colander and run cold water over it until it is cool to the touch. Drain thoroughly and pat with paper towels to remove excess moisture. Toss with the artichokes, tomatoes, and the mayonnaise mixture. Line 4 plates with the lettuce, if you wish, and mound the pasta on top. Serve immediately.

Yield: 4 side-dish servings

When using pasta for a salad, be sure to drain it thoroughly, or the water will dilute the salad dressing. Some pasta shapes, such as spirelli, hold water in their twists, so be especially careful with them. Since farfalle is almost completely flat, it drains more easily. Pat moist pasta dry with a paper towel, if necessary.

Pears and Cashews with Blue Cheese Vinaigrette

Blue cheese provides a sharp contrast to buttery cashews and pears in this salad. It's a fast, very satisfying replacement for a time-consuming salad of poached, cooled pears and triple-cream Cambozola. Substitute hazelnuts for the cashews, if you prefer, and use half hazelnut oil, half olive oil to embellish the nutty flavor. When available, use red Bartlett pears for their surprising, bright red skin color.

> 1/2 cup olive oil
> 2 tablespoons raspberry vinegar
> 1/4 cup crumbled blue cheese (about 2 ounces)
> 6 cups lightly packed torn leaf lettuce
> 2 pears, halved, cored, and diced
> 1/2 cup cashews
> salt and freshly ground pepper, to taste

Blend the oil, vinegar, and blue cheese in a large salad bowl. Add the lettuce, pears, and cashews and toss thoroughly. Adjust the seasoning with salt and pepper, if needed, and serve immediately.

Yield: 4 side-dish servings

Fanning out pears, just like avocados, provides a dramatic touch. Once you've done it a time or two, you'll find it easier than dicing. Slice the pear in half and remove the core and seeds. Leave the stem attached to one half. If fanning avocados, cut them in half, remove the pit, and peel.

Place the halves flat on a cutting board, and hold the stem end as a base, make 1/4-1/2-inch slices with a sharp knife, taking care not to cut through the base. Apply gentle pressure to spread the slices.

Comice pears are ideal for salads or eating out-of-hand. Their skin should be green to yellow, possibly with a red blush. It should be smooth and thin, requiring no peeling. On the other hand, Bosc pears are ideal for cooking because they hold their shape well when heated. Their coarse brown skin is best peeled.

Warm Cajun Seafood Salad

Full of feisty flavors, this spicy, colorful salad makes a marvelous luncheon or dinner salad, accompanied by crusty bread. The list of ingredients may seem long, but it's fast to put together, and most of the ingredients should be close at hand. Use a commercially prepared Cajun spice blend, if you prefer, but unless you have it in your pantry, blending it yourself is faster than shopping for it.

2 teaspoons paprika
1 teaspoon freshly ground black pepper
1 teaspoon ground red pepper (cayenne)
1/2 teaspoon salt
8 ounces small-medium, shelled, deveined shrimp
8 ounces bay scallops
1/2 cup olive oil, divided
3 tablespoons Dijon mustard
3 tablespoon red wine vinegar
2 tablespoons mild honey
4 plum tomatoes, diced
1 head romaine or iceberg lettuce or a combination,
   torn or shredded
salt and freshly ground pepper, to taste

Combine the paprika, black pepper, red pepper, and salt in a large salad bowl. Add the shrimp and scallops and toss to coat evenly. Heat 2 tablespoons olive oil in a medium saucepan over medium-high heat and stir in the shrimp and scallops, sautéing until opaque and barely cooked, about 3-4 minutes.

Remove the pan from the heat. Whisk the remaining oil, mustard, vinegar, and honey in the salad bowl and add the cooked seafood. Top with the tomatoes and lettuce, and toss together thoroughly. Adjust the seasoning with salt and pepper, if needed, and serve immediately.

Yield: 4 entrée-size servings

Romaine and iceberg lettuce need very little cleaning, a boon to quick-cooking. Remove the tough leaves and stem of romaine, and some people insist on trimming off about 4 inches of the ribs. If any of the leaves are dirty, wipe them clean. Iceberg lettuce has rescued me too many times to count, since its keeping qualities, if not its flavor, are outstanding. And it requires practically no cleaning. Trim off the stem end and remove any unattractive outer leaves. Chop with a large knife.

Tuscan Tuna and Cannellini Salad

A rendition of this substantial salad was served to me once on focaccia, the soft, leavened bread which is becoming a staple in American kitchens as it has been in Italian ones for centuries. It was made with fresh grilled tuna that was meaty, smoky, and succulent. If you have time, substitute 4 small tuna steaks for the canned tuna, grill them, and serve hot or cool in the salad. This recipe makes a colorful, well-balanced meal, comprised of a satisfying variety of textures, colors, and flavors.

For maximum freshness, store fresh herbs, such as basil, dill, cilantro, oregano, and parsley with their stems in a glass of water in the refrigerator loosely covered with plastic wrap.

> 2 15-ounce cans cannellini beans
> 2 7-ounce cans water-packed tuna
> 1 cup pitted Kalamata or Niçoise olives
> 3/8 cup extra virgin olive oil
> 1/4 cup fresh or bottled lemon juice
> 2 cloves garlic, minced
> 1 tablespoon fresh oregano leaves or 1 teaspoon dried
> 4 plum tomatoes, diced
> 3 scallions, sliced
> salt and freshly ground pepper, to taste
> 4 cups lightly packed curly endive leaves

Drain the beans, tuna, and olives together. Whisk the olive oil, lemon juice, garlic, and oregano in a medium salad bowl. Toss with the cannellini mixture, tomatoes, and scallions. Adjust the seasoning with salt and pepper, if needed.

Make a bed of endive on 4 serving plates and top with the salad. Alternatively, toss the endive with the other ingredients and serve immediately.

Yield: 4 entrée-size servings

Warm Potato Salad with Roquefort and Watercress

Instead of spending the time carefully picking off watercress leaves, which can be painstaking, remove only the toughest of stems. Line each plate with whole sprigs, top with the accompaniments, and serve with a knife and fork. Be sure to reserve the tougher stems for another use (Watercress Triangles, page 46), (Arugula Butter, page 220).

The quintessential American potato salad, considered plain good food, takes a long time to prepare. This comparatively elegant update takes 25 minutes maximum. For those of us in a hurry, warm potatoes straight from the heat absorb more flavor from a dressing and provide an interesting contrast in temperature to cool ingredients. (Grandmother's potato salad had to cool for an hour before dressing with gobs of mayonnaise.) If not serving right away, chill the potatoes in the dressing and bring them to room temperature before continuing.

> **1 1/2 pounds tiny new potatoes**
> **3 tablespoons white wine, tarragon, or cider vinegar**
> **1 tablespoon Dijon mustard**
> **1/2 teaspoon freshly ground black pepper**
> **1/2 cup olive oil**
> **1 cup crumbled Roquefort cheese (about 8 ounces)**
> **4 scallions**
> **salt and extra freshly ground pepper, to taste**
> **2 small bunches watercress**

Place the potatoes in a large pot of lightly salted water and bring it to a boil. Simmer about 15 minutes, or until barely tender when pierced with a knife.

While the potatoes are cooking, whisk the vinegar, mustard, and pepper in a large bowl. While whisking, drizzle in the olive oil in a thin stream. If not pre-crumbled, break up the Roquefort over the dressing, and slice the scallions.

When the potatoes are tender, drain them. When cool enough to handle, slice them in half (or quarters, if large) and toss them with the vinaigrette and the scallions. Adjust the seasoning with salt and pepper, if needed.

Trim the watercress (see sidebar) and arrange on individual plates. Spoon the potatoes onto the center of each plate and serve immediately.

Yield: 4 entrée-size servings

Asparagus, Sun-Dried Tomatoes, and Prosciutto with Pasta

This red, white, and green salad makes a stunning, balanced meal. Substitute farfalle, or bow-tie pasta, if you like, for a fanciful shape. It's possible to add the asparagus to the pasta while it's cooking, if ample water is boiling and if you have a close idea how fast the asparagus will cook. For instance, if you've bought pencil-thin asparagus, you could add it during the last 3 minutes of cooking the pasta and then drain both together. I often cook vegetables and pasta together, but some experience in timing is critical.

> 8 ounces spirelli
> 12 ounces asparagus
> 1/2 cup sun-dried tomatoes packed in oil
> 4 thin slices prosciutto
> 1 shallot
> 1 clove garlic
> 1/4 cup olive oil + 2 teaspoons, divided
> 2 tablespoons balsamic vinegar
> 1/2 teaspoon salt and freshly ground pepper, or more,
>   to taste

In a large pot, bring 2 quarts of lightly salted water to boil. Add the pasta, stir, and cook until *al dente*, about 8 minutes.

While the pasta cooks, trim the ends of the asparagus (see page 184) and slice into 1" lengths. Drain the sun-dried tomatoes and slice each into 1/4" pieces. Slice the prosciutto into thin strips. Peel and mince the shallot and garlic together. Blend them in a small bowl with 1/4 cup olive oil, the vinegar, and salt and pepper.

When cooked, drain the pasta and run cold water over it until it reaches room temperature. Place in a large bowl and, if not using immediately, toss with 2 teaspoons olive oil.

Fill the same pot with 2 inches of lightly salted water. Bring it to a boil. Add the asparagus and cook about 3-5 minutes or until just tender. Drain the asparagus and run cold water over it briefly. Toss the pasta with the asparagus, tomatoes, prosciutto, and dressing. Adjust the seasoning, if needed, and serve immediately.

Yield: 4 entrée-size servings

Running cold water over a cooked vegetable does more than help retain its bright green color. Keeping the water running until the vegetable becomes cold allows the cook to serve cooked vegetables cold in minutes. Another alternative is dropping vegetables in ice water. It's effective, but troublesome.

If small cooked shrimp smell fishy or taste salty, run them under cold water a minute, then drain well. Pat them dry with paper towels, if needed, so they don't dilute the salad dressing.

Curried Chickpeas and Shrimp

This wonderful balance of hot and sweet flavors invites variety. Use cooked lamb or poultry instead of the shrimp, diced apples or red grapes for the green, more grapes for the raisins, or different nuts. The olive oil gives yogurt a sheen, which is particularly appealing in a salad dressing. Mince all of the ingredients together fine, if you like, and blend lightly with some of the dressing for an unusual sandwich spread.

> 1 cup plain yogurt
> 2 tablespoons curry powder
> 1 tablespoon sugar
> 2 tablespoons olive oil
> 2 cloves garlic, minced
> 4 scallions, sliced
> 1 cup slivered almonds, preferably lightly toasted
> 1 cup seedless grapes
> 1/2 cup raisins
> 1 pound canned chickpeas, drained
> 2 cups tiny cooked shrimp
> salt and freshly ground pepper, to taste
> 4-8 large lettuce leaves

In a large bowl, whisk the yogurt, curry, sugar, olive oil, and garlic until the curry and sugar dissolve. Add the scallions, almonds, grapes, raisins, chickpeas, and shrimp to the bowl and toss thoroughly. Season with salt and pepper, if needed.

Arrange lettuce leaves on individual plates. Spoon the curried salad onto the leaves and serve immediately.

Yield: 4 entrée-size servings

Ham and Warm Lentil Salad

You can serve this full-meal salad warm—straight from cooking—or cover and chill it to serve cold. Tomatoes add a pleasant acidity, the ham a bit of saltiness, and the oregano a pleasant aroma for the bland backdrop of nutritious lentils. Be careful not to overcook them, or they'll turn mushy, a texture unbecoming to a salad. The addition of lemon juice helps them retain their bright, carrot-like color.

1 cup red lentils
2 1/2 cups chicken or beef stock or broth
1 teaspoon fresh or bottled lemon juice
1/4 cup olive oil
1/4 cup red wine vinegar
2 teaspoons Dijon mustard
8 ounces cooked ham
4 ripe plum tomatoes
1 tablespoon fresh oregano leaves or 1 teaspoon dried
salt and freshly ground pepper, to taste
4 large lettuce leaves (optional)

Place the lentils, stock, and lemon juice in a heavy medium saucepan, and bring to a boil. Cover and simmer until the lentils are tender but firm, about 6-8 minutes, stirring occasionally. Drain them thoroughly, if they have not absorbed all the liquid.

While the lentils cook, blend the oil, vinegar, and mustard in a medium salad bowl. Dice the ham and tomatoes and add to the dressing with the lentils. Blend in the oregano, adjust the seasoning with salt and pepper, and serve immediately on lettuce leaves, if desired.

Yield: 4 entrée-size servings

Red or Egyptian lentils are smaller and do not contain the seed coat of the typical French or European lentil, so they need no presoaking and only brief cooking. Red lentils can be found in some supermarkets and many specialty shops. If making a special stop for them, stock up— they'll keep for at least 6 months at room temperature.

When a recipe calls for un-specified fresh greens, con-sider using one of the blends available washed and pre-pared in resealable plastic bags. Continental blends variously include an attrac-tive mixture of arugula, curly endive, radicchio, oak leaf lettuce, spinach, chervil, and mâche.

Croutons baked on a wire rack will crisp on both sides simultaneously. When put on baking sheet, the undersides steam instead of bake.

Grilled Chicken Salad with Pesto and Goat Cheese Croutons

Smoky chicken warm from the grill tops a bed of fresh greens tossed with a pesto-spiked vinaigrette in this full-meal salad. If you don't have toasted pine nuts, brown them in the oven while making the croutons, and sauté the chicken breasts in a bit of oil, if you prefer not to grill them. The chicken will lack the smoky flavor, but will be delicious nonetheless.

> **8 slices French bread**
> **4 boneless skinless chicken breast halves**
> **4 ounces mild goat cheese, such as Montrachet**
> **1/2 cup olive oil**
> **3/8 cup prepared pesto**
> **3 tablespoons red wine vinegar**
> **salt and freshly ground pepper, to taste**
> **3 quarts lightly packed torn fresh greens**
> **1/4 cup pine nuts, lightly toasted**
> **8 goat cheese croutons (see recipe below)**

Preheat a grill, if using an outdoor one, or set up a stove-top grill. Preheat the oven to 325 degrees. Arrange the bread in a single layer on a wire rack. Place in the oven to dry out about 8 minutes.

Place the chicken in a single layer on the grill, adjust the heat to medium-high (see pages 122, 142), and cook until just done, about 4-5 minutes on each side. When cooked, remove the chicken to a cutting board.

Remove the bread from the oven and spread the goat cheese evenly over each slice. Place in the oven until warmed through, but not brown. Hold in a barely warm (200-degree) oven, if necessary.

Meanwhile, whisk the olive oil, pesto, and vinegar in a large salad bowl. Adjust the seasoning with salt and pepper, if needed, and reserve. Toss the greens with the vinaigrette and place on individual plates. Slice the chicken and arrange it in the center of each plate. Garnish with a sprinkling of pine nuts and 2 crou-tons.

Yield: 4 entrée-size servings

Easy Entrées:
Fish, Poultry,
and Meat

Recipes

The stove-top cooking of entrées affords the cook the utmost in convenience and speed. It poses the opportunity to make a sauce in the same pan used to cook fish or meat, taking advantage of every bit of flavor left in the pan and cutting down on cleanup time. The cook gains comforting control as well, since all the cooking goes on within earshot, sight, and smell, and even within range of easy tasting. Those senses can guide you to perfectly sautéed, pan-fried, and stir-fried entrées, avoiding the ticklish timing of roasts and questionable temperature thermometers. Stove-top cooking also allows for convenient creativity, since tasting and doctoring are within comfortable reach. Adding a splash of this and a dash of that is at hand.

When pan-frying or sautéing, be sure to allow enough room between the pieces of meat, fish, or poultry, otherwise they'll steam instead of sear. Searing meat heightens its flavor, gives it an appealing brown color, and creates browned bits of intense flavor in the bottom of the pan that can be the basis for a marvelous, easy pan sauce.

To create a pan sauce, remove the fish or meat, but leave the pan or return it to the heat. Deglaze the pan by pouring in a liquid, such as stock, vinegar, wine, cream, milk, water, or a combination of liquids, while stirring. This will release the solids on the bottom of the pan as well as add flavor and substance. The liquid will boil or simmer down to thicken, intensify flavors, and create a sauce. Herbs and spices, cheeses, diced fruits and vegetables, and prepared condiments can contribute their unique textures and aromas. Once you've practiced this fast, simple technique a few times and explored its possibilities, you'll realize you can cook every entrée, complete with interesting sauce, in one pan without fail in minutes.

Sautéing, unjustly, has taken on a bad name of late. Because the process is French in origin does not mean it's laden with butter. On the contrary, food can be sautéed quickly in a minimum of fat over fairly high heat. Nonstick skillets can even be used, but I prefer a well-seasoned pan, since it requires little fat but still produces flavor-filled browned bits on the bottom of the pan.

Fish and Shellfish

No ingredient is more sensitive to timing than fish. A minute can make the difference between a perfectly cooked, moist fish and a dry, tough, tasteless one. For fish over one inch thick, cook it ten minutes per inch of thickness, regardless of the fish or the cooking method. For thinner fish, sight and touch are the best tests of doneness. When cooked, the fish should have just acquired an opaque look and feel firm, but not rubbery. Test it by lifting the thickest part of it. If it flakes, it's cooked.

Mussels, scallops, and clams are cooked when their shells open plus 30 seconds extra cooking time, and any that do not open should be discarded. Oysters are cooked when their edges curl, and shrimp are ready to eat when they turn opaque and firm.

Buy fish that is cut into fillets or steaks no more than one inch thick for the quickest cooking. Select shelled and deveined shrimp, shucked scallops and oysters, and find farmed mussels to avoid time-consuming scraping of their shells and debearding.

Poultry

Chicken is the most versatile poultry. Its bland flavor lends it to amazingly diverse flavors and cooking techniques, as cuisines from all over the world can attest. Since we've become more health-conscious, chicken and turkey have acquired new prestige as valuable sources of protein that are low in fat and cholesterol. As poultry has gained in popularity, grocers have supplied the convenience of chickens and turkeys cut into every part imaginable, thereby shortening preparation and cooking times significantly for the home cook. In most groceries, poultry parts that have been boned and skinned are available. In some, chicken breasts cut up for stir-frying are available, so take some time to seek out the convenience you need. It's probably there for the asking and for some little added cost.

Turkey breasts make an excellent alternative to chicken breasts, and they're usually less expensive. They need to be sliced before cooking, since they are large, and both types of breasts benefit from brief pounding to tenderize them and even out their thickness. Since both cook so quickly, about 4-5 minutes maximum per side for chicken and even less for turkey, if part of the breast is thicker than another, the fatter part will undercook while the thinner dries out. Allow 1 pound turkey breast for 4 people. Slice it into 8 even pieces, pound it lightly to flatten it and even out its thickness, and sauté it for a *total* of 5 minutes. Substitute turkey for any chicken breast recipe in this chapter.

Duck breasts are also a quick alternative, although in some parts of the country, it's difficult to find them sold without the rest of the bird intact. Quail, most often found frozen and partly boned, are easily broiled or grilled in a flash. Although expensive, they make an elegant offering for a special, easy dinner.

Pork

Pork has benefited from improved technology and breeding. It's 50% leaner today than it was 20 years ago, and it needs to be cooked only to 140 degrees, yielding a moister meat compared to when 180 degrees was considered safe to ensure that trichinosis bacteria were killed. Some cuts of pork today are actually leaner than chicken. However, since pork lacks the marbling of beef, which renders moisture during cooking, it's a bit drier.

The following recipes are cooked quickly until the pork is just cooked without allowing it time to dry out, and all are accompanied by interesting sauces to lend moisture and flavor to the meat.

Beef, Veal, and Lamb

The quintessential American meat, beef is rich in flavor and texture, due to the streaks of fat running through it. Its fat content, however, has caused many of us to lower the amount of meat in our diets due to health concerns. But there are times when nothing but the real thing will satisfy the craving for a thick steak or a perfectly cooked hamburger. Ground beef and well-marbled, tender steaks about one inch thick are best for quick-cooking, since they require only about 10 minutes total cooking time whether pan-fried, broiled, or grilled.

Veal, meat from a young calf, is delicate in texture and flavor, making it a blank canvas, similar to chicken breasts, for the creative cook. Both veal scallops and calf's liver make ideal meats for quick-cooking, since they require only about two minutes of cooking per side.

Lamb is particularly complex in flavor, offering a lightly musky undertone and rich texture. Tender steaks and chops no thicker than 1 inch can be cooked quickly, like beef, requiring 10 minutes total cooking per inch of thickness. In choosing beef, veal, and lamb, keep in mind that cuts from younger animals are lighter in appearance and will be more tender than those from older animals.

Sausages vary dramatically in flavor and contents, but all are convenient and cook quickly. Many are available today made with less fat, and some are based entirely on chicken and turkey. Often they're packed with enough flavor to need little time-consuming adornment.

If using a stove-top grill, there's no need to preheat it, since it heats so quickly, especially over a gas flame. I typically assemble the grill, pour water into it, and place the fish or meat on the grill at room temperature while I'm making the salsa. All that's left to do is turn on the burner when I'm ready to cook the fish, and, in the meantime, it's warming up from its stay in the refrigerator.

Yellowfin Tuna with Pineapple-Mint Salsa

This brightly colored salsa is equally vivid in flavor with the sweet acidity of pineapple and tomato, the heat of green chilies, and the refreshment of spearmint. These counterbalance the roastiness of sesame oil and soy. If you prefer, substitute swordfish, marlin, shark, king mackerel, or another tuna for the reddish yellowfin meat. Use one or two serrano chilies, depending upon your heat tolerance. You can always make the salsa with one chili, taste it, and add more chili if you like. Making the salsa by hand is easy, but whether using a food processor or working by hand, buy pineapple prepped at the grocery, if possible. Since yellowfin doesn't store well, use it immediately.

1/2 cup olive oil
1/4 cup sesame oil
1/4 cup soy sauce
4 6-ounce yellowfin tuna steaks, about 1" thick
1-2 serrano chilies, stemmed
1/2 medium red onion (about 3 ounces)
1/2 cup fresh mint leaves, tightly packed
3 1/2" thick pineapple slices
1 plum tomato
2 tablespoons red wine vinegar
2 tablespoons olive oil

Preheat a grill or broiler. Blend the olive oil, sesame oil, and soy sauce in a shallow glass dish. Turn the steaks in the marinade to coat and let them rest while preparing the salsa.

In a food processor, mince the chilies, red onion, and mint. If not already prepared, peel, core, and remove the eyes from the pineapple. Cut into 1/2-inch thick slices and quarter each. Quarter the tomato and place in the processor with the pineapple. Chop coarsely. Pulse to blend in the vinegar and olive oil, and reserve.

Remove the fish from the marinade and grill or broil until barely cooked, about 4-5 minutes per side. Transfer to serving plates and top with the salsa. Serve immediately.

Yield: 4 servings

Bronzed Red Snapper

Bronzing, as opposed to the blackening cooking method, allows the home cook to enjoy juicy, tender, spice-encrusted fish without an accompanying smoke alarm. Since blackening requires a cast iron skillet to reach at least 500 degrees, it creates a blinding amount of smoke that only a commercial vent can handle. The tamer bronzing method requires only 350 degrees, a reasonable alternative. Another advantage to bronzing is that all the fillets can be cooked at once; blackening requires that one fillet be cooked at a time, wiping out the skillet in between. If you like, substitute any firm-fleshed fish, such as tuna, salmon, walleye, pompano, or tilefish in this recipe.

> 2 teaspoons mild paprika
> 1 1/2 teaspoons dried thyme
> 1 1/2 teaspoons dried oregano
> 1 teaspoon salt
> 1/2 teaspoon freshly ground black pepper
> 1/4 teaspoon ground red pepper (cayenne)
> 6 ounces unsalted butter
> 4 6-8 ounce red snapper fillets, each 3/4" thick,
>   skinned, room temperature, if possible

In a small bowl, blend the paprika, thyme, oregano, salt, and ground peppers thoroughly. Melt the butter in a small skillet and keep over low heat.

Place a large cast-iron skillet over medium-high heat. Pat the fillets dry. When the skillet is very hot, dip the fillets in the butter and sprinkle both sides evenly with the spice mixture. Place immediately in the skillet (do not place on another surface or the spices will be lost) and cook about 3 minutes. Turn and cook the other side about 2 minutes, depending upon its thickness. Remove the fish to a warm serving plate.

Pour the remaining warm butter into the cast-iron skillet, scraping up any browned bits and spices that may have accumulated on the bottom. Pour over the fish and serve immediately.

Yield: 4 servings

If the fillets have a long thin end, as they sometimes do, turn the thin end over onto part of the remaining fillet to form a mass of even thickness. Since fish is cooked so quickly, it's critical that it be evenly thick; otherwise, the thinner part of the fish will dry out and the fatter part remain partly undercooked.

To remove the skin from a cooked fish, cut the skin neatly at the head and the tail. With the point of a knife or the tines of a fork, lift the skin off carefully. It should come off in one piece per side of fish. If you like, scrape off any dark oily flesh before serving.

Salt-Baked Trout

Encased in salt and baked in the hottest possible oven, small whole fish retain all their juices and inherent flavor without interference from extraneous ingredients. Use this simple technique with any small, particularly oily, fine-grained fish. If you can't find trout that weigh 8 ounces, adjust the baking time by 2-3 minutes. For a beautiful, dramatic presentation, remove the skin between the head and the tail of each trout after baking. It takes no more than 30 seconds per fish, since, once cooked, the skin slides off easily.

5 pounds coarse kosher salt
4 8-ounce whole trout, cleaned
1/4 cup olive oil
1 fresh lemon, cut into wedges (optional)
freshly ground pepper, to taste (optional)

Preheat the oven to 500 degrees. Pour about 2/3 of the salt onto a large shallow baking pan. Spread the salt fairly evenly and place in the oven for about 5 minutes.

Clean the trout, if not already prepared, and wipe them dry. Carefully remove the pan from the oven and arrange the trout on the salt so that they do not touch one another. Cover the fish with the remaining salt and bake 15 minutes.

With metal spatulas, crack off the salt from the trout. Brush off all remaining salt and drizzle with olive oil. Serve immediately with a wedge of lemon and a grating of pepper, if desired.

Yield: 4 servings

Halibut with Ginger-Scallion Sauce

Asians have long used fresh ginger to mask fishy odors and, as this recipe exemplifies, used well-balanced flavors in a simple sauce to enhance fish. The ginger and scallion are most assertive, but sweet red bell pepper tames them a bit and adds bright color. Available year-round, halibut is white, lean, and large-flaked, varying with the size of the catch. Substitute red snapper, cod, or grouper for the halibut, if you like, although grouper needs a slightly longer cooking time.

> 2 tablespoons peanut oil
> 4 halibut steaks, about 6 ounces each, about 1" thick
> 4 scallions
> 1 2-inch slice fresh ginger (about 1/4 cup minced)
> 1/4 red bell pepper
> 1/4 cup soy sauce
> 2 tablespoons sherry
> 1 tablespoon sugar

Heat the oil in a heavy large skillet, preferably nonstick, over medium-high heat. Arrange the fish in a single layer and cook 4-5 minutes. Turn and cook another 4-5 minutes.

While the fish cooks, mince the scallions with the ginger and bell pepper, and reserve. Blend the soy sauce, sherry, and sugar, and reserve.

When the fish is done, remove the steaks to a warm plate. Add the scallions and ginger to the skillet and stir-fry about 1 minute. Pour in the soy sauce mixture, allow it to simmer 10-15 seconds, and serve immediately over the fish.

Yield: 4 servings

Your first consideration when buying fish should be freshness. If a recipe you want to try calls for a particular fish that looks questionable, make substitutions that are similar in fat content, texture, and intensity of flavor. Fish with similar characteristics follow: salmon and tuna; shark and swordfish; cod, flounder, orange roughy, halibut, haddock, sea bass, and sole; red snapper, grouper, pike, pollack, and pompano.

Salmon Steaks with Black Butter Sauce

Brown (page 218) and black butter sauces are among the fastest and simplest that we borrow from French cuisine. Brown butter sauce, or *beurre noisette*, owes its name to the nutty aroma that the protein and sugar in the milk content of butter give off when they caramelize in the pan. This black butter sauce is cooked a few seconds longer, delivering a stronger flavor that's perfect with assertive fish, such as salmon. The steps for the sauce have been shaved here. Unlike the classic French sauce, which calls for reducing the vinegar by half and cooling the butter, this simplified version works without delay.

8 tablespoons unsalted butter, divided
4 6-8-ounce salmon steaks, about 1" thick
2 tablespoons drained capers
1/4 cup red wine, balsamic, or sherry vinegar
salt and freshly ground pepper, to taste

Melt 2 tablespoons butter in a large heavy skillet over medium heat. When the butter foams, arrange the salmon steaks in the pan without crowding. Cook 4-5 minutes on each side, or until the fish flakes easily with a fork.

Remove the salmon to a warm plate, wipe the skillet dry, and return it to medium-high heat. Add the remaining butter and the capers, swirling the pan occasionally, until the butter just turns brown. Pour in the vinegar, scraping up any browned bits that have accumulated on the bottom of the pan. Let simmer one minute.

Adjust the seasoning with salt and pepper, if needed, and serve the sauce immediately over the salmon.

Yield: 4 servings

Sole with Pine Nuts and Capers

Dotted with piquant green capers and golden brown nuts, this recipe for delicately flavored sole is peaked with lemon and vermouth. Look for Dover or Channel sole. It's fine-textured, lean, and consistent in quality. In this recipe, the nuts are browned in butter in the pan used to cook the fish, thereby saving the trouble of toasting the nuts separately. If you have toasted pine nuts on hand (see page 93), eliminate sautéing the nuts first.

> 1/4 cup unsalted butter
> 1/4 cup pine nuts (about 1 ounce)
> 4 fillets of sole, about 4 ounces each
> all-purpose flour, for dredging
> 1/2 cup vermouth or dry white wine
> 2 tablespoons fresh or bottled lemon juice
> 2 tablespoons drained capers
> salt and freshly ground pepper to taste

Cooked nuts yield more flavor and crunch than raw ones. If you don't have toasted nuts on hand (see page 93), and you want to add them to an entrée which you are going to pan-fry, toast them in the pan with or without oil or butter prior to cooking the fish, poultry, or meat to save cleaning an extra dish.

Melt the butter in a heavy large, preferably nonstick, skillet over medium-low heat. Add the pine nuts to the skillet and cook, shaking the pan occasionally, to toast the nuts evenly. Remove them to a paper towel as soon as they are golden brown.

Dredge the fillets in the flour, shaking off any excess. Place the fillets in the pan in a single layer. Cook 1-2 minutes, shaking the pan occasionally to keep them from sticking. Turn the fillets, and cook the other side until barely done, another 1-2 minutes. The fish should just be opaque and should flake easily. Remove it to a warm plate.

Add the vermouth over medium-high heat. Stir up any browned bits which may have accumulated on the bottom of the pan while reducing the amount of liquid by approximately half, about 2 minutes. While the sauce reduces, stir in the lemon juice, capers, and the reserved pine nuts. Adjust the seasoning with salt and pepper, if needed, and serve immediately with the fish.

Yield: 4 servings

Avocado and Shellfish with Indian Spices

Rambunctious and rich, this eye-catching combination of scallops, shrimp, and avocado is deceptively simple to make, thanks to the condiment, Indian pickle in oil. Among other ingredients, it contains lime, mango, green chili, karonda, ginger, mustard oil, fenugreek, turmeric, and asafoetida—not your typical pantry pickings. Avocados tame the feisty spices a bit, and if you prefer them warm, microwave them while making the sauce. The lesser amount of cream coats the shellfish and distributes the spices nicely, and the greater amount of cream creates a pool of sauce, calorie-free, of course.

> **2 tablespoons Indian pickle in oil**
> **1/2-3/4 cup cream**
> **2 ripe avocados, preferably Haas**
> **2 tablespoons olive oil**
> **12 medium shrimp, peeled and deveined**
> **12 medium sea scallops**
> **salt and freshly ground pepper, to taste**

Purée the pickle mixture with the cream in a small food processor, blender, or with an immersion blender, and reserve. Halve, pit, and peel the avocados. Fan them out (see page 109), if desired, arrange on serving plates, and reserve.

Heat the oil in a heavy large saucepan over medium-high heat. Add the shrimp and scallops, sautéing until just opaque and cooked through, about 4-5 minutes. Remove the shellfish to a warm plate and drain off any remaining oil.

Lower the heat and add the reserved cream to the pan, stirring until blended and slightly thickened. Add any juices exuded from the shellfish to the pan and reduce, if needed. Return the shellfish to the pan, adjust the seasoning with salt and pepper, if desired, and serve immediately with the shellfish and avocado.

Yield: 4 servings

West Coast Crab Cakes

These red and green-flecked crab cakes contain just enough binding to hold them together, making them luxurious and tender. The bell pepper and scallions are pre-cooked in the same pan used for the crab cakes, thereby saving a pan to clean and coating it with a bit of moisture for the delicate cakes. Serve them with tartar sauce, lemon wedges, Brown Butter Sauce (page 218), Processor Aïoli (page 229), or Cajun Mayonnaise (page 228).

4 tablespoons unsalted butter, divided
1 red bell pepper, stem removed, seeded, minced
3 scallions, sliced thin
2 eggs
1 pound cooked, picked-over crabmeat
1 tablespoon fresh or bottled lemon juice
1 1/2 cups fresh white bread crumbs
1 tablespoon Worcestershire sauce
salt and freshly ground pepper, to taste

Melt 1 tablespoon of the butter in a heavy large, preferably nonstick, saucepan over medium-low heat. Stir in the pepper and scallions. Cook, stirring occasionally, until softened, about 5 minutes.

Meanwhile, beat the eggs lightly in a medium bowl. Blend the crabmeat, lemon juice, bread crumbs, Worcestershire, and the cooked vegetable mixture with the eggs. Adjust the seasoning, if needed (see sidebar). Form into patties about 1/2" thick.

Melt the remaining butter in the pan used to cook the bell pepper. Sauté the cakes, turning carefully once, 4-5 minutes on each side, and serve immediately.

Yield: 4 servings

Cooked, picked-over crab-meat commands a high price, but having caught, cooked, and cleaned hundreds of them, I consider the convenience worth every penny. Lump meat is the most expensive. It comes out in large, solid pieces from the body of the crab. Flake meat also comes from the body but in smaller pieces, and the stringy, darker meat comes from the claws. Both of these less expensive types make fine pickings for crab cakes.

When binding wet and dry ingredients, the amounts needed may vary, depending upon the amount of moisture in them. Eggs, crab, fresh breadcrumbs, and vegetables, among many other foods, contain different amounts of water, depending upon their age, the season, and how the ingredients have been transported and stored.

To taste a blend of raw food, pinch off part of it, and microwave it for a few seconds until barely cooked. Taste it, and adjust the seasoning, if needed. Repeat until the seasoning is correct. If you don't microwave, sauté a bit of the mixture briefly in a pan, preferably nonstick, so that neither butter nor oil changes its flavor.

Mussels Steamed with Garlic and Lemon Grass

Mussels make a stunning, quick-cooking feature for a meal. Their long, shiny-black shells dotted with creamy-tan meat always look sophisticated. They take just minutes to cook, but provide a rich, flavorful entrée to linger over. The mussels create a broth reminiscent of the seaside, complemented by citrusy lemon grass and pungent garlic. Enrich the liquid, if you like, with 4 tablespoons of unsalted butter or 1/2 cup cream.

2 quarts mussels
2 tablespoons unsalted butter
2 cloves garlic, minced
1 large onion, coarsely chopped
3 stalks of lemon grass, tough stalks removed, minced
1 cup vermouth or dry white wine
salt and freshly ground pepper, to taste

Scrub and debeard the mussels, if necessary. In a heavy 4-quart saucepan, melt the butter over medium-low heat.

Stir in the garlic, onion, and lemon grass. Cook, stirring occasionally, until the onion is softened, about 5 minutes.

Pour in the vermouth and mussels, increase the heat to high, and cover partially. Cook, shaking the pan frequently, until the shells open, about 5 minutes, depending upon their size. Cook for another 30 seconds. Taste the cooking liquid for salt and pepper and adjust the seasoning, if needed. Serve the mussels with the cooking liquid in warm soup bowls with crusty French bread.

Yield: 4 servings

Scallops with Orange Cream

Bay scallops are sweet, tender morsels typically 3/8 inch thick in diameter, and they need the briefest of cooking time. Here they are complemented with a creamy sauce of shallots, sherry, and orange. Stove-top cooking is ideal for small scallops, since you'll need to keep a close eye on them to be sure they don't overcook and toughen. They're ready as soon as they turn opaque, and they're small enough that the lucky cook can test one or two while sautéing.

I like to serve these with a simple recipe for asparagus (Roasted Asparagus, page 185), since the slender green stalks offer a beautiful contrast in color and the orange sauce highlights the flavor of both scallops and asparagus.

> **2 tablespoons unsalted butter**
> **1 1/4 pound bay scallops**
> **2 large shallots, minced**
> **1/2 cup dry sherry**
> **1/2 cup orange juice**
> **3/4 cup fish stock or clam juice**
> **1/2 cup cream**
> **freshly grated zest of 1 orange or**
> ** 2 teaspoons dried orange zest**
> **salt and freshly ground pepper, to taste**

Melt the butter in a heavy large skillet over medium-high heat. Add the scallops, shake the pan occasionally, and cook until they turn opaque. Remove the scallops to a warm plate. Add the shallots to the pan off the heat, and cook, stirring frequently until softened, about 2 minutes.

Return the pan to the stove and pour in the sherry and orange juice. Cook until the liquid reduces to a glaze, about 2 minutes. Add the stock, cream, and orange rind. Allow the liquid to boil down until thickened, about 5 minutes.

Return the scallops and any accumulated liquid to the pan. Warm through, adjust the seasoning with salt and pepper, if needed, and serve immediately.

Yield: 4 servings

Scallops and shrimp freeze beautifully, rarely losing any of their texture or flavor, and since they contain no waste, they take up little freezer space. Stock up when they're on sale. You can defrost them in minutes by floating them in cold water, separating them as they defrost. Pat them dry with paper towels before cooking, or they will steam instead of sauté.

Many sauces appear thinner while hot than when served, as frequently happens with reduced sauces. As soon as the sauce hits a cool plate, it becomes more viscous. If you're concerned about the precise thickness of a sauce, remove a spoonful to a small plate to judge whether it should reduce further (to thicken it) or whether it needs more liquid (to thin it). Be especially careful when reducing cream sauces, since they can boil over quickly and burn on the bottom of a pan.

To save time, buy shrimp already shelled and deveined. If there's any liquid left in a container of shrimp, blot them dry with paper toweling before cooking. If you can't buy them ready to cook, invest in a shrimp peeler. They cost very little, consume only a tiny amount of storage space, and go straight into the dishwasher. They'll peel and devein shrimp of all but the tiniest size with one quick stroke.

Sweet and Spicy Shrimp

The sweetness of honey and the heat of cayenne do a lively balancing act in this dish. Play with those two ingredients, if you like, after making the shrimp once, so you can suit your own palate. Toothpick each shrimp, if you like, to use as hors d'oeuvre, and leftovers are marvelous in a salad or sandwich. Be sure to use mild honey, since strong ones can overwhelm a dish.

3 tablespoons unsalted butter
4 cloves garlic, minced
1/2 teaspoon ground turmeric
1/2 teaspoon ground cinnamon
1/4 teaspoon freshly grated or ground nutmeg
1/4 teaspoon ground red pepper (cayenne)
1/4 cup fresh or bottled lemon juice
1/4 cup vermouth, dry white wine, or fish stock
2 pounds shrimp, shelled and deveined
2 tablespoons mild honey
salt and freshly ground pepper, to taste

Melt the butter in a large sauté pan or wok over medium-low heat. Stir the garlic, turmeric, cinnamon, nutmeg, and red pepper into the butter, and cook gently until the garlic softens, about 4 minutes.

Increase the heat to high and stir in the lemon juice, vermouth, and shrimp. Sauté, turning frequently, until the shrimp are barely cooked. They will look bright pink and opaque when done. If there are more than 2 tablespoons liquid in the pan, remove the shrimp with a slotted spoon or spatula to a warm oven, reduce the liquid in the pan to a syrupy glaze, and return the shrimp to the pan.

Toss the shrimp with the honey until it melts and glazes the shrimp. Season with salt and pepper, if needed, and serve immediately.

Yield: 4 servings

Oysters à la Meunière

This simple French classic delivers pure oyster flavor with a hint of lemon. Fillet of sole is often cooked à la Meunière, and you can use this same treatment with any fish fillet or steak. The quality of the shellfish is critical, since its taste is unadorned by many other ingredients. For variety, add a few capers, minced sun-dried tomatoes, or chopped parsley or tarragon. Be sure to save the oyster liquor for Oyster Stew (page 71).

24 small shucked oysters
2 eggs
all purpose flour, for dredging
1/4 cup unsalted butter
1/2 cup vermouth, fish stock, or clam juice
2 tablespoons fresh or bottled lemon juice
salt and freshly ground pepper, to taste

Drain the oysters of their liquor. Place the oysters on a couple of layers of paper towels and pat the tops dry. Lightly beat the eggs in a small bowl and place the flour on a paper towel close to the eggs.

Melt the butter in a heavy large sauté pan over medium heat. Dip each oyster in the egg and then in the flour, shaking off any excess. As the oysters are coated, add them to the butter. When the oysters turn golden on the bottom, turn them to cook the underside. When cooked through and golden on both sides, remove them to a warm plate.

Pour in the vermouth and lemon juice, scraping up the browned bits on the bottom of the pan. Simmer until slightly thickened, adjust the seasoning with salt and pepper, if needed, and serve immediately over the oysters.

Yield: 4 servings

Double-dipping food in eggs and flour can be messy. Line up the oysters, eggs, and flour next to the stove to avoid a lot of drips and dust. Put the flour on a paper towel instead of a dish that'll need washing. The towel can be thrown away when finished.

Anytime you're cooking a lot of small ingredients that need to be turned once (as opposed to stir-frying, where ingredients are continually turned), place them in a set pattern as you add them to the pan, such as clockwise from the top, so you can turn them quickly and efficiently as they cook.

Whenever you need to mince parsley and garlic to add to a recipe together, mince them together. If you are mincing them by hand, the dry parsley will help keep moist garlic from sticking to your knife, and if mincing in a food processor, the parsley will help keep the garlic from sticking to the sides of the workbowl.

Scampi

I never tire of this simple recipe. It provides the perfect balance of garlic, butter, and lemon. Sometimes mistaken for jumbo prawns, scampi are technically small members of the lobster family. In America, the Venetian term *scampi* has come to mean any type of shrimp cooked in butter, garlic, and wine. Add a couple of teaspoons of fresh herbs, such as oregano, basil, or rosemary, if you like, to vary the recipe.

1/4 cup unsalted butter
6 sprigs parsley
3 cloves garlic
2 pounds large shrimp, shelled and deveined
1/2 cup vermouth or dry white wine
1/4 cup fresh or bottled lemon juice
salt and freshly ground pepper, to taste

Heat the butter in a large wok or skillet over medium heat. Meanwhile, mince the parsley and garlic together. When the butter bubbles, add the shrimp and parsley mixture. Cook, tossing the mixture occasionally, until the shrimp turn pink and opaque. Be careful not to overcook.

Remove the shrimp to a warm plate and pour in the vermouth and lemon juice over high heat. Let the liquid simmer until it reduces by approximately one-half, about 5 minutes.

Return the shrimp to the pan and toss them in the wine mixture. Season with salt and pepper, if needed, and serve immediately.

Yield: 4 servings

Chicken with Dijon and Blueberry Vinegar

Fruit-based vinegar and pungent mustard create a pleasing balance of flavors in this creamy sauce. Mustard helps thicken it, as does the flour used for dredging, so the sauce takes on a creamy consistency with the addition of just milk, no cream. Use raspberry or another fruit-flavored vinegar, if you prefer. If you have fresh berries on hand, dot the finished sauce with them and barely warm through before serving.

> 2 tablespoons unsalted butter
> 4 skinless, boneless chicken breast halves
> all-purpose flour, for dredging
> 1/4 cup blueberry vinegar
> 3 tablespoons Dijon mustard
> 1 cup milk
> salt and freshly ground pepper, to taste

Melt the butter in a heavy large skillet or sauté pan over medium-low heat. Dredge the chicken in the flour, shaking off any excess. Increase the heat to medium-high and arrange the chicken in the pan in a single layer. Cook 4-5 minutes on each side, or until tender and golden. Remove the chicken to warm plates.

Pour in the vinegar, scraping up any browned bits that may have accumulated on the bottom of the pan. Reduce the vinegar to a glaze. Whisk in the mustard and milk, and reduce until slightly thickened. Adjust the seasoning with salt and pepper, if needed, and serve the sauce immediately over the chicken.

Yield: 4 servings

Pounding chicken breasts cuts down a bit on their cooking time and, most importantly, it evens out their thickness so that all the meat cooks in the same amount of time. Since thinner meats cook faster, the thickest part of a chicken breast will remain undercooked while the thinner part overcooks and dries out. I usually remove the small tenderloin that separates naturally from the breast before pounding. You can pound the remaining meat between two sheets of waxed paper, if you prefer, or on a cutting board. Gently pound the meat out and down from the center until evenly flattened. Cook the tenderloins alongside the breasts in the same pan, but remove them sooner. Since they're so small, they require only 2-3 minutes per side.

Lemon and Sage-Flavored Chicken

Sprightly lemon offsets the pleasantly musky flavor of sage in this easy chicken dish, and Worcestershire and cumin add complexity. Sage is underappreciated in this country, where it's usually relegated to holiday stuffing for poultry. On the other hand, Europeans take full advantage of this Mediterranean herb, using it sparingly in pastas, poultry, meat, and cheese dishes. Too much sage is overwhelming. However, there may be no more useless herb than dried sage that's in decline. It looks, and tastes, like dust.

> **3 tablespoons olive oil**
> **4 skinless, boneless chicken breast halves, lightly pounded**
> **all-purpose flour, for dredging**
> **6-7 large fresh sage leaves**
> **1/2 cup chicken stock**
> **1 tablespoon fresh or bottled lemon juice**
> **1 teaspoon Worcestershire sauce**
> **1/4 teaspoon ground cumin**
> **salt and freshly ground pepper, to taste**
> **3 tablespoons chopped fresh chives (optional)**

Heat the oil in a heavy large, preferably nonstick, skillet over medium-high heat. Dredge the chicken in the flour, shaking off any excess. Arrange the chicken in the pan in a single layer and cook, turning once, about 4-5 minutes on each side. If the chicken browns too quickly, reduce the heat during cooking. Both sides should be golden.

While the chicken cooks, mince the sage and blend it with the stock, lemon juice, Worcestershire, and cumin in a small bowl or glass measure. When the chicken is done, remove it to a warm plate. Pour the stock mixture into the pan, scraping up any browned bits on the bottom of the pan, and reduce it slightly.

Adjust the seasoning, if needed, with salt and pepper. Pour over the chicken, sprinkle with chives, if using, and serve immediately.

Yield: 4 servings

Unless it's burned, a sauce that has reduced too much can almost always be reconstituted with water. Never add stock or wine to reconstitute a sauce, since it can leave an unappealing concentration of its flavor. Pour a bit of water into the pan and whisk to regain the character of the sauce. Add more water, as necessary. If you've added too much water, simmer to reduce it again, watching carefully. Keep in mind that the wider the skillet and the higher the heat, the faster a sauce reduces.

Instead of using another bowl, use a measuring cup to gauge the basic liquid for a recipe (here, the stock) and blend the remaining herbs, condiments, and flavorings in the measuring cup.

Chicken with Mushrooms and Madeira

Madeira adds a caramel, smoky flavor to the earthiness of mushrooms. It ranges from sweet to dry and from pale blonde to dark and tawny. If you don't have Madeira on hand, however, substitute dry Marsala or sherry for different, but interesting nuances. By all means use wild mushrooms, if you can get them.

4 skinless, boneless chicken breast halves
all-purpose flour, for dredging
4 tablespoons unsalted butter
2 cloves garlic
2 cups sliced mushrooms
1/2 cup dry Madeira
salt and freshly ground pepper, to taste

Dredge the chicken in the flour, shaking off any excess. Melt the butter over medium heat in a heavy skillet large enough to hold the chicken in a single layer without crowding. When the butter melts, add the chicken and cook until golden on both sides, about 4-5 minutes per side.

While the chicken is cooking, mince the garlic. If you didn't buy pre-sliced mushrooms, slice them now.

When the chicken is barely cooked, remove it to a warm plate. Add the garlic and mushrooms to the pan and sauté until softened, about 4 minutes. Pour in the Madeira over medium-high heat, stir the browned bits from the bottom of the pan into the liquid, and simmer until slightly thickened. Season with salt and pepper, if needed, and serve immediately over the chicken.

Yield: 4 servings

Dredging chicken, fish, or meat in flour gives the meat an attractive golden color, adds crispness to the exterior, and thickens sauces a bit. Some of the flour is left in the pan and it cooks with the butter or oil as the meat cooks. When adding liquid to the pan, especially over high heat, count on some thickening power from the flour used for dredging.

To cut chicken into chunks quickly, stack two breast halves at a time and make slices every 3/4 inch. Turn the chicken or your cutting board ninety degrees and repeat. The time spent cutting the chicken is made up for in reduced cooking time.

Five-Spice Glazed Chicken

This full-flavored, 10-minute recipe is an adaptation of one that took hours of marinating and roasting. With the availability of five-spice powder and hoisin sauce, both available in supermarkets, a lot of work has been done for the cook. Five-spice powder often contains more than 5 spices, but it's typically an intriguing blend of cinnamon, clove, fennel, star anise, and Szechuan peppercorns (fagara). Sometimes licorice root and ground ginger, rarely used for any other purpose in China, are included. Any leftovers do nicely in a salad.

> 2 tablespoons hoisin sauce
> 2 teaspoons sesame oil
> 1 tablespoon sugar
> 3/4 teaspoon five-spice powder
> 2 tablespoons corn or peanut oil
> 2 cloves garlic, minced
> 4 scallions, cut into 1" lengths
> 4 skinless, boneless chicken breast halves,
>   cut into 3/4-inch chunks

In a small bowl, blend the hoisin sauce, sesame oil, sugar, and five-spice powder and reserve.

Heat the oil in a large wok or skillet over medium-high heat. Add the garlic and scallions and stir-fry 30 seconds. Add the chicken and toss until the chicken starts to turn white, about 2 minutes. Add the reserved sauce mixture and stir-fry until the chicken is opaque and the sauce heated through, about 2 minutes. Serve immediately.

Yield: 4 servings

Indonesian-Flavored Chicken Fingers

Many hurried cooks think Asian cooking is too time-consuming to take seriously at home, but carefully chosen recipes are as fast as cooking can be. This exciting balance of spicy, sweet, and nutty flavors is simplified by peanut butter, which flavors and thickens simultaneously, and red chili paste, which contains fresh red chili peppers, vinegar, sugar, and salt. Often sold as Sambal Oeleck, the blend provides convenience, giving foods roundness and depth of flavor with little effort. This recipe provides enough sauce to moisten rice or noodles as well as the chicken.

> 4 skinless, boneless chicken breast halves
> 4 scallions
> 1/2 cup chicken stock or broth
> 1/3 cup smooth peanut butter
> 1 tablespoon honey
> 1 tablespoon soy sauce
> 1 teaspoon ground red chili paste (Sambal Oeleck)
> 2 tablespoons corn or peanut oil

Slice the chicken into 3" x 1/2" "fingers" or "threads" (see page 147). Slice the scallions into 1-inch lengths. Whisk the stock, peanut butter, honey, soy sauce, and chili paste with 1/4 cup water in a measuring cup or a small bowl and reserve (the mixture will smooth out completely when cooked).

Heat the oil in a heavy large wok or skillet over medium-high heat. Add the chicken and scallions and cook until the chicken turns white and opaque on all sides, about 5 minutes.

Pour the peanut mixture into the pan and simmer, whisking, until smooth and slightly thickened. When the chicken is cooked through, about 2 minutes, serve immediately over rice or noodles.

Yield: 4 servings

If meats and poultry have been frozen and need to be sliced, keep in mind that partially defrosted meat can be sliced more easily and neatly than completely defrosted or fresh. This is particularly helpful if you need thin shreds or a small dice of meat.

An accurate, easy way to measure a solid ingredient such as peanut butter is to pour liquid into a glass measure up to an easily measurable quantity, then add the solid ingredient, and measure by displacement. In recipes where a substantial amount of liquid is called for, measure the liquid first, and then add the solid ingredient to measure it.

Honey and Ginger-Glazed Roast Chicken

To save on preparation time, buy chicken already cut into pieces. You can pick your favorite cuts or buy a complete chicken in serving pieces. If you buy small pieces, such as wings or drumettes (which make perfect hors d'oeuvre), you can cut the cooking time in half. Remove any large pieces of fat from chicken before baking. Although the fat bastes the chicken as it cooks, its removal makes degreasing easier, and the meal healthier.

Aside from delicious sweet-warm flavor and a beautiful glaze, the amazing thing about this dish is its ease of preparation. The orange juice mixture bastes the chicken during cooking and boils down to make its own simple sauce. If you don't have molasses handy, double the amount of honey. The chicken will be lighter in color and have less depth of flavor, but wonderful nonetheless. This recipe is an exception in this book, since it needs a full hour of cooking, but it's a prime example of how effortlessly a meat can roast, forming its own sauce without attention from the cook.

2 cloves garlic
1 1/2-inch slice fresh ginger (about 1 tablespoon minced)
1 cup orange juice
2 tablespoons honey
2 tablespoons molasses
1 tablespoon Dijon mustard
1 3 1/2 to 4-pound chicken, cut into 4 equal serving pieces
salt and freshly ground pepper, to taste

Preheat the oven to 375 degrees. Mince the garlic and ginger together. Place in a baking pan with the orange juice, honey, molasses, and mustard (see first tip, page 42). Whisk to blend the ingredients.

Dip the chicken quarters in the liquid and turn to coat them. Bake about 50-60 minutes, depending upon the thickness of the pieces. Turn and baste them at least once during cooking.

Remove the chicken to a warm plate. Skim off as much fat as possible from the cooking juices, place over high heat, and bring the liquid to a boil. Reduce until syrupy, season with salt and pepper, if needed, and serve over the chicken.

Yield: 4 servings

Duck Breast Dijon with Raspberries

Complemented by a sweet and sour sauce, these succulent duck breasts, sliced on the diagonal before serving, are punctuated with glistening raspberries. This is a sophisticated entrée made in 15 minutes flat. Use the sauce for chicken or pork, as well, and adjust the sugar to your taste. This one is on the sweet side.

4 boneless duck breast halves
3 cloves garlic
1/2 cup chicken stock or broth
2-4 tablespoons sugar
1/4 cup raspberry vinegar
2 tablespoons Dijon mustard
2 teaspoons Worcestershire sauce
2 tablespoons unsalted butter (optional)
1 1/2 cups fresh or flash-frozen raspberries
salt and freshly ground pepper, to taste

Delicate fruits, such as raspberries, are ideal for quick-cooking. If cooked longer than it takes to just heat them through, they'll fall apart in the sauce, losing their beautiful appearance and texture.

Preheat the oven to 350 degrees.

Trim the breasts of excess fat and make 5 or 6 diagonal slices just through the skin across each breast half. Place the breast skin side down in a heavy large skillet over medium-high heat and cook, running a spatula sharply under the skin occasionally, until the skin is golden and some fat has exuded from the skin, about 3-5 minutes.

Use 1 tablespoon of the fat to grease a foil-lined baking sheet. Place the breasts skin side up and roast about 10 minutes, or until the meat is pink and firm. It should register 125 degrees for rare on an instant-read thermometer.

While the duck roasts, pour off all but 1 tablespoon of fat, mince the garlic, and add it to the fat in the skillet over medium-low heat. Cook until just softened, about 3 minutes. Pour in the stock, sugar, vinegar, mustard, and Worcestershire over medium heat, and reduce until slightly thickened. Swirl in the butter, if using, without letting it melt. Add the raspberries and cook just to heat through. Adjust the seasoning with salt and pepper, if necessary, and reserve.

When the duck is cooked, remove it to a cutting board, and following the diagonal cuts on its skin, slice each breast into 5-6 pieces. Serve immediately with the sauce.

Yield: 4 servings

If you are using an outdoor grill, you can test its heat without special equipment. If you can keep an open palm at the cooking level for 2 seconds, the grill is hot; for 3 seconds, medium hot; for 4 seconds, medium; and for 5 seconds, low.

Butterflied Quail in Plum Sauce

Quail make a pleasant, slightly gamy, all-dark meat alternative to chicken breasts. If you cannot find fresh whole quail, use frozen boned ones, which are easier to find. Many come partially boned and flattened. If you own a heavy cleaver, the blade will cut through the backbone of small birds and the flat side will flatten them. If you prefer, grill the quail skin side up, 4-6 inches above a bed of hot coals. Baste and turn occasionally until the breast meat is still pink at the bone, about 8-10 minutes total.

> **4 quail, about 6 ounces each whole or 4 1/2-5 ounces each boned, thawed, if frozen**
> **1 8-ounce jar golden plum sauce**
> **1 tablespoon low-sodium soy sauce**
> **1 teaspoon sesame seed oil**
> **3/4 teaspoon crushed red pepper flakes (optional)**
> **2 tablespoons toasted sesame seeds (optional)**

Preheat the broiler. If not already split, cut through the backbone of each bird with a heavy knife or poultry shears. Place them skin side up on a flat surface and press down firmly until they lie flat. Line a baking sheet with foil and arrange the quail in a single layer.

In a small saucepan, whisk the plum sauce, soy sauce, and sesame seed oil, and red pepper, if using, and place over medium heat. Brush the quail with the mixture and broil 5 inches from the heat for 4-5 minutes. Turn and baste the birds with more plum sauce, and broil another 4-5 minutes. Remove the quail to warm plates.

Pour about 2 tablespoons of water in the baking pan and stir to dissolve any juices or sauce sticking to the foil. Pour the juices over the quail, sprinkle with sesame seeds, if using, and serve immediately. Pass the extra warm plum sauce.

Yield: 4 servings

Asian-Flavored Pork Sauté

This colorful western-style sauté, dotted with red chilies and green scallions, is highlighted with Asian flavors. Fresh ginger and dried chilies provide heat, and orange juice lends a bit of sweetness. Substitute chicken breasts for the pork, if you prefer.

1/4 cup minced fresh ginger (about 1 2-inch slice)
4 scallions, cut in 1" lengths
8 dried red chilies
1 cup orange juice
2 tablespoons low-sodium soy sauce
2 tablespoons sherry
2 tablespoons corn or peanut oil
4 boneless pork loin steaks, 4 ounces each, 1/2-3/4" thick

Combine the ginger, scallions, and chilies and reserve. Combine the orange juice, soy sauce, and sherry and reserve.

Heat the oil in a heavy large skillet over medium heat. Add the pork in a single layer and cook 4 minutes. Turn the meat and cook another 4-5 minutes. Remove the meat to a warm plate and drain off all but 1 tablespoon fat from the pan.

Add the ginger mixture and stir-fry until fragrant, about 30 seconds. Pour in the orange juice mixture, increase the heat, and simmer until thickened slightly, about 3 minutes. Nap the pork with the sauce and serve immediately.

Yield: 4 servings

When cooking and serving whole dried red chilies, be sure no one eats them. They impart heat to the sauce and are typically left whole in Chinese dishes, but beware their blazing potential. You can substitute crushed dried red chili flakes, if you like, as a safe alternative.

Gingered Pork Medallions with Orange and Wine

Dry red wine and balsamic vinegar lend their complex undertones to make a sophisticated, lightly herbed, sauce for boneless pork loin. If you can find fresh lemon thyme to use in place of regular, it will add a pleasant, but strong, citrusy aroma to the dish.

> **4 slices boneless pork loin, about 4 ounces each, 1" thick**
> **1/3 cup dry red wine**
> **1/4 cup orange juice**
> **1 teaspoon sugar**
> **1 teaspoon balsamic vinegar**
> **1 1/2 teaspoons fresh thyme or 1/2 teaspoon dried**
> **3 tablespoons unsalted butter, divided**
> **1 1/2-inch slice fresh ginger (about 1 tablespoon minced)**
> **1 large shallot**
> **salt and freshly ground pepper, to taste**

Trim the pork of any excess fat, if necessary. In a small bowl, blend the wine, orange juice, sugar, vinegar, and thyme and set it aside.

Heat one tablespoon of the butter in a heavy medium sauté pan, preferably nonstick, over medium-high heat. Place the meat in the pan without crowding. Cook about 4-5 minutes, turn, and cook another 4-5 minutes, or until the meat is lightly browned on both sides. Meanwhile, mince the ginger and add it to the wine and orange juice mixture. Mince the shallot and reserve. Reduce the heat, continue to cook another two minutes, and remove the meat to a warm platter.

Add the shallot to the pan and sauté until softened, about 2 minutes. Increase the heat and pour in the wine and orange juice mixture, scraping up any browned bits that may have accumulated on the bottom of the pan. Allow the sauce to simmer, reducing it to about 3/4 of its original volume. Whisk in the remaining butter without letting it melt, adjust the seasoning with salt and pepper, and serve immediately.

Yield: 4 servings

When measuring a number of liquid ingredients that will be added to a recipe simultaneously, choose a cup measure large enough to hold the total of the combined liquids. Pour one into another, measuring additional ones from where the previous one left off. If there are other ingredients that will be added to the recipe with the liquid, such as herbs, garlic, or ginger, add them to the liquid, so you don't have to scramble for them and measure them out while cooking.

When sautéing meat, most of us try to use as little fat as possible. If the meat appears to be sticking to the pan, run a metal spatula sharply underneath it to keep it loosened. Because of health concerns, pork has been bred to be leaner than in past decades. Most of its fat surrounds the meat, instead of being marbled through it, as with beef. Since it has little of its own fat to release, it tends to stick to pans more than other meats.

Thai Pork with Red Curry

The well-rounded heat of curry paste and peanut butter make this stir-fry appealing to children as well as adults. Red curry paste is a versatile ingredient traditionally used for Thai satays, sauces, and peanut dressings. It can be made at home with lemon grass, chili peppers, garlic, shallots, lemon, and galanga root, but, for convenience, buy it prepared. The canned curry paste will keep indefinitely in the refrigerator if removed to a glass jar and kept tightly covered. Leftovers of Thai Pork reheat well in the microwave, or serve them cold in a salad.

> **1 1/2 pounds boneless pork loin chops, about 1/2-inch thick**
> **1 1/2 teaspoons freshly grated or dried lemon zest**
> **2 cups frozen green peas (1 10-ounce package)**
> **1/4 cup oyster sauce**
> **2 tablespoons unsalted smooth peanut butter**
> **2 tablespoons sugar**
> **3 tablespoons peanut or corn oil**
> **1 1/2 tablespoons red curry paste**

Remove any excess fat from the pork, stack 2 chops at a time, and slice into 1/4" strips. If you are using fresh lemon zest, grate the lemon and reserve. Place the peas in a strainer and run cold water over them briefly to begin defrosting them. In a small bowl, blend the oyster sauce, peanut butter, sugar, and 1/2 cup cold water and reserve.

In a large wok or heavy skillet, blend the oil and curry paste over medium-high heat. When the mixture sizzles, add the pork and lemon zest and stir-fry until the meat is no longer pink, about 5 minutes. Stir in the reserved oyster sauce mixture and cook, stirring, another 3-4 minutes. Stir in the peas and cook until just heated through. Serve immediately.

Yield: 4 servings

Frozen green peas are usually tastier than what we can buy fresh. I consider them a great convenience product—they defrost quickly under running water, they only need to be heated through to be cooked, and they scatter throughout a dish adding color, nutrition, and pleasing flavor.

A citrus zester makes easy work of removing rind. It digs into the fruit just far enough to remove the flavorful zest, while leaving the bitter white pith. Typically, citrus zest removed this way needs no further grating or chopping.

Pork Tenderloin with Port and Apricots

Fruit and pork are a traditional combination, and dried fruit provides even more concentrated sweetness and flavor than fresh. Apricots are at their best dried, thankfully, since fresh ones are available for such a short season. Substitute all or part prunes or dried apples for the apricots, if desired. Port adds further sweetness to this intriguing, simple sauce, and plumps the dried fruits as they simmer.

> *Cooking dried fruits with a liquid plumps them, making their texture more appealing, and using wine or fruit juice lends them added flavor. The liquid will permeate the fruit most quickly if the fruit is chopped and then heated with the liquid.*
>
> *Pork, chicken, and beef roasts will remain juicier if allowed to rest for a few minutes before slicing. This conveniently allows the cook time to concoct a quick sauce in the roasting pan while the meat rests just prior to carving.*

4 ounces dried apricots (about 3/4 cup)
1/2 cup port
2 boneless pork tenderloins, about 1 1/2 pounds total
all-purpose flour, for dredging
2 tablespoons olive oil
1 cup chicken stock or broth
2 tablespoons unsalted butter
salt and freshly ground pepper, to taste

Preheat the oven to 500 degrees. Stack the apricots a few at a time and slice thin. Pour the port into a 2-cup glass measure, add the apricots, and reserve. Trim the tenderloins of any exterior fat and dredge them in the flour.

In an ovenproof skillet, heat the olive oil over medium-high heat. Add the pork and cook, turning as needed to brown the meat evenly, about 5 minutes. Place the pan in the oven and cook until the pork reaches 145 degrees, about 10-12 minutes. Turn once during roasting.

Remove the meat to a warm plate, pour off the fat from the pan, and return it to the stove over medium-high heat. Pour in the port and apricots, stirring to scrape up any browned bits from the bottom of the pan. Simmer until the liquid is reduced to a few tablespoons.

Pour in the stock and simmer until reduced by half. Meanwhile, slice the pork on the bias. Take the skillet off the heat and swirl in the butter without letting it melt. Adjust the seasoning of the sauce, if needed, and serve immediately over the pork.

Yield: 4 large servings

Pork Threads in Black Bean Sauce

This striking entrée is slightly hot, but it gets most of its intriguing flavor from Chinese fermented black beans. With plain white rice as an accompaniment, it makes a complete, colorful meal. Fermented black beans are unlike any Occidental seasoning. They are pungent and salty, so small amounts go a long way, and they'll keep at room temperature indefinitely. Don't confuse them with Western black beans—there's little similarity. Buy prepared broccoli florets, if you like, to save a bit of time.

3/4 pound pork tenderloin
1 small red bell pepper
2 scallions
2 cups broccoli florets
1 15-ounce can baby corn
3 tablespoons fermented black beans
3 tablespoons dry sherry
1/2 teaspoon crushed red pepper flakes
2 tablespoons corn or peanut oil
salt and freshly ground pepper, to taste

Bring 3 inches of water to boil in a heavy wok. Meanwhile, slice the pork into 1/2" strips (see below). Quarter and seed the bell pepper, and slice it into 1/2" strips. Slice the scallions thin and reserve. Stir the broccoli into the water and cook 2-3 minutes. Drain and run cold water over the broccoli to set the color. Drain the corn.

Blend the beans, sherry, and pepper flakes with 2 tablespoons water. Heat the oil in the wok over medium-high heat. When hot, stir-fry the pork and bell pepper 2-3 minutes. Add the broccoli, scallions, corn, and beans and stir-fry another 2-3 minutes, or until the sauce is slightly reduced. Adjust the seasoning, if needed, with salt and pepper, and serve immediately.

Yield: 4 servings

To quickly cut pork tenderloin into Asian "threads" or western "fingers," cut across the pork, forming 1/2-inch slices. Stack a few of them and cut downward into 1/2-inch slices. For chicken, stack two chicken breast halves and hold them steady while slicing crosswise into 1/2-inch sections. Since the halves are about 3 inches across, half your work was done by the chicken.

Steak au Poivre with Green Peppercorns

The soft texture and lively flavor and color of green peppercorns packed in brine makes this pepper steak a cut above. Using green peppercorns instead of the traditional dried black ones relieves the cook of the chore of pounding whole peppercorns and makes it easy to increase or decrease the amount of spice to suit your taste. Sprinkle in a few more, or dredge a few out, as needed. Green peppercorns are typically sold next to capers in a similar jar. Take care not to confuse them.

Incorporating butter into a sauce by swirling it in without letting it melt into a pool enriches a sauce and gives it a satiny appearance. Usually only a tablespoon or two is used, so the basic character of the sauce remains unchanged and its flavors intact.

> **4 6-ounce sirloin strip steaks, about 1" thick**
> **2 tablespoons corn or vegetable oil**
> **2 large shallots**
> **4 teaspoons green peppercorns, or more, to taste**
> **1/2 cup dry red wine or cognac**
> **1/2 cup beef stock or broth**
> **2 tablespoons unsalted butter**
> **salt and freshly ground pepper, to taste**

Trim the steaks of any excess fat. Heat the oil in a heavy large skillet or sauté pan over medium-high heat and add the steaks in a single layer. Cook about 5 minutes on both sides for medium-rare.

While the steaks cook, mince the shallots and drain the peppercorns. When the meat is cooked, remove it to a warm plate. Pour off all but 2 tablespoons fat and reduce the heat to medium-low. Add the shallots and peppercorns to the pan, and sauté about 3 minutes, or until barely softened.

Pour in the wine and simmer over medium-high heat, stirring up any browned bits that may have accumulated on the bottom of the pan. When the wine is reduced to a glaze, pour in the stock. Simmer, reducing by about half.

Remove the pan from the heat and swirl in the butter, incorporating it into the sauce without allowing it to melt. Adjust the seasoning for salt and pepper, if needed, and serve the sauce over the steaks immediately.

Yield: 4 servings

Steak Diane

Steak Diane, a so-called French classic, may be purely an American chef's invention. What it lacks in authenticity, however, it makes up for in its appetizing blend of flavors. In restaurants, Steak Diane is often cooked at the tableside and it's usually costly, but it can be made quickly and relatively inexpensively at home. If beef fillet is outrageously expensive, substitute another steak or even lean ground beef for the fillets. Be sure the meat is an inch thick or adjust the cooking time accordingly.

> 1 tablespoon unsalted butter
> 1 tablespoon corn or vegetable oil
> 4 beef fillet steaks, each about 1 inch thick
> 1 large shallot
> 1/2 cup brandy, sherry, or dry red wine
> 2 tablespoons Worcestershire sauce
> 2 tablespoons sour cream
> 1/2 teaspoon Dijon mustard
> salt and freshly ground pepper, to taste

Melt the butter and oil in a heavy large skillet over medium-high heat. Add the steaks without crowding, cooking 5 minutes on each side for medium-rare. Meanwhile, mince the shallot. Remove the meat, cover it loosely with foil, and place on a warm plate or in a warm oven while making the sauce.

Pour off all but 1 tablespoon of fat. Add the shallot to the skillet and sauté over medium-low heat until softened, about 3 minutes. Increase the heat to high and deglaze the pan by pouring the brandy over the shallots and stirring to scrape up any browned bits that have accumulated on the bottom of the pan. Whisk in the Worcestershire, sour cream, and mustard. Cook one minute more to heat through.

Season with salt and pepper, if necessary. Remove the steaks to warm plates, nap with the sauce, and serve immediately.

Yield: 4 servings

Cook beef steaks or ground beef over medium-high heat ten minutes per inch of thickness for medium-rare. Cook a minute longer per side for medium. Whether broiling, grilling, or pan-frying, the timing is the same.

Since butter has a low burning point, it will often start to smoke and blacken before meat is cooked. Oils have higher smoking points, so their addition to butter makes pan-frying easier. Sautéing or pan-frying with butter and oil raises the smoking point of the fat, while retaining the flavor of butter.

Bockwurst with Shallots and Dijon

This sausage is so full of flavor that a simple mustard sauce is all that's needed to enhance it. The bockwurst is a spicy German mixture of pork or beef with veal flavored with coriander, ginger, nutmeg, pepper, and garlic. It's surprisingly light in texture. If you have leftovers, either freeze the sausage with the sauce or chill it for delicious sandwiches, salad, or soup additions.

1 tablespoon olive oil
4 bockwurst, about 1 pound total
2 large shallots
2 teaspoons dried rosemary (optional)
1/2 cup low-salt beef stock or broth
2 tablespoons Dijon mustard
salt and freshly ground pepper, to taste

Heat the olive oil in a heavy medium skillet over medium heat. Meanwhile, align the bockwurst side to side and score the meat with 1/4" deep slices about 1/2" apart. Turn the sausages over and repeat.

Place the wurst in the skillet and cook until nicely browned on the underside, shaking the pan occasionally. Turn the sausages over and repeat. Meanwhile, mince the shallots. Remove the meat to a warm plate and cover loosely with foil.

Pour off all but 1 tablespoon of fat from the pan, add the shallots and rosemary, if using, and return it to medium-low heat. Sauté the shallot mixture a minute and deglaze the pan by pouring in the beef stock and mustard, scraping up any browned bits from the bottom of the pan. Simmer until reduced and slightly thickened, about 5 minutes.

Return the meat to the pan, turning to coat it with the sauce. Season with salt and pepper, if needed, and serve immediately.

Yield: 4 servings

When cooking with salty ingredients, such as sausages and mustard, use low-salt or unsalted stock or broth, since using unsalted ingredients gives you more control over the final seasoning of a dish. Unsalted broth is available canned, and unsalted stock can be found frozen in some parts of the country. When serving an entrée you know is on the salty side, serve a light fruit salad with it. It's ideal for cutting through saltiness.

Burgers with Roquefort and Rosemary

The piney, woodsy aroma of crushed rosemary combined with the sharp taste of Roquefort transforms ground beef into a special-occasion dish. To make it more elegant, substitute beef tenderloin for the hamburger, if you like. Stilton, Gorgonzola, and Danish Blue make reasonable substitutes for Roquefort, since all three are firm blue cheeses that crumble easily for use in salad dressings and sauces.

2 tablespoons olive oil
1 pound lean hamburger
2 shallots
1 tablespoon fresh or dried rosemary
1 cup dry white wine or vermouth
2 tablespoons milk
4 ounces Roquefort (about 1 cup crumbled)
salt and freshly ground pepper, to taste

Heat the olive oil in a heavy, preferably nonstick, large skillet over medium heat. Meanwhile, form the hamburger into 4 1/2-inch rounds and add them to the pan without crowding. Cook, running a spatula under the meat occasionally to keep it from sticking, 5 minutes on each side for medium rare.

While the meat is cooking, mince the shallots and rosemary. Remove the burgers to a warm plate and pour off all but 2 tablespoons of fat from the pan.

Over medium-low heat, stir in the shallot and rosemary. Cook about 2 minutes, or until softened slightly. Pour in the wine over high heat, and let the mixture simmer while scraping the browned bits from the bottom of the pan. When the wine is reduced almost to a glaze, lower the heat and stir in the milk and cheese. If the cheese is in a solid block, break it up with a spatula as it cooks.

When the cheese is completely melted, season it with salt and pepper, if needed. Whisk in water, extra milk, or extra wine if the sauce thickens too much. Nap the burgers with the sauce, and serve immediately.

Yield: 4 servings

> To save a bit of time, buy blue cheese already crumbled. Most foods that are crumbled, ground, or chopped do not keep as well as those in a solid mass, since so much more of their surface is exposed to air. Crumbled blue cheese, thankfully, is an exception, lasting for weeks if chilled and tightly covered. Freeze it if you're saving the cheese for more than a month. When cooking a crumbly cheese in a pan, to save time add it in a block and break it up with a spoon or spatula as it cooks.

For convenience, have your butcher pound veal scallops. They have the right equipment and plenty of experience. If you have meat that needs to be pounded, but no special equipment, use a rolling pin or the heel of your hand. Gently pound the meat from the center outward to achieve an even thickness.

Veal Piccata

Lemon and sprightly capers enliven this Italian veal dish, giving it a light, fresh flavor. Veal scallops are ideal for quick-cooking. They're delicate, tender, and so thin that they cook in a couple of minutes. Young, milk-fed veal should be creamy in color, since a darker color indicates that the cut was taken from an older, tougher animal. Plume de Veau and Provimi Delft Blue are top-quality veals to buy. You may buy veal scallops, scallopini, or medallions and receive the same small cut of meat from the loin.

> **4 veal scallops, about 1 1/4 pounds total**
> **1/4 cup dry white wine or vermouth**
> **1 tablespoon fresh or bottled lemon juice**
> **2 tablespoons capers, drained**
> **3 tablespoons unsalted butter**
> **all-purpose flour, for dredging**
> **salt and freshly ground pepper, to taste**
> **1/4 cup fresh Italian parsley, chopped (optional)**

If not already pounded, flatten the veal with a meat pounder until evenly thin. Blend the wine, lemon juice, and capers, and reserve.

Melt the butter in a heavy large skillet over medium heat. Dredge the veal in the flour, shaking off any excess. When the butter bubbles, add the scallops to the pan, making certain not to crowd them. Sauté about 1 minute on each side, remove to a platter, and keep warm.

Deglaze the pan with the wine mixture, scraping the bottom of the pan to loosen any browned bits left from the meat. If needed, adjust the seasoning with salt and pepper, and stir in the parsley, if using.

Pour the sauce over the veal and serve immediately.

Yield: 4 servings

Calf's Liver with Bacon, Garlic, and Sage

Bacon and onion are traditional accompaniments to calf's liver, but onion benefits from slow cooking to release its natural sweetness. Garlic, closely related to the onion, provides a quick-cooking substitute and sage adds a musty, minty aroma. Although calf's liver may be the youngest and mildest liver available, its flavor is strong enough to handle assertive accompaniments nicely. Since it toughens with overcooking, calf's liver is ideal for quick-cooking, needing only about two minutes per side.

> 4 slices bacon
> 1 tablespoon chopped fresh sage
> 2 cloves garlic
> 4 slices calf's liver, about 1 1/4 pounds total
> all-purpose flour, for dredging
> 3/4 cup dry white wine
> salt and freshly ground pepper, to taste

Arrange the bacon in a single layer in a heavy, preferably nonstick, skillet large enough to hold the liver without crowding. Place over medium heat and cook the bacon, turning as needed, until crisp. Meanwhile, mince the sage and garlic together and reserve. Remove the bacon and drain off all but 2 tablespoons fat.

Rinse the liver slices, pat them dry, and dredge in the flour, shaking off any excess. Place the meat in the remaining bacon fat without crowding and cook over medium-high heat 2-3 minutes on each side. The liver should remain pink inside. Remove the meat to a warm platter.

With the pan on medium-high heat, add the wine, garlic, and sage. Scrape the browned bits on the bottom of the pan into the boiling wine, and reduce the mixture until it is slightly thickened. Taste for salt and pepper, and adjust the seasoning, if needed. Pour the sauce over the liver, top with the reserved bacon, and serve immediately.

Yield: 4 servings

Since calf's liver is sliced so thin, your eyes make the best thermometer as it cooks. Its underside will begin to curl under a bit, and beads of moisture will appear on the uncooked side when it's ready to turn. After turning it, the underside will begin to curl under a bit and lose its pink color. It should be ready, still pink inside, in no more than 4 minutes total cooking.

Butter can burn after a few minutes of cooking. By removing the cooked butter and starting with fresh to make the sauce, you can enjoy the flavor of butter and use all the flavor-packed browned bits in the bottom of the pan, creating a wonderful sauce. If you remove the butter by wiping out the pan with a paper towel, be sure not to disturb the flavorings in the bottom of the pan.

Capered Calf's Liver

Liver is a favorite of mine to vary a streak of ordinary menus, and this recipe includes capers and vinegar, which provide sharp contrast to the flavor of liver. Calf's liver is especially subtle in flavor and tender in texture. It freezes well, there's no waste to speak of, and it cooks quickly. If you're not a liver lover, use this recipe for veal scallopini, or use it for chicken breasts, increasing the cooking time to 4-5 minutes per side.

> **4 tablespoons unsalted butter, divided**
> **4 slices calf's liver, about 1 1/4 pounds total**
> **all-purpose flour, for dredging**
> **1/4 cup drained capers**
> **1/4 cup veal stock or chicken broth**
> **2 tablespoons balsamic vinegar**
> **salt and freshly ground pepper, to taste**

Melt 2 tablespoons of the butter over medium heat in a heavy large skillet. Rinse the liver and pat dry with paper towels. Dredge the slices in flour, shaking off the excess. Arrange the liver in a single layer in the butter, and cook about 2 minutes. Turn and cook about another 2 minutes. Remove the slices to a warm plate and discard the butter in the pan.

Melt the remaining butter in the same pan. Add the capers and cook over medium-high heat until they are lightly browned. Pour in the stock and vinegar, scraping up any browned bits that may have accumulated on the bottom of the pan. Season with salt and pepper, if needed, and serve immediately over the liver.

Yield: 4 servings

Lamb Noisettes in Fresh Basil

Spring lamb and fresh summer basil are both, thankfully, available year-round. Basil is the herb of choice with tomatoes, and its pungent flavor, combined with tomatoes' pleasant acidity, make an ideal foil for lamb. Meltingly tender noisettes, or medallions of lamb, are cut from the tenderloin, boned rolled tenderloin, or the short saddle section. They're usually cut 3/4 to 1 inch thick and need only brief cooking.

> 2 tablespoons olive oil
> 8 lamb noisettes or 4 lamb sirloin steaks or loin chops,
>   each about 1 inch thick
> 1/3 cup lightly packed fresh basil leaves
> 2 plum tomatoes
> 1/3 cup sherry or Madeira
> 3/4 cup cream
> salt and freshly ground pepper, to taste

Heat the oil in a heavy large skillet over medium-high heat and add the lamb to the pan without crowding. Sauté each side about 4-5 minutes for medium-rare. While the lamb is cooking, chop the basil and tomatoes and reserve. Remove the lamb from the pan, and cover it loosely with foil to keep it warm.

Drain off all but 1 tablespoon of the fat. Pour in the sherry over medium-high heat and let the liquid boil, reducing it to a glaze. Add the cream, basil, and tomatoes, and reduce until the sauce thickens slightly. Adjust the seasoning with salt and pepper, if needed, and serve immediately with the noisettes.

Yield: 4 servings

For most of the year, plum tomatoes have much more flavor than larger varieties. They're also meatier, containing fewer seeds and pockets that contain liquid. Quick-cooking is especially kind to tomatoes, since it retains their texture and fresh taste.

Fresh herbs retain their flavor
best if left whole and cooked
only briefly. Many begin to
lose their flavor as soon as
they are chopped, and the
taste of others may be un-
pleasantly changed. If you
must chop herbs, do so at the
last possible minute and use
a sharp knife to avoid crush-
ing them, which releases their
flavor prematurely.

Lamb Chops
with Garlic and Balsamic Vinegar

Balsamic vinegar, intensely sweet and pungent, teams with succulent lamb in this
satisfying entrée. The traditional accompaniments of garlic and mint are included
here as well, and both are added late in cooking to retain their pronounced fresh
flavors.

> 2 tablespoons olive oil
> 4 4-ounce lamb chops
> 3 cloves garlic
> 1/2 cup fresh spearmint leaves
> 1 cup beef stock or broth
> 1/4 cup balsamic vinegar
> salt and freshly ground pepper, to taste

Heat the olive oil in a heavy large sauté pan over medium-high heat and arrange
the lamb in the pan without crowding. Cook 4-5 minutes, turn, and cook another
4-5 minutes for medium-rare. While the meat cooks, mince the garlic and mint
and reserve.

When cooked, remove the meat to a warm platter and pour off all but 1
tablespoon fat. While the pan is off the heat, cook the garlic in the fat 30 seconds,
stirring.

Return the pan to the heat, pour in the stock and vinegar, and simmer,
scraping up any browned bits that may have accumulated on the bottom of the
pan. Reduce the sauce by approximately half, about 4 minutes. Add the mint to
the sauce, adjust the seasoning with salt and pepper, if needed, and serve immediately over the lamb.

Yield: 4 servings

Fast-Paced
Pastas, Beans,
and Grains

Recipes

Tenderloin of spaghetti was the result of my first attempt at pasta. The instructions didn't specify an amount of water required to boil the 10 x 3-inch package that I'd bravely purchased, so I carefully laid all of the noodles in a pot of boiling water. Ten minutes later, I removed the pasta to find a tidy, gummy, 10 x 3-inch mass of spaghetti, ready to be cut into solid slices. My gracious guests didn't complain.

Since then I've learned there's a critical proportion of water to pasta that makes it palatable and easy to cook. Always bring a large pot of water to boil first. Since 1 pound of dried pasta serves four as an entrée, you'll need 3 quarts of water for each main course recipe in this chapter and half that for side dishes. Once you're familiar with the amount, you can eyeball it without measuring. You'll also find most of the preparation of each dish takes place while the water comes to a boil or while the pasta cooks.

Once water begins to steam, cover the pot with a lid to hasten boiling, since it retains all the heat in the pot. If you're dashing madly for ingredients, put the water on to boil first thing. The cover won't save you any time until the water begins to evaporate, so you have a while to unearth a lid. If you're shaving seconds from cooking time, add salt after the water boils, since salt inhibits boiling.

In many recipes in this chapter, I've used the same pot the pasta cooks in to make a quick sauce while the pasta drains. Pasta needs a few minutes to drain (and it retains heat quite nicely), the pot is hot so it needs no reheating, and most fresh ingredients need little time to cook, thereby saving their character and nutrients. This also saves the quick-cook a pot to clean. If necessary, pasta, beans, and grains reheat beautifully in the microwave, retaining their texture, flavor, and color.

Cooking fresh pasta is always faster than cooking commercially dried, but it will not necessarily be better. Dried pasta is made with semolina flour and will retain its bite with proper cooking. Most fresh pastas are made with softer wheat which makes for softer cooked pasta. Chunky sauces, vegetables, and meats and seafoods are most appropriate with dry pasta and its chunkier shapes that trap heavy ingredients. Fresh, thin pastas are perfect with thinner sauces and more delicate ingredients. For especially easy sauces, use one of the compound butters on pages 220-224.

Although we've come to accept pasta as a substantial dinner, grains and legumes can also serve as the mainstay of a meal. Risottos and polentas, long-time standards in Italy, have come into culinary vogue in this country of late. As versatile as pasta, both can serve as a first course, side dish, or entrée when enriched with vegetables and bits of meat, fish, or poultry.

In the last few years, grains that used to be found only in specialty shops have made their way to supermarket shelves. Quinoa, an ancient Peruvian grain, and kasha, a Russian staple, keep company with barley, bulgur, and a staggering array of rices today. Fava beans, cannellini, black beans, chickpeas, canned lentils—legumes that used to be troublesome to find—are available in most super-markets. The invasion of grains reflects our growing health concerns and our reluctance to continue a diet based on meat. As an additional bonus, many grains and legumes lend themselves to quick cooking.

Couscous with Garlic, Mint, & Tomatoes

The finest cut of pasta made with semolina, couscous is a staple of North African cooking. Its blandness makes an ideal backdrop to highlight other ingredients in salads and side dishes, and it can be served hot, cold, or at room temperature. In this side dish, the tomatoes and mint provide a refreshing contrast in color, temperature, and flavor to the warm couscous. Cherry tomatoes are especially festive, but if time demands, use plum tomatoes instead. Chill any leftovers for a delightful salad.

1 1/2 cups chicken stock or water
2 teaspoons olive oil
2 cloves garlic
1 1/2 cups couscous
8 cherry tomatoes or 2 plum tomatoes
1/4 cup fresh mint leaves, tightly packed
salt and freshly ground pepper, to taste

In a heavy medium saucepan with a secure lid, combine the stock and olive oil. Bring to a boil and meanwhile mince the garlic. Stir in the couscous and garlic and remove the pan from the heat.

Cover and let stand 5 minutes. Meanwhile, cut the cherry tomatoes into slivers or chop plum tomatoes coarsely. Mince the mint. Uncover the couscous and fluff with a fork to separate the grains. Stir in the tomato and herb. Adjust the seasoning with salt and pepper, if needed, and serve immediately.

Yield: 4 side-dish servings

Fresh mint, like fresh basil (see page 79), should be chopped just prior to using, since the cut edges will blacken quickly. If you must chop mint early, add a dribble of olive oil to the chopped mint, so the oil will coat the cut surfaces, sealing them off from air.

Sesame-Scented Chinese Noodles

These silky noodles are a passion of mine. I eat them piping hot, well-chilled, and at every temperature in between. There's something satisfying about their slippery texture, and once water has come to a boil, they take all of 3 minutes to cook. Asian sesame oil lends a deep, nutty aroma to the noodles, and occasionally I add a quarter-teaspoon of chili oil for heat. It's easy to adjust the noodles to your taste, since none of the seasonings have to cook. Sprinkle 1/4 cup toasted sesame seeds over the noodles, if you like.

> **14 ounces fresh Chinese-style egg noodles or 1 pound dry**
> **3 scallions (optional)**
> **2 tablespoons low-sodium soy sauce, or more, to taste**
> **2 tablespoons sesame oil, or more, to taste**

Bring 2 1/2 quarts of water to boil in a large saucepan. If you choose to garnish the noodles with scallions, slice them thin while the water is coming to a boil.

When the water boils rapidly, add the noodles and stir to separate them. Bring the water back to a boil and reduce the heat so that the water bubbles but will not boil over. When the noodles are tender, in about 3 minutes, drain them briefly in a colander or large strainer.

Remove the noodles to a serving dish and toss with the soy sauce and sesame oil. Sprinkle with the scallions, if using, and serve immediately or cool for later use.

Yield: 4 large side-dish servings

If you have any noodles left, add them chilled to salads, or treat yourself to a pan-fried noodle pancake: drizzle a bit of peanut oil in a nonstick skillet and arrange the noodles evenly in the pan over medium heat. Cover and cook until golden on the bottom. Carefully turn the pan over, so that the pancake is on the lid. Return the skillet to the heat and slide the uncooked side of the pancake onto the skillet. Cook until golden on the bottom, and serve. The golden crusts provide crunchy contrast to the velvety interior.

Pasta with Sun-Dried Tomatoes and Garlic

Since this sauce doesn't cook, the full flavors of all of the ingredients are strong and lively. Extra virgin olive oil, which typically loses some of its valued fruitiness when cooked with competing ingredients, is wonderfully aromatic in this pasta. The sun-dried tomatoes lend a chewy sweetness, and the garlic is sharp and pungent. Add sliced prosciutto or drained olives to the basic combination, if you like.

1 cup sun-dried tomatoes packed in oil
1 cup Italian parsley leaves, lightly packed
4 cloves garlic
1 cup freshly grated Parmesan cheese (about 4 ounces)
3/4 cup olive oil, preferably extra virgin
4 teaspoons fresh or bottled lemon juice
1 pound thin pasta (cappellini, spaghettini, or vermicelli)
salt and freshly ground pepper, to taste

Bring 3 quarts of lightly salted water to boil over high heat. While the water comes to a boil, drain the tomatoes and slice into thin strips, mince the parsley and garlic together, and grate the cheese, if not pre-grated. Place in a large bowl with the olive oil and lemon juice.

Add the pasta to the boiling water and cook according to the package directions. When the pasta is cooked, drain it well and toss with the prepared mixture. Adjust the seasoning with salt and pepper, if needed, and serve immediately.

Yield: 4 entrée-size servings

Garlic should be peeled and minced just before using. Whole peeled cloves sold in refrigerated jars are convenient, but they don't deliver sharp garlic flavor. Using a garlic press that stores peeled garlic in the refrigerator liquefies garlic cloves on its first use, destroying their texture. Store garlic in a cool, dark, dry place and, unless roasted or poached and glazed (see page 39), peel and mince it just prior to using.

great ✓

When tossing cooked, drained pasta with a sauce made in the same pan the pasta was cooked in, be sure the sauce coats the pan well. Otherwise, the pasta may stick to the sides of the pan.

Spirelli with Pine Nuts and Prosciutto

Sweet green peas and pine nuts punctuate this beautiful dish, providing a pleasant contrast to the saltiness of prosciutto and Parmesan. Spirelli, or corkscrew pasta, is available in a multi-hued variety made with vegetable dyes, but I prefer the plain pasta for this dish, since it shows off the accompanying ingredients.

2 cups frozen green peas
4 thin slices prosciutto
4 scallions
1/2 cup freshly grated Parmesan cheese (about 2 ounces)
1 pound spirelli or farfalle
1/4 cup olive oil
1/2 cup pine nuts, lightly toasted
salt and freshly ground pepper, to taste

Bring 3 quarts of lightly salted water to boil in a large saucepan. While the water heats, place the peas in a colander and run cold water over them to separate and begin defrosting them. Stack the slices of prosciutto and cut into slivers. Mince the scallions and, if not using pre-grated Parmesan, grate it now and reserve.

When the water boils, cook the pasta according to package directions, about 8 minutes. During the last minute of cooking, stir in the peas. When the water comes back to a boil, drain the pasta and peas in the colander and return the pan to medium heat.

Pour the olive oil into the pan. If you don't have pine nuts already toasted, add them to the oil and cook, stirring occasionally, until golden. Stir in the scallions and sauté briefly, about 2 minutes. Return the pasta and peas to the pan, top with the Parmesan and prosciutto, and toss thoroughly. Adjust the seasoning with salt and pepper, if needed, and serve immediately.

Yield: 4 entrée-size servings

Sun-Dried Tomato and Shrimp Linguine

This dish is light, colorful, and addictive. The convenience of shelled and cooked shrimp and flavor-packed sun-dried tomatoes makes this one-dish meal simple and fast. Add some fresh herbs, such as oregano or tarragon, for variety, or cloves of roasted garlic (see page 39), if you have them on hand.

5 scallions
2 cloves garlic
16 sun-dried tomatoes, packed in oil (about 1 cup)
1 cup freshly grated Parmesan (about 4 ounces)
12-16 ounces fresh or dried linguine
3 tablespoons olive oil
1 pound small shelled, cooked shrimp
salt and freshly ground pepper, to taste

Bring 3 quarts of lightly salted water to boil in a heavy large saucepan or wok over high heat. Meanwhile, chop the scallions, mince the garlic, drain and slice the tomatoes, and grate the Parmesan, if you haven't bought it pre-grated.

When the water comes to a rolling boil, add the pasta and stir to separate it. Cook according to the package instructions, or until tender but still firm to the bite. Drain the pasta and return the pan to medium heat.

Add the olive oil to the pan and stir in the scallions, garlic, tomatoes, and shrimp. Stir briefly to heat through, add the drained pasta and Parmesan, take off the heat and toss thoroughly. Season with salt and pepper, if needed, and serve immediately.

Yield: 4 entrée-size servings

Whether using fresh or dried pasta, cooking times should start when the water comes back to a boil after adding the pasta. Stir it occasionally to keep it from sticking. You'll probably need to reduce the heat during the cooking time, since the water can boil over quickly. Sometimes fresh pasta will release a lot of foam in the water. This indicates soft-wheat flour has been used in making it and care must be taken not to overcook it, otherwise it will become mushy and pasty.

Orzo Santa Fe

Rice-shaped orzo takes on Southwestern flavors in this mildly peppery side dish. While the orzo drains, tomato, onion, and jalapeño cook quickly, retaining their fresh flavors and textures. Cheddar cheese rounds out the toppings, but substitute Monterey Jack or mozzarella, if you prefer.

> **8 ounces orzo (about 1 cup)**
> **2 ounces cheddar cheese (about 1 1/4 cups)**
> **1 large tomato or 2 plum tomatoes**
> **1/2 jalapeño chili**
> **1 small onion**
> **1 tablespoon corn or peanut oil**
> **1 teaspoon ground cumin**
> **salt and freshly ground pepper, to taste**

Bring 1 1/2 quarts lightly salted water to boil in a heavy large pot. Stir in the orzo and boil until barely tender, 8-10 minutes.

Meanwhile, grate the cheese in a food processor and remove it to a paper towel. Without washing out the bowl, coarsely chop the tomato in the processor, remove it to a serving dish, and reserve. Trim the chili and remove the seeds. Mince it in the processor. Peel and quarter the onion, add it to the chili, and chop it coarsely.

When the pasta is cooked, drain it in a colander. Return the pot to medium-low heat and add the oil. Stir in the chili and onion, and cook until softened, about 4 minutes. Add the cumin, tomato, orzo, and cheese. Toss all together and adjust the seasoning, if needed, with salt and pepper. Serve immediately.

Yield: 4 side-dish servings

Fettucine with Poblano Pesto

This takeoff on traditional Genoan pesto is smoky with roasted chili flavor balanced by the freshness of cilantro. Be sure to use well-toasted pine nuts, since their delicate flavor can get lost with competing ingredients. The recipe makes 4 large side-dish portions, but with the addition of 2 cups of leftover or cooked fish, chicken, or turkey, the fettucine will make a one-dish meal. The pesto is also delicious spread thin on flour tortillas and baked until the bases are crisp.

1 clove garlic
1/4 cup pine nuts, well-toasted
1 7-ounce can diced peeled green chilies
1/2 bunch cilantro, leaves and tender stems only
  (about 2 cups, lightly packed)
3 tablespoons olive oil
1 tablespoon fresh or bottled lime or lemon juice
12 ounces fettucine
salt and freshly ground pepper, to taste

Pesto can be made in minutes with a food processor. Not only will it be fresher and much less expensive than what you can buy prepared, but the possibilities for pesto offer interesting variety. Use roasted garlic (see page 39), sun-dried tomatoes, cilantro, nuts, or black or white beans as a base for this uncooked, nubby-textured sauce.

Bring 3 quarts of lightly salted water to boil in a large saucepan over high heat.

Drop the garlic through the feed tube of a food processor with the motor running. Add the pine nuts and mince until finely textured. Add the chilies, cilantro, olive oil, and lime juice, and process to a uniformly nubby, but creamy texture.

When the water comes to a rolling boil, add the fettucine and stir to separate. Cook according to the package directions, stirring occasionally. Drain the pasta and remove it to a shallow bowl. Add the pesto and toss thoroughly. Season with salt and pepper, if needed, and serve immediately.

Yield: 4 large side-dish servings

Cappellini with Quick Clam Sauce

This quick clam sauce, thanks to the convenience of whole baby clams out of the shell, cooks in just about the same amount of time it takes to prepare cappellini, one of the fastest pastas to cook. Substitute thin spaghetti, or spaghettini, if you prefer—the thin, briny clam sauce needs a delicate pasta to accompany it. Anchovy paste eliminates the need to mince whole fillets, but if you have only fillets on hand, add them to the pan with the wine and break them up with a spoon. They'll melt right into the sauce.

Using canned whole baby clams eliminates scrubbing shellfish and discarding the shells once used. Cans of minced clams often contain larger, older clams that have been chopped to an appropriate size, but they maintain their tough texture. For special occasions, buy baby clams in glass jars. You can see exactly what size clams you're buying, ensuring that they are small and tender.

2 cloves garlic
1 shallot
1/4 cup olive oil
1 pound cappellini
1/2 cup dry white wine
1 tablespoon fresh or bottled lemon juice
1 teaspoon anchovy paste
2 10-ounce cans whole baby clams
1/2 cup lightly packed fresh Italian parsley (optional)
salt and freshly ground pepper, to taste

Bring 3 quarts of lightly salted water to boil in a large pot. Meanwhile, mince the garlic and shallot. Heat the olive oil in a heavy medium saucepan over medium-low heat, stir in the garlic and shallot, and sauté until softened, about 4 minutes. When the water boils, stir in the cappellini and cook according to package directions.

Pour the wine, lemon juice, anchovy paste, and the liquid from the clams into the shallot mixture. Bring to a boil and let simmer about 5 minutes. Mince the parsley, if using. Stir in the clams, heat through, and adjust the seasoning with salt and pepper, if needed.

Drain the cappellini and divide between four plates or shallow bowls. Top with the clam sauce and serve immediately.

Yield: 4 entrée-size servings

Pasta Puttanesca

Straight from the pantry, this powerful sauce can cook in the time it takes to boil the fettucine. Even when cooked briefly, the robust aromas of garlic, anchovies, imported olives, and capers give the impression of slow-simmering. It will be delicious on the spot, but if you have time, start cooking the sauce and let it simmer up to an hour to let its flavors meld. This is one of a few pasta dishes I prefer not to toss. The red, black, and dots of green look stunning atop plain pasta.

1 pound fettucine or linguine
1/4 cup olive oil
3 cloves garlic
2 2-ounce cans anchovies
1 28-ounce can crushed Italian tomatoes
2 4.5-ounce jars pitted imported black olives (about 2 cups)
1/4 cup capers
salt and freshly ground pepper, to taste

Bring 3 quarts of lightly salted water to boil in a large heavy pot. When the water boils, stir in the pasta and cook according to the package directions.

Meanwhile, heat the olive oil in a heavy large skillet or sauté pan over medium heat. Mince the garlic, drain the anchovies, and stir them into the olive oil. Stir the anchovies so they melt into a paste in the pan. Blend in the tomatoes. Drain the olives and capers, blend with the tomatoes, and simmer while the pasta cooks. Adjust the seasoning, if needed, with salt and pepper.

When the pasta is barely tender, drain it, and mound it in a shallow bowl or divide it between 4 individual plates. Top with the puttanesca sauce and serve immediately.

Yield: 4 entrée-size servings

Italians often serve pasta in shallow bowls to make optimum use of sauces. The pasta is scattered in the bowl and the sauce is poured over it. If tossed, the sauce cannot be lost as it sometimes is when tossed in a deep bowl. Thin sauces with finely textured ingredients may be enjoyed more easily as a topping to pasta.

Nutmeg grinders and graters preserve fresh nutmeg flavor, allowing the cook to grate the spice on the spot and in the precise amount needed. Ground spices lose their potency quickly, but whole ones, such as peppercorns and nutmeg, retain their flavor indefinitely. I prefer the grinders, since they're quick to use and you're not likely to lose your fingertips when grating the last bit of the nutmeg.

Couscous with Harissa Sauce

Harissa is a fiery sauce made with red chilies, garlic, cumin, and caraway. Tunisians traditionally serve it with couscous, soups, and stews, and often it's used as a condiment. The pasta's blandness, along with sweet-scented cinnamon and nutmeg, make a perfect foil for the harissa's heat. It's available in cans and jars at specialty shops and better supermarkets. This side dish is ideal when served with a meat accompanied with ample sauce to moisten the couscous.

2 cups chicken stock or broth
1/2 teaspoon ground cinnamon
1/4 teaspoon crumbled saffron threads
1/4 teaspoon freshly grated or ground nutmeg
1 1/2 cups couscous
1 teaspoon harissa sauce
salt and freshly ground pepper, to taste

Blend the broth, cinnamon, saffron, and nutmeg in a heavy medium saucepan and bring it to a boil over high heat. Stir in the couscous, cover, and simmer 5 minutes. Uncover, top with the harissa, and toss to fluff the couscous and blend in the sauce. Adjust the seasoning, if needed, with salt and pepper, and serve immediately.

Yield: 4 side-dish servings

Cannellini Purée

I think of this white kidney bean purée as an Italian version of Mexican refried beans. White wine adds a depth of flavor to the garlic-scented cannellini, and green flecks of parsley contribute visual interest. The purée can stand in for refried beans in quesadillas, enchiladas, tostadas, and most things Mexican.

2 15-ounce cans cannellini beans
4 cloves garlic
8 sprigs fresh parsley
2 tablespoons olive oil
1/3 cup dry white wine or vermouth
salt and freshly ground pepper, to taste

In a colander or large strainer, rinse the beans and drain them thoroughly. Pat them dry with paper towels. Mince the garlic in a food processor, remove it and reserve. Remove the thick, tough stems of parsley and place the remaining stems and leaves in the processor. Mince the parsley, add the beans, and purée.

Heat the olive oil in a heavy medium nonstick skillet over low heat. Add the garlic and cook until it softens, about 3 minutes. Do not allow it to brown.

Pour in the wine, bring it to a boil over high heat, and cook it down to about 2 tablespoons. Reduce the heat to low and scrape the beans into the pan, stirring occasionally to blend the mixture well. Adjust the seasoning with salt and pepper, cover, and heat through. Serve immediately.

Yield: 4 side-dish servings

Nonstick pans are invaluable at times. When a recipe calls for one, use it, or opt for trouble. Nonstick surfaces have been greatly improved over the last few years, including some aluminum pans that are anodized, resulting in a harder surface and greater bonding between the surface and the pan. Many of the best quality nonstick surfaces will brown foods better than before and come with a guarantee of up to twenty years.

Confetti Bean Sauté

This healthy, flavorful bean dish looks like a carnival of color. Black and white beans are speckled with fresh bits of tomato and bright green cilantro leaves. The earthy flavor of beans is piqued by lemon juice and tomatoes, and Tabasco supplies heat to this satisfying, nutritious side dish. Add bits of ham or cooked poultry to extend it to a one-dish meal.

> 1 15-ounce can black beans
> 1 15-ounce can cannellini beans
> 1 tablespoon olive oil
> 2 cloves garlic
> 4 plum tomatoes
> 2 tablespoons fresh or bottled lime or lemon juice
> 1/4 teaspoon Tabasco Sauce, or more, to taste
> salt and freshly ground pepper, to taste
> 1/4 cup cilantro leaves

Rinse and drain the black and cannellini beans together and reserve. Heat the olive oil in a heavy medium saucepan over medium-low heat, mince the garlic, and stir it into the oil. Cook, stirring occasionally, until just softened, about 3 minutes.

While the garlic cooks, dice the tomatoes and add them to the pan with the beans, lime juice, and Tabasco. Cook, stirring occasionally, until just warmed through, about 5 minutes. Adjust the seasoning, if needed, with salt and pepper, and serve immediately scattered with the cilantro leaves.

Yield: 4 side-dish servings

Combining colorful foods is a simple way to add visual and flavor interest to dishes. Combine food with similar cooking requirements, such as broccoli and cauliflower, carrots and parsnips, yams and sweet potatoes, red and green bell peppers, and multi-hued beans, so recipes don't need to be altered.

Keep your eyes and nose tuned into garlic as it cooks. If it browns, it turns bitter and gives off a burned smell. You'll need to discard it and begin again. Unless combined with other insulating ingredients, I never cook garlic on heat higher than medium-low. Thankfully, stovetop cooking allows the cook to see and smell any early signs of trouble, as well as easy access to rescue browning garlic from the heat.

Southwestern Barley

This is a zesty, colorful dish, spicy with the heat of cumin and red pepper, and sweet with corn, which provides a pleasing contrast to feisty spices. Barley, with its bland flavor and soft texture, is as receptive a backdrop to diverse ingredients as pasta. Use part or all frozen green peas instead of the corn, if you prefer, and parsley instead of cilantro. Extend the dish with leftover poultry or cooked sausage to make a satisfying one-dish meal.

2 teaspoons olive oil
1 clove garlic, minced
1 medium onion, chopped
2/3 cup pearl barley
1 14 1/2-ounce can stewed tomatoes
1 1/4 cups chicken stock or broth
1/2 teaspoon ground cumin
1/4 teaspoon ground red pepper (cayenne)
1 small bunch cilantro (optional)
1 cup frozen corn
salt and freshly ground pepper, to taste

Pour the olive oil in a large heavy saucepan over medium heat. Stir in the garlic and onion and cook, stirring occasionally, until softened, about 5 minutes.

Stir in the barley, tomatoes, broth, cumin, and ground red pepper. Bring to a simmer, cover, and cook 25 minutes. Meanwhile, mince the cilantro, if using. Blend in the corn and cilantro, cover, and cook another 5 minutes. Adjust the seasoning with salt and pepper, if needed, and serve immediately.

Yield: 4 side-dish servings

If you prefer canned stewed or whole tomatoes chopped finer than the manufacturer provides, break them up with a wooden spoon in the pan while the dish cooks, saving the time and mess of chopping them on a cutting board.

Lemon and Mint Tabbouleh

Refreshing lemon and mint highlight this tabbouleh, a Middle Eastern specialty based on bulgur. It's typically served cold, but this version is cooked quickly and served at room temperature, so it can be relished right away. If you have time for it to rest to let the flavors meld, do so. Since it's best at room temperature, it's a convenient dish for entertaining.

1 cup medium-grain bulgur
1 clove garlic
1 cup lightly packed fresh parsley leaves
1/2 cup fresh mint leaves
1/2 small red onion (about 1 cup chopped)
4 plum tomatoes
1/2 cup olive oil, preferably extra virgin
1/3 cup fresh or bottled lemon juice
salt and freshly ground pepper, to taste
1/4 cup lightly toasted pine nuts (optional)
8 romaine lettuce leaves (optional)

Bring 1 quart lightly salted water to boil in a heavy medium saucepan over high heat. Stir in the bulgur and cook 15 minutes, stirring occasionally.

While the bulgur cooks, mince the garlic, parsley, and mint in a food processor. Remove it to a salad bowl or serving dish and reserve. Without washing the workbowl, coarsely chop the onion and add to the parsley mixture. Quarter the tomatoes, chop them in the processor, and add to the parsley.

When the bulgur is tender, place it in a colander and run cold water over it until the grains feel cool to the touch. Drain thoroughly and pat dry with paper towels. Add to the tomatoes and toss with the olive oil and lemon juice. Adjust the seasoning with salt and pepper, and sprinkle with pine nuts, if using. Surround the tabbouleh, if desired, with lettuce leaves to use as scoops for the grain.

Yield: 4 servings

Tomato-Basil Risotto

Risotto is as satisfying to me as pasta, and it's equally versatile and healthy. The microwave oven, thanks to innovative cookbook author, Barbara Kafka, brings this northern Italian specialty within the reach of the hurried cook. Traditionally risottos have to be stirred constantly over the stove, but the microwave frees your hands, so you can prepare ingredients while the food is cooking. This one is redolent with garlic, onion, and basil. Use a decorative microwave-proof dish to cook the risotto, and it will double as a serving dish, if you like.

> **4 cloves garlic**
> **2 leeks, white part only, or 1 medium mild onion**
> **2 tablespoons olive oil**
> **3/4 cup arborio rice**
> **4 plum tomatoes**
> **1 1/2 cups chicken stock or broth**
> **1/4 cup freshly grated Parmesan (about 1 ounce)**
> **2 tablespoons fresh basil or 2 teaspoons dried**
> **salt and freshly ground pepper, to taste**

Mince the garlic, chop the leeks, and reserve. Microwave the oil in a 9" glass pie plate or soufflé dish 2 minutes on full power. Stir in the garlic, leeks, and rice, coating them with the oil, and cook uncovered 3 minutes.

While the rice is cooking, dice the tomatoes. Stir in the tomatoes and broth and cook, uncovered, 8 minutes. Stir and cook another 8 minutes. Meanwhile, grate the Parmesan, if not pre-grated, and mince the basil.

Stir in the Parmesan and basil. Season with salt and pepper, if necessary, and serve immediately.

Yield: 4 side-dish servings

When adding fresh tomatoes to a dish that requires a precise amount of liquid, such as risotto, you may need to adjust the amount of liquid depending upon the juiciness of the tomatoes. Plum tomatoes, with their fat, meaty walls, are the most consistent in flavor and texture.

Risotto, like pasta, should be cooked al dente, maintaining a bite within each grain. All sorts of leftovers, fresh or frozen vegetables, meats, and fish can be added to the basic dish. To transform leftover risotto into a crisp first course or hors d'oeuvre, pack it down evenly in a 1/2" thick layer. When cold, cut it into serving sizes, and pan-fry it in a nonstick skillet with a bit of olive oil.

Herbed Olivada Risotto

Fragrant with olives and oregano, this exotic-looking side dish is awash with the purplish color of black olivada, a prepared purée of olives, olive oil, lemon juice, vinegar, and herbs. Olivada makes a handy, flavor-packed spread for crostini (page 41), a simple sauce for pastas, and a flavor enhancer for vegetables (Tomato-Speckled Zucchini with Olivada, page 192). Add 2 diced plum tomatoes to the risotto with the broth, if you like, for interesting color and pleasing acidity.

2 tablespoons olive oil
1 large shallot
3/4 cup arborio rice
1/4 cup freshly grated Parmesan (about 1 ounce)
2 1/2 cups chicken stock or broth
1-2 tablespoons black olivada, to taste
2 tablespoons fresh oregano leaves or 2 teaspoons dried
salt and freshly ground pepper, to taste

Microwave the oil in a 9" glass pie plate or soufflé dish 2 minutes on full power. Meanwhile, mince the shallot and add it to the dish with the rice, stirring to coat them with the oil, and cook uncovered 3 minutes.

While the rice is cooking, grate the Parmesan, if not pre-grated. Stir in the broth and cook, uncovered, 8 minutes. Stir and cook another 8 minutes.

Stir in the Parmesan, olivada to taste, and oregano. Season with salt and pepper, if necessary, and let rest 3-4 minutes before serving.

Yield: 4 side-dish servings

Saffron and Cinnamon-Scented Basmati Rice

This is a fragrant, colorful adaptation of an Indian recipe that required soaking the rice 1 hour, roasting the saffron, and grinding spices on the spot. It's fragrant with the enticing combination of saffron, cinnamon and basmati rice. Although powdered saffron can be added straight into a liquid, its expensive fragrance is often lost if stored too long. In this recipe, adding saffron threads requires no more steps or time than powdered saffron.

> 2 tablespoons unsalted butter
> 1 1/2 cups basmati or long-grain rice
> 5 cardamom pods (optional)
> 2 3-inch long cinnamon sticks
> 3 cups chicken stock or broth
> 1/2 teaspoon crumbled saffron threads
> salt and freshly ground pepper, to taste

Melt the butter in a heavy medium saucepan over medium heat. Stir the rice, cardamom, if using, and cinnamon in the butter 1 minute. Blend in the stock and saffron, bring to a simmer, and cook covered about 18 minutes. Remove the lid and fluff with a fork. Remove the cardamom pods, adjust the seasoning, if needed, and serve immediately.

Yield: 4 side-dish servings

Saffron threads are typically crushed and soaked in hot water to release their aroma before adding to other cooking ingredients. If a liquid needs to simmer to cook a food such as rice, add it early in cooking to avoid the extra step of soaking. Too much saffron in a dish can be unpleasant to your palate and your pocketbook, so use it judiciously to avoid a harsh aroma and unneeded expense.

Polenta with Garlic and Parmesan

If you ask eight Italian cooks how to prepare polenta, or cornmeal, you will hear eight different answers. Some call for a full ninety minutes of cooking, some require constant stirring, and those who are pinched for time resort to the microwave. For this 20-minute version, a nonstick or well-seasoned pan is helpful, but not necessary. Since polenta is typically bland, it's an easy, nutritious companion, like pasta, for other interesting flavors. This recipe is perfumed with the aroma of mellow garlic and the salty nuttiness of Parmesan. Use the relatively attention-free twenty minutes of cooking to prepare a salad or entrée.

3 1/2 cups chicken stock or broth
2 cloves garlic
1 cup yellow cornmeal
1/4 cup freshly grated Parmesan (about 1 ounce)
2 tablespoons unsalted butter
salt and freshly ground pepper, to taste

In a heavy medium saucepan, bring the stock to a boil. Meanwhile, mince the garlic and add it to the stock. When boiling, pour the cornmeal in a steady stream while stirring continuously to prevent lumps. Reduce the heat to low, and cook for 20 minutes, stirring occasionally, to prevent the mixture from sticking to the bottom of the pan. When almost cooked, the polenta will start to pull away from the sides of the pan.

Meanwhile, if the Parmesan isn't grated, do so while the cornmeal cooks. Stir in the Parmesan, butter, and salt and pepper, to taste, and serve immediately.

Yield: 4 side-dish servings

If not using the polenta immediately, pour it onto a baking sheet and smooth it out to about 1/2 inch of thickness. Cover and chill until ready to use. Heat a bit of oil in a heavy, preferably nonstick skillet. Cut the polenta into usable shapes (3 x 4 inches for an entrée base, 2 x 3 for a side dish) and with a spatula transfer the cornmeal to the skillet. Pan-fry until golden on the underside. Flip and repeat, and serve immediately with a savory topping or as is.

Middle Eastern-Flavored Quinoa

Quinoa is a natural whole grain, providing the highest and most complete balance of protein in any grain, since it contains all eight essential amino acids. It can be used as rice, in salads, and as a breakfast cereal. Tiny and bead-shaped, quinoa is finding its way into more and more supermarkets and is almost always available in boxes in specialty stores.

This dish is slightly sweet from dates, stewed tomatoes, and green peas. Add cooked ham, poultry, or shrimp for a complete meal, if you like. Reheat leftovers in the microwave or use them to make an unusual salad base.

1 cup quinoa
1 14 1/2-ounce can stewed tomatoes
1 1/2 cups chicken stock or broth
1/2 cup raisins, dried currants, or chopped dates
1/4 teaspoon crumbled saffron threads
10 ounces frozen peas
salt and freshly ground pepper, to taste

Rinse the quinoa under cold running water and drain it. Blend it in a heavy medium saucepan with the tomatoes, stock, raisins, and saffron. Bring to a boil, cover, and simmer until almost all the liquid is absorbed, 12-15 minutes.

Stir in the peas and cook until they are just heated through. Adjust the seasoning with salt and pepper, if needed, and serve immediately.

Yield: 4 side-dish servings

If you've ever bought whole dates, you know how difficult they are to pit. Pitted dates are convenient, but chopped ones are even more so. However, some chopped dates are coated with so much sugar that they make savory dishes too sweet. Place them in a strainer and shake them over a sink to get rid of excess sugar.

Kasha with Mushrooms

Kasha, the Russian specialty of hulled, crushed buckwheat groats, has a subtle, nutty taste with a slightly bitter edge. Although it has a stronger taste than many grains, it easily accepts accompanying ingredients, such as ham, red bell peppers, mushrooms, and herbs. It's available in boxes in fine, medium, and coarse grains, the finest cooking the fastest.

1 egg
1 cup kasha
2 tablespoons unsalted butter
8 ounces mushrooms, sliced
2 shallots, minced
2 cups beef stock or broth
1/2 cup freshly grated Parmesan cheese (about 2 ounces)
1/4 cup minced fresh parsley (optional)
salt and freshly ground pepper, to taste

Beat the egg lightly in a heavy 9-inch skillet or saucepan. Add the kasha and blend thoroughly until all the grains are well coated. Place the pan over medium heat and stir until the grains dry and separate. Transfer it to a serving plate and reserve.

Return the empty pan to medium heat and add the butter. When melted, stir in the mushrooms and shallots. Sauté until softened, about 5 minutes. Blend in the stock and kasha, separating it, if necessary. Cover, and simmer 8-12 minutes, or until the kernels are tender and the liquid is absorbed. Meanwhile, grate the Parmesan, if not pre-grated.

Toss the Parmesan and parsley, if using, with the kasha. Adjust the seasoning with salt and pepper, if needed, and serve immediately.

Yield: 4 side-dish servings

Tossing kasha with beaten egg before heating, although not absolutely necessary, helps keep the grains separate while it cooks. You can use egg white only, but the kernels will not separate quite as well. Blending the grain and egg in the skillet before heating it saves washing an extra bowl.

Very Easy Vegetables

Recipes

Once when I was in New York dining on tender-crisp asparagus and baby artichokes, my sister remarked that the vegetables that I would be eating two days from now on an upcoming trip to the South were probably already cooking. She was right. The menu included greens turned gray from looking at the inside of a pot too long, creamed corn simmered until the texture of vegetable and sauce became identical, and green beans boiled beyond recognition with salt pork. Luckily for the quick cook and the nutrition-conscious, the tradition of long-simmering vegetables has made a quick, if not universal, turnabout.

The knowledgeable cook can transform vegetables into exciting side-dish fare in minutes. The youngest specimens will be most tender, deliver the freshest flavor, and cook the fastest. Older vegetables make ideal ingredients, delivering maximum flavor, for the soup and crock pot, but not for the cook with time constraints.

Take advantage of frozen vegetables. Corn, lima beans, green beans, and green peas are among the frozen vegetables that outshine fresh ones most of the year. Picked at the peak of the season and packaged with the latest technology, they contain more flavor and nutrients than fresh ones we buy out of season. And they provide tremendous convenience as well. Pearl onions, requiring parboiling and individual peeling when fresh, arrive ready to use when frozen. Spinach, needing careful rinsing to rid it of sand and individual stemming of tough, older leaves, is ready to cook. Peas and beans are shelled, corn is shucked, and brussels sprouts are completely trimmed.

Before using frozen vegetables, rinse them in a colander or strainer first to remove the ice crystals that sometimes give them that freezer off-odor. This will improve their flavor and start their defrosting as well. Some frozen vegetables, such as green peas and corn, need only to come to a boil to be ready to eat.

Canned tomatoes are ideal for use in sauces, soups, stews, and casseroles. Perhaps one month out of the year fresh tomatoes will out-perform commercially canned ones. Canned chilies have been roasted and peeled, freeing the quick cook from two time-consuming chores. Beets, typically needing trimming, peeling, and slow cooking, are conveniently canned pickled and plain, shredded, whole, and sliced. Artichokes enjoy a short season fresh, but canned, jarred, and frozen ones provide a ready-to-use, year-round substitute. Utilize combinations of fresh, frozen, and canned vegetables to suit your taste and time constraints.

To slice long vegetables, such as asparagus, carrots, celery, and parsnips quickly and evenly, align them side-by-side before slicing. You'll get 3 or 4 times as many slices per chop. If carrots and parsnips are tapered, place a fat end next to a thin one to bunch them together evenly.

Almond-Lemon Asparagus

The ease of this recipe reminds me of the first time I cooked asparagus. The instructions told me to peel each stalk, and, not knowing any different, I did, all six pounds of it. This is a fast, simple, and interesting treatment for this luxurious vegetable, complemented by crunchy almonds. The almonds and lemon provide pleasing contrast and eliminate the longing for a time-consuming sauce.

1 pound asparagus
2 tablespoons unsalted butter
1/2 cup slivered almonds
2 tablespoons fresh or bottled lemon juice
salt and freshly ground pepper, to taste

Holding the tips of the asparagus together, break off and discard the tough, silvery bottom ends. Align the stalks and cut crosswise into 1" pieces.

Melt the butter in a large heavy skillet or wok over medium-high heat. Add the almonds to the pan. Toss them occasionally, until they are evenly golden. With a slotted spoon or spatula, remove the almonds to a paper towel to drain. Add the asparagus to the pan and sauté 3-4 minutes.

Add 2 tablespoons water, cover, and steam until tender, about 5 minutes. Add the almonds, lemon juice, and toss together. Season with salt and pepper, if needed, and serve immediately.

Yield: 4 servings

Roasted Asparagus

Roasting vegetables, lightly coated with oil, brings out pure vegetable flavor. It's delicious, easy, healthy, and different from run-of-the-mill vegetable treatments. Choose asparagus that is firm, bright green, and with tightly closed tips, indicating that it's young and tender. Especially for roasted asparagus, try to find stems that are about the same thickness. Otherwise, the thinner ones will overcook before the thicker stalks have become tender.

> **1 pound asparagus**
> **1-2 tablespoons olive oil**
> **salt and freshly ground pepper, to taste**

Preheat the oven to 500 degrees. Align the tips of the asparagus on a cutting board and cut off the thick, tough ends. Place the asparagus in a roasting pan in a single layer and brush with olive oil. Sprinkle with salt, if desired.

Roast in the upper third of the oven about 12 minutes, depending upon the thickness of the stalks, or until tender. Season with extra salt and pepper, if needed, and serve immediately.

Yield: 4 servings

If not using asparagus right away, store the spears upright in an inch or two of water covered loosely with plastic to retain their moisture. When ready to use, break or cut off the woody ends of each stalk and, if sandy, rinse in water.

Hot Sesame-Ginger Broccoli

This delightful balance of Asian flavors with fresh broccoli may be served hot, room temperature, or cold. Do without the chili oil entirely, if desired, to eliminate the heat. Serve the florets with toothpicks alongside to make an intriguing, healthy hors d'oeuvre. Choose bright green, firm broccoli with buds that are tightly closed. Old, yellowing buds should send up a warning flag to avoid them at all costs.

1 pound broccoli (1 medium bunch)
1 1-inch slice fresh ginger (about 2 tablespoons minced)
2 cloves garlic
2 tablespoons soy sauce
1 teaspoon sesame oil
1/2 teaspoon sugar
1/4 teaspoon hot chili oil, or to taste
2 teaspoons toasted sesame seeds (optional)

Bring 3 quarts of water to boil in a large pot. Cut off the broccoli florets and reserve. Slice the stems of the broccoli into 1/2" cross sections. Drop the stems into the water and cook 2 minutes. Drop the florets into the water and continue to cook another 3 minutes.

While the broccoli cooks, mince the ginger with the garlic and reserve. Drain the broccoli in a colander. Blend the ginger and garlic mixture, soy sauce, sesame oil, sugar, chili oil, and sesame seeds, if using, in the pot the broccoli was cooked in. Add the broccoli and toss thoroughly.

Yield: 4 servings

Broccoli florets can act as a sponge, soaking up the water that they have been cooked in, so, depending upon the broccoli's role in cooking, you may want to squeeze the florets dry in a colander or with paper towels before using, so that they won't dilute a sauce or salad dressing.

Carrot Coins with Orange and Ginger

Orange juice, butter, and vegetable juice cook down in this dish to create a slightly sweet, effortless sauce. The carrots can be set up and ready to cook ahead of time, except for a last-minute tasting for salt and pepper.

Buy carrots that are loose, and choose those that are small, firm, and bright orange in color. Especially avoid the orange-tinged plastic packages that may disguise carrots that are dried out, limp, or cracked. Parsnips are delicious raw or, combined with carrots as they can be here, they add color and flavor interest. Substitute parsnips entirely for the carrots in this recipe, if you like.

> **1 1/4 cups orange juice**
> **2 tablespoons unsalted butter**
> **1 teaspoon ground ginger**
> **1/4 teaspoon ground cinnamon**
> **6 medium carrots (or a combination of carrots and parsnips)**
> **salt and freshly ground pepper, to taste**

In a heavy medium saucepan over medium-high heat, blend the orange juice, butter, ginger, and cinnamon. Stir occasionally until the butter melts.

Meanwhile, peel the carrots and cut them into 1/4" rounds. Add them to the orange mixture, stir well, and bring the mixture to a boil. Simmer rapidly uncovered until almost all the liquid is absorbed and the carrots are tender, about 15 minutes. Season with salt and pepper, if needed, and serve immediately.

Yield: 4 servings

Buying baby carrots that are peeled will shave off 5 minutes from the preparation time in this recipe. They're available in 1- and 2-pound plastic bags in the produce section of most supermarkets. For carrots with the freshest flavor, buy them with the green tops intact. When you get them home, remove the tops before refrigerating.

Mushrooms Glazed with Port

These mushrooms take on the sweetness of port and honey, but retain their earthy flavor, so they're ideal to serve with roast chicken or ham. They positively glisten with a mahogany color. If you're cooking a number of dishes that require your attention, glaze the mushrooms, cap side down. Take them off the heat, flip them, and reheat 4 or 5 minutes just before serving. Watch the mushrooms carefully when first cooking, since they can burn, due to the sugar in the port and honey. Use only common cultivated mushrooms for this recipe. Wild varieties, such as morels and chanterelles, have too many irregular surfaces to glaze easily. Try to buy equally sized mushrooms, so they'll cook in the same amount of time. Sprinkle the mushrooms with chopped prosciutto and Italian flat-leaf parsley, if you like, and use as an individual hors d'oeuvre or as part of an antipasto platter.

1 pound mushrooms
3 tablespoons port
2 tablespoons olive oil
1 1/2 tablespoons balsamic vinegar
1/2 teaspoon honey or sugar
salt and freshly ground pepper, to taste

Remove the mushroom stems and reserve for another use (Herbed Mushroom Soup, page 76). Combine the port, olive oil, vinegar, and honey in a heavy large skillet over medium heat. Bring the mixture to a boil, stirring. Once the mixture simmers, reduce the heat slightly and add the mushrooms, cap side down.

Shake the pan occasionally, until mixture becomes syrupy and the caps are glazed, about 5 minutes. Turn the mushrooms over and cook another 3-5 minutes, depending upon their size. Spoon some of the glaze over each serving, and season with salt and pepper, if needed. Serve the mushrooms immediately.

Yield: 4 servings

Roasted New Potatoes and Garlic

I always make more of these potatoes than I need. They're a bite-size snack food from the fridge, or, tossed with Caper Vinaigrette (page 226), leftovers make a unique potato salad with a toasty aroma. Sprinkle the potatoes with a teaspoon of crumbled rosemary during the last 15 minutes of cooking for an added woodsy aroma, if desired.

1 pound baby new potatoes
2 cloves garlic
3 tablespoons olive oil
1/4 teaspoon salt, or more, to taste
1/4 teaspoon black pepper, or more, to taste

Preheat the oven to 350 degrees. Line a shallow baking dish or jelly roll pan with foil and spray with a nonstick vegetable spray. Slice the potatoes into quarters, peel and halve the garlic, and toss them with the olive oil, salt, and pepper directly on the prepared pan.

Bake until tender, 30-40 minutes, depending upon their size. Turn once to promote even browning. As the garlic begins to turn brown, remove it. Season with extra salt and pepper, if needed, and serve the potatoes immediately or hold briefly in a warm (200 degree) oven.

Yield: 4 servings

Tossing a vegetable directly on a baking pan saves a bowl and greases the pan at the same time. Human hands are often the fastest tools for blending solids with a sauce or coating them with oil. Using ten fingers at once is most effective, compared to a single spoon or spatula.

If you've bought potatoes in webbed plastic, wash them by holding the opening closed and rubbing the potatoes back and forth under running water. Shake the sack over the sink to eliminate most of the water.

Crunchy Winter Squash Purée

Acorn or butternut squash bakes in the oven as effortlessly as a potato. If you don't have the hour required to cook the squash until tender, microwave it. Both squashes are difficult, at best, to slice in half and seed raw, as many recipes call for. Bake them whole instead, so that they'll slice easily. Since steam builds up in the vegetable as it cooks, pierce it in a few places to avoid an explosion in the oven.

Lightly spiced and sweetened, this purée's aroma reminds me of fall, when winter squashes are plentiful and inexpensive—they'll keep 2 weeks or more in a cool, dry place. When possible, buy them young since old ones may be fibrous and dry. Leftover squash makes an elegant, velvety soup (Pumpkin Soup with Curry (page 74). Or add chicken or vegetable stock and milk or cream to the purée and heat through.

Substitute maple syrup or honey for the brown sugar, if you like, and add it according to your sweet tooth. When I'm in a desperate dash for dinner, I double one spice and eliminate the others. The combination is delightful, but each works well individually.

> **2 1/2-3 pounds acorn or butternut squash**
> **4 amaretti (optional)**
> **2 tablespoons unsalted butter**
> **2 tablespoons brown sugar**
> **1/2 teaspoon ground ginger**
> **1/4 teaspoon ground cinnamon**
> **1/4 teaspoon freshly grated or ground nutmeg or mace**
> **salt and freshly ground pepper, to taste**

Preheat the oven to 350 degrees. Prick each squash in 3-4 places with a sharp knife. Place on a shallow baking dish and cook one hour, or until tender. Alternatively, place on a microwave-proof dish and cook at full power until tender, about 15 minutes. If you're not using a carousel in the microwave, turn once during cooking.

While the squash cooks, place the amaretti, if using, in a food processor. Mince with on-off turns and remove to a paper towel. Place the butter, sugar, and spices in the processor.

Slice the squash in half and remove the seeds and strings. Scoop out the flesh and purée in the processor until the butter melts and the squash is smooth. Adjust the seasoning with salt and pepper, if needed, and sprinkle each serving with the crushed amaretti. Serve immediately.

Yield: 4 servings

Double Summer Squash
and Bell Pepper Mélange

This stunning side dish delivers vibrant color and pure vegetable flavor, since the squashes and peppers cook in their own juices. Substitute all of one type of pepper or squash, if all aren't available. Any leftovers are terrific cold in a salad or as part of an antipasto platter. Choose small- to medium-size summer squashes that are firm and unblemished, since large ones can be tough and mealy.

> 2 tablespoons olive oil
> 2 cloves garlic, minced
> 1 green bell pepper, sliced
> 1 red bell pepper, sliced
> 1 crookneck yellow squash, sliced
> 1 zucchini, sliced
> 1 teaspoon dried oregano or 1 tablespoon minced fresh
> salt and freshly ground pepper, to taste

Heat the olive oil in a heavy large wok or sauté pan over medium-low heat. Add the garlic and cook until fragrant, about 1 minute.

Stir the vegetables and oregano into the pan and sauté, tossing occasionally, over medium-high heat about 3 minutes. Lower the heat, cover tightly, and cook until tender, about 7 minutes. Adjust the seasoning with salt and pepper, if needed, and serve immediately.

Yield: 4 servings

Bell peppers need very little cleaning. Discard only the stems and seeds, since the membranes contain valuable nutrients. Place one trimmed half on top of the other to cut slicing time in half. Or better yet, cut the peppers into quarters lengthwise, stack the quarters, and slice. Always choose shiny, unblemished, firm peppers, and for most dishes, I prefer red ones since they're sweeter than green. When peppers are plentiful in a rainbow of colors, don't be fooled by the black ones for cooking, since they lose their exotic color and turn green when heated.

Many foods that have been broiled can be successfully held in a warm oven. Once the food is nicely browned, turn off the heat and close the oven door. If your broiler retains a lot of heat, lower the food to a more distant, cooler wire rack.

Tasting for seasoning can be trickier than it seems. Food to be served cold needs more seasoning, and a stuffing for bland ingredients may require more, since the container for the stuffing hasn't been seasoned. If sprinkling cheese on top of a stuffing, remember the cheese will contribute saltiness.

Tomato-Speckled Zucchini with Olivada

Creamy and redolent with olives, this simple dish can be cooked and stuffed a day ahead and broiled just prior to serving. If you don't care for a strong olive aroma, omit the olivada—the recipe works beautifully without it. Many vegetables make ideal containers for stuffing, but most require a lot of time to cook. Zucchini and yellow summer squash, which can be substituted for the zucchini, are exceptions, since they need only about ten minutes to become tender and both are fairly bland, lending them to a variety of cuisines and tastes. Small, young vegetables cook most quickly. If you have a 3-pound zucchini, save it for bread or soup.

2 medium zucchini (about 12 ounces total)
1 scallion
1 plum tomato
1/2 cup freshly grated Parmesan (about 2 ounces)
1/4 cup prepared mayonnaise
1 tablespoon olivada
salt and freshly ground pepper, to taste

Preheat a broiler and place a rack about 6 inches from the heat. Bring 2 inches of water to boil in a large skillet. Add the zucchini to the water and simmer 10 minutes, or until tender when pierced with a sharp knife. While the zucchini cook, mince the scallion and dice the tomato. Grate the Parmesan, if it is not pre-grated, and blend it in a medium bowl with the Parmesan, mayonnaise, and olivada.

When the zucchini are tender, drain and slice them in half lengthwise. Leaving a quarter-inch shell, scoop out the flesh with a melon baller or small spoon and chop it coarsely. Blend it with the mayonnaise mixture and adjust the seasoning with salt and pepper, if needed. Pack it lightly into the zucchini shells and broil until lightly browned, about 5 minutes.

Yield: 4 servings

Parsnips with Cranberries and Orange

This colorful dish of pale parsnips dotted with scarlet cranberries is perfect for a festive occasion. Cranberries provide tart flavor and a pleasing contrast to mildly sweet parsnips, but substitute carrots for an equally tasty dish, if you prefer. Be sure to buy medium or, preferably small, parsnips. Old ones tend to be tough and woody.

        16-20 ounces small parsnips, trimmed, peeled
        1 cup orange juice
        2 tablespoons unsalted butter
        3/4 cup fresh or frozen cranberries
        salt and freshly ground pepper, to taste
        2 tablespoons minced fresh chives (optional)

Slice the parsnips into 1/4-inch slices and place in a heavy medium saucepan with the orange juice and butter. Bring to a boil, cover, and simmer the parsnips 5 minutes.

Add the cranberries and cook on medium-high heat uncovered, stirring occasionally, until the berries have popped, the parsnips are tender, and the orange juice has thickened. Adjust the seasoning, if needed, and sprinkle with chives, if using. Serve immediately.

Yield: 4 servings

If you can only find large parsnips, which are disproportionately large at the stem ends, cut the oversized pieces into quarters lengthwise and then slice crosswise. Making the size of pieces of vegetables even equalizes the amount of cooking time they'll need to reach tenderness.

Cranberries, due to their small size, will defrost quickly in a simmering liquid, so there's no need to defrost them ahead of time.

Defrosting spinach in a colander set inside a larger bowl allows it to drain while warming to room temperature. Run cool water over it in a sink to hasten defrosting or microwave on the defrost cycle.

Ginger-Sesame Spinach

For those who are not enthusiastic about the taste of spinach, try this Asian-flavored recipe. For the die-hard quick cook, frozen spinach is convenient and reliable. Pre-washed and dried spinach in bags makes a viable alternative for cooking, but it, too, needs sorting through, and most of the leaves are tough and old. Add a drained 5-ounce can of sliced water chestnuts to this dish, if desired, for an easy counterpoint in texture and flavor.

1 pound frozen spinach
3 scallions
1 1/2-inch slice fresh ginger (about 1 tablespoon minced)
1 clove garlic
2 tablespoons soy sauce
1 teaspoon sesame oil
1/2 teaspoon sugar
1 tablespoon vegetable oil
1 5-ounce can sliced water chestnuts, drained (optional)
2 tablespoons toasted sesame seeds (optional)

Defrost and drain the spinach (see sidebar). Mince the scallions, ginger, and garlic together. Blend the soy sauce, sesame oil, and sugar in a small bowl and reserve.

Heat the vegetable oil in a large wok or skillet over medium-high heat. Add the minced ginger mixture and stir-fry 1 minute. Add the spinach and cook, turning frequently, until barely cooked, about 3 minutes.

Drizzle the soy sauce mixture over the spinach and add the water chestnuts and sesame seeds, if using. Toss the mixture well and serve immediately.

Yield: 4 servings

Sautéed Yams with Pecans

Using a combination of yam and sweet potato makes this dish beautiful with rounds of pale yellow and bright orange, studded with pecans. It's an unusual treatment where the cut slices caramelize to a golden brown and steam simultaneously, enhancing the natural sweetness of the vegetables. Substitute hazelnuts for the pecans, if you prefer. Cooking the yams is so simple that, assuming you have a tight-fitting lid so that steam doesn't escape, you'll be free to prepare other foods while the vegetables cook.

> **2 yams (or 1 yam, 1 sweet potato)**
> **2 tablespoons unsalted butter**
> **2 tablespoons maple syrup (optional)**
> **1/4 cup chopped pecans (optional)**
> **salt and freshly ground pepper, to taste**

Peel the yams and cut them into 1/2" slices. In a heavy large, preferably nonstick, skillet, melt the butter over medium-low heat. Arrange the yams in a single layer, cover, and cook slowly, shaking the pan occasionally, until lightly golden on the underside, about 15 minutes.

Turn the yams, cover, and cook the other side until golden and tender, 10-15 minutes, depending upon their thickness and age. Remove the slices to a warm plate. Add the maple syrup and the pecans to the pan, if using. When warm, pour over the yams, adjust the seasoning with salt and pepper, if needed, and serve immediately.

Yield: 4 servings

Peeling and slicing all vegetables, but particularly root vegetables, cuts their cooking time into fractions. Heavy-duty peelers are available for yam, sweet potato, and butternut squash skins, which are usually too tough for common vegetable peelers.

Sautéing an accompaniment to a vegetable while it drains saves dishes and labor. If the vegetable has cooled too much while draining, reheat it when returned to the pan or microwave it.

Shredded Escarole with Peas

The French often cook peas with shreds of lettuce, but escarole, a member of the endive family, adds a slightly bitter counterpoint to sweet green peas, as well as a contrast in texture. It has slightly curved, broad green leaves, and it's available all year long. Add minced fresh mint, if available, to the peas just before serving.

> 1 small head escarole (about 2 cups shredded)
> 2 cups frozen tiny green peas (1 10-ounce package)
> 1 tablespoon unsalted butter
> 1 teaspoon sugar
> salt and freshly ground pepper, to taste

In a heavy medium sauté pan, bring an inch of water to boil. Meanwhile, shred the escarole into a fine chiffonade (see page 98).

Add the peas to the water and bring it back to a boil, stirring occasionally to break up the peas. Drain them and return the saucepan to medium-low heat.

Melt the butter and sauté the escarole until just softened, about 2 minutes. Sprinkle with the sugar, return the peas to the pan, and heat through. Adjust the seasoning with salt and pepper, if needed, and serve immediately.

Yield: 4 servings

Tomato Gruyère Gratin

Broiled tomatoes may be the fastest cooked vegetable on record. All this lightly-crusted, showy side dish requires is to be topped with a few flavorful ingredients and to be broiled quickly at the last minute until golden. It lends a pleasant acidic flavor and bright color contrast to dress up almost any plate. It's especially appealing in late summer, when large beefsteak tomatoes are in season.

2 ripe large tomatoes or 4 plum tomatoes
1/4 cup fresh bread crumbs
1 ounce Gruyère cheese (about 1/4 cup grated)
1/4 cup lightly packed fresh parsley
2 tablespoons olive oil
salt and freshly ground pepper, to taste

Preheat the broiler and arrange a rack about 8 inches from the heat. Slice the tomatoes in half lengthwise. Remove any tough core, should there be any. Place on a baking sheet lined with foil. If the tomatoes will not sit flat, slice a tiny piece off the bottom of each (see page 57).

If you do not have fresh breadcrumbs on hand, place a slice of bread in a food processor and mince. Measure out 1/4 cup. If not pre-grated, mince the cheese in the processor and add to the bread. Repeat with the parsley. Blend the bread crumbs, cheese, parsley, and olive oil together. Adjust the seasoning, if needed, with salt and pepper.

Spread the mixture over the tomato halves, place under the broiler, and close the oven door part way, so the underside of the tomatoes warm. Cook until the tops are golden, about 4-6 minutes. Hold in a warm oven for a few minutes, if needed, before serving.

Yield: 4 servings

Whenever possible, buy vegetables loose, not packed airtight. They need air circulation to fend off mold and remain firm. Buying them loose allows you to pick each vegetable individually, so you can be certain each is unblemished and wrinkle-free. Vegetables should feel heavy for their size. The stem ends of tomatoes, melons, and pineapple should reveal their fragrance when ripe.

Broccoli Purée with Parmesan

This soothing dish achieves the impossible—it satisfies those of us who want their green vegetables bright green and those who still think they should be cooked long enough to slice with a fork. It makes use of every bit of broccoli without having to peel its tough stems, and it can be made ahead, or even frozen, to be reheated in the microwave. Set aside 4 cooked florets before puréeing for an optional garnish, or sprinkle with extra cheese before serving.

Don't be tempted to fudge on the cooking time when making a purée. If the vegetable isn't well-cooked, even a food processor won't smooth its texture. Despite the fact that they are cooked until soft, green vegetables will retain their bright green color if cooked uncovered at a rolling boil and then cooled under cold running water. Be sure to drain vegetables thoroughly when making a purée. Otherwise, the dish will be so diluted it won't hold its shape.

> **1 medium bunch broccoli (20-24 ounces)**
> **1/4 cup freshly grated Parmesan (about 1 ounce)**
> **1/4 cup unsalted butter**
> **freshly grated or ground nutmeg, to taste**
> **salt and freshly ground pepper, to taste**

Bring a large pot of lightly salted water to boil. Meanwhile, cut the broccoli stems into 1" pieces and break the top into florets. When the water comes to a rolling boil, add the stems and cook 6 minutes. Add the florets and cook another 6 minutes, or until the broccoli is very tender.

While the broccoli cooks, mince the Parmesan in a food processor, if you haven't bought it pre-grated. Add the butter and about 1/8 teaspoon nutmeg to the workbowl. Drain the broccoli thoroughly, place in the processor, and purée, scraping down the sides of the bowl as needed. Adjust the seasoning with salt and pepper, if necessary, and serve immediately.

Yield: 4 servings

Baby Bok Choy with Bell Peppers

This is a stunning side dish prepared in 3-5 minutes. Most recipes call for cooking the stems and leaves of bok choy separately, since they cook at different rates. Here, it's all done in one step, providing pleasing differences in texture. The bok choy stems provide white celery-like crunchiness and the leaves a deep green color and fuller flavor. Sweet, tender red bell peppers are the perfect counterpoint. If you can get black sesame seeds, do. They dot the dish with exotic bits of color.

1 tablespoon corn or peanut oil
1 clove garlic, minced
1 pound baby bok choy, sliced into 1/2-inch diagonal pieces
1/2 red bell pepper, trimmed, seeded, quartered,
 and sliced thin
2 tablespoons soy sauce
1 teaspoon sesame seed oil
1/2 teaspoon black sesame seeds (optional)

Heat the oil in a large wok or skillet over medium-high heat. Add the garlic and cook a few seconds. Stir in the bok choy and pepper and stir-fry about 5 minutes. Add the soy sauce, sesame seed oil, and sesame seeds, if using. Toss until warmed through and serve immediately.

Yield: 4 servings

There are a bewildering number of varieties of bok choy available today, and, although they have different cooking times, they are interchangeable. If you like a change of texture in a dish, the stems and leaves can be cooked together for the same amount of time.

To slice long fruits or vegetables on the diagonal, align them side by side and push them gently so that each end is 1/2-1 inch ahead of the other. Slice across them on the angle.

When glazing vegetables, it's best to use a pan that can hold them in a single layer with a bit of room to spare, so the vegetables have room to roll around in the glazing mixture. Ideally, the vegetables should be about the same size and a shape that can roll. Whole chestnuts couldn't be better designed for glazing, but vegetables such as carrots and turnips have to be turned, or carved into small torpedo-shapes so they can roll easily.

Brown Sugar-Glazed Chestnuts

Whole chestnuts add a touch of elegance to a special dinner. They're subtly sweet and nutty, and treasured for their delicate starchiness. Be sure to relish that first sweet aroma when opening a jar—it's intoxicating, just like opening a container of coffee beans. Blend these with cooked brussels sprouts, carrots, or pearl onions, if you like, or splurge and serve them as is. Granulated sugar or mild honey can be used in place of the brown sugar.

> 1 16-ounce jar prepared whole chestnuts
> 3/4 cup chicken stock or broth
> 2 tablespoons unsalted butter
> 2 tablespoons brown sugar
> salt and freshly ground pepper, to taste

Drain the liquid, if there is any, from the jar of chestnuts. Heat the chestnuts and chicken broth in a heavy medium saucepan over medium heat. Simmer to heat through, about 5 minutes. Drain the chestnuts and return the pan to medium heat.

Melt the butter, add the chestnuts, and sprinkle with the sugar. Cook, stirring or shaking the pan occasionally, until glazed, about 3-4 minutes. Adjust the seasoning, if needed, with salt and pepper, and serve immediately.

Yield: 4 servings

Green Beans with Pancetta and Garlic

Frozen green beans, picked at the peak of their season, provide great convenience, since all the trimming has been done for you. Regardless of convenience, I find fresh green beans too often dull in color and tough and fibrous, and no amount of cooking will tenderize them. Chinese long beans make trimming easy but they have less crispness and can be difficult to locate. When you shop for fresh green beans, look for small, crisp ones that snap when bent.

> 1 pound fresh or frozen green beans
> 4 ounces pancetta or bacon
> 3 cloves garlic
> 1 tablespoon fresh or bottled lemon juice
> salt and freshly ground pepper, to taste

Bring a large pot of lightly salted water to a boil and, if you've bought fresh green beans, trim them while the water heats. Add them to the boiling water and simmer until barely tender, about 5-10 minutes, depending upon their size and age. Meanwhile, dice the pancetta, mince the garlic, and reserve. Drain the beans and set aside. Return the pan to medium heat.

Add the pancetta to the pan and cook until crisp, stirring occasionally. Transfer to paper towels and drain off all but 1 tablespoon fat. Off the heat, blend the garlic with the fat and stir briefly, about 1 minute.

Add the beans and lemon juice. Toss thoroughly and reheat covered, if necessary. Stir in the pancetta, adjust the seasoning with salt and pepper, if necessary, and serve immediately.

Yield: 4 servings

Making a sauce directly in the cooking pan for a vegetable saves a dish to be cleaned. Often, however, a pot will be too hot for a temperature-sensitive ingredient, such as garlic or shallots. In that case, remove the pan briefly from the heat to cook the garlic, and then return it to the heat with insulating ingredients. Once the sauce is made, return the vegetable to the pot, toss, and reheat, covered, if necessary.

When draining canned vegetables, beans, or fruit, completely cut through the lid of the can. Use the lid, pressing down lightly onto the contents of the can, to drain its liquid and retain the solids, thereby avoiding the use of a colander or strainer. If draining while preparing other ingredients, set the loose lid and can upside down at an angle over the drain of a sink. The contents will drain while you pursue another activity.

Beets Grand Marnier

A delicate orange-flavored sauce glazes perfectly shaped, deep purple beets in this beautiful dish. The convenience of canned beets means no long cooking and messy peeling of beets that bleed when skinned. Add some fresh orange zest (see page 104) for more intense citrus flavor or a tablespoon of orange marmalade for those with a sweet tooth.

1 1-pound can medium whole beets
2 tablespoons unsalted butter
1/4 cup Grand Marnier or other orange-flavored liqueur
salt and freshly ground pepper, to taste

Drain the beets and place them with the butter and liqueur in a heavy medium saucepan over medium-high heat. Cover and cook until the beets are heated through, about 3 minutes.

Uncover and cook, shaking the pan occasionally, until the liquid reduces to a glaze, about 3 minutes. Adjust the seasoning, if needed, with salt and pepper, and serve immediately.

Yield: 4 servings

Jalapeño-Glazed Plantains

Plantains make an unusual side dish for roast pork or chicken. The jalapeño jelly speckles the rosy flesh of plantains with hot green flecks, and a sprinkling of brown allspice, which combines the flavors of cinnamon, nutmeg, and clove, adds a warm undertone. Less sweet than bananas, plantains are starchy and firm. Botanically they are a fruit and can be eaten raw, but typically they're cooked and served like a vegetable, as an accompaniment to another dish.

> **4 ripe plantains (about 2 1/2 pounds)**
> **1/2 cup orange juice**
> **1/4 cup jalapeño jelly**
> **2 tablespoons unsalted butter**
> **1 teaspoon ground allspice**
> **salt and freshly ground pepper, to taste**

Peel the plantains, align them side by side, and cut into 1/8-1/4" rounds. In a heavy medium, preferably nonstick, skillet over medium heat, stir the orange juice, jelly, butter, and allspice until the mixture is smooth.

Stir in the plantains and cook until tender and glazed, about 5 minutes, turning them occasionally with a spatula. Adjust the seasoning, if needed, with salt and pepper and serve immediately.

Yield: 4 servings

Be prepared for the plantain to hold tenaciously to its skin. Use a sharp paring knife to make two lengthwise cuts through the skin. Then run your thumbs under the skin, peeling it away from its flesh.

In most cooking, but especially quick cooking, it's important to use a tight-fitting lid, since steam from food escapes, thereby drying out the food and reducing the temperature in the pan.

Asian Eggplant Rounds

Asian varieties of eggplant will cook in half the time of the bulbous western types. They're smaller, less bitter, contain fewer seeds, and have more tender skin. Most recipes call for peeling, salting, rinsing, and baking Western eggplants. This treatment of the Japanese variety, although unorthodox, is the fastest I've ever cooked. It needn't be peeled, and slicing it into thin rounds shaves the cooking time. The eggplant is a bit peppery from fresh ginger and has a nutty aroma from sesame seed oil. Eggplants of all types should be smooth, firm, and unblemished. Choose those that feel heavy for their size, since lighter ones can be mealy in texture.

4 thin Japanese eggplants (about 1 pound)
2 scallions
1 1/2-inch slice fresh ginger (about 1 tablespoon minced)
2 tablespoons sugar
2 tablespoons low-sodium soy sauce
4 teaspoons mild vinegar, preferably rice vinegar
1 tablespoon sherry
1 teaspoon sesame seed oil
3 tablespoons corn or peanut oil

Cut off and discard the stem ends of the eggplants, align them, and slice crosswise into 1/8-1/4" rounds. Mince the scallions and ginger together, and reserve. Blend the sugar, soy sauce, vinegar, sherry, and sesame oil in a small bowl and reserve.

Heat the oil in a heavy large wok or skillet over medium-high heat. Add the rounds and toss thoroughly. Add 1/2 cup water, cover tightly, and cook until tender, stirring occasionally, about 5 minutes. Add more water, if necessary.

Stir in the scallions and ginger and cook until aromatic, about 20 seconds. Blend in the soy sauce mixture. Stir until the sauce coats the eggplant. Serve immediately or at room temperature.

Yield: 4 servings

Wild Mushroom Sauté

Wild mushrooms are so dear in price and subtle in flavor that it seems unkind to complicate their delicate nature by long cooking or extraneous ingredients. Their varying textures, flavors, and colors (see Wild Mushroom Salad with Walnut Vinaigrette, page 94) are so striking that they speak well for themselves with little adornment.

> 1 pound assorted wild mushrooms (about 2 quarts)
> 2 tablespoons unsalted butter
> 1 tablespoon olive oil
> 3 shallots, minced
> salt and freshly ground pepper, to taste

Clean, trim, and slice the mushrooms, if large (leave oyster mushrooms and other small varieties whole).

Melt the butter and oil in a heavy large sauté pan or wok over medium heat. Stir in the mushrooms and shallots, and sauté until tender, about 8 minutes. Adjust the seasoning with salt and pepper, and serve immediately.

Yield: 4 servings

Since mushrooms continue to breathe after they're picked, always store them in paper, not plastic. In paper, they'll keep up to a week, if chilled.

When combining vegetables that require various types of cooking and different amounts of cooking time, plan ahead so they can be cooked in the same pot. Start with vegetables that require the longest amount of cooking, adding more tender ones toward the end. In this recipe the onions need to boil to cook through, and both the onions and the peas benefit from glazing (see page 208) in the reduced onion cooking liquid. Peas require so little cooking that they'll be tender in the time it takes to glaze them.

Sugar Snap Peas with Pearl Onions

Peeling a lot of pearl onions is tedious, at best, so frozen ones provide much-needed convenience. Their tiny size dresses up dishes, such as stews and soups, that chopped large onions are lost in. Crisp, small, bright green sugar snap peas are easier to prepare than snow peas, since, they rarely need any trimming. If you should see any visible strings, remove them. Look for small pods—the larger, pale ones tend to be tough and stringy. Try to use them the day you buy them, since, like corn, their natural sweetness starts turning to starch the moment they're picked.

> 1 10-ounce package frozen pearl onions
> 1 cup chicken stock or broth
> 3/4 pound sugar snap peas
> 2 tablespoons unsalted butter
> 1 teaspoon sugar
> salt and freshly ground pepper, to taste

Place the onions in a colander and run warm water over them. Pour the stock in a heavy medium saucepan, add the onions, and bring to a boil over high heat. Cover and cook until the onions are tender, about 5 minutes.

Uncover and stir in the peas, butter, and sugar. Cook until glazed, shaking the pan occasionally, about 6 minutes. Season with salt and pepper, if needed, and serve immediately.

Yield: 4 servings

Herbed New Potatoes

Baby new potatoes, red-skinned and no more than an inch and a half in diameter, are available all year round. They cook quickly and need the simplest of enhancement: here, a few herbs and butter. To provide variety and to make this recipe even easier, use one of the compound butters on pages 220-224, instead of the butter, thyme, and oregano used here.

> **1 pound baby new potatoes**
> **2-3 tablespoons unsalted butter**
> **1 tablespoon fresh oregano or 1 teaspoon dried**
> **1 1/2 teaspoons fresh thyme or 1/2 teaspoon dried**
> **salt and freshly ground pepper, to taste**

Place the potatoes in a shallow pan large enough to hold them in one layer. Pour cold water to cover them by one inch. Bring to a boil and simmer until tender when pierced with a sharp knife, about 12-15 minutes, depending upon their size. Drain the potatoes and return the pan to medium heat.

Melt the butter in the pan. Add the herbs, potatoes, and salt and pepper, shaking the pan occasionally until well coated and heated through. Serve immediately.

Yield: 4 servings

Using unpeeled, uncut potatoes is not only the quickest and easiest way to cook potatoes, but the most nutritious, since cut potatoes lose vitamin C in the cooking liquid. For those who don't care for potato skin, the skin on baby new potatoes is delicate and paper-thin.

Sweet Potatoes Glazed with Curry and Cashews

This golden, mahogany-colored combination of sweet potatoes and cashews is slightly sweet and slightly hot. The curry powder contributes subtle but complex flavor and its characteristic striking yellow-orange color makes it particularly appealing for fall. Sweet potatoes normally take a long time to cook. Peeling and slicing the potatoes cuts the required cooking time to about 15 minutes, more than making up for a few minutes of preparation time. Buy smooth, unblemished sweet potatoes to make peeling them easy. Use a food processor, if you prefer, to reduce the time spent slicing.

> **2 medium sweet potatoes**
> **1 cup orange juice**
> **2 tablespoons low-sodium soy sauce**
> **1 teaspoon curry powder**
> **1 teaspoon mild honey**
> **3/4 cup cashews**
> **salt and freshly ground pepper, to taste**

Trim off and discard the ends of the potatoes. Peel the vegetables and quarter them lengthwise. Align two lengths of potato together and slice them crosswise into quarter-inch pieces. Repeat until all the lengths are cut.

Blend the orange juice, soy sauce, curry, and honey in a heavy large skillet over high heat. Add the potato slices and toss them with the liquid. Cover, reduce the heat, and simmer until tender when pierced with a sharp knife, about 10 minutes.

Uncover, add the cashews, and cook, stirring occasionally, over medium-high heat until the liquid thickens and glazes the potatoes, about 3-4 minutes. Adjust the seasoning with salt and pepper, if needed, and serve immediately.

Yield: 4 servings

Glazing vegetables gives them a shimmering, jewel-like appearance. Root vegetables, individual cloves of garlic, shallots, carrots, turnips, pearl onions, and peeled and cooked whole chestnuts make excellent candidates. A light glaze is achieved with water or stock and sugar, and darker glazes can be made using rich brown stock. Regardless of color, the simple process of cooking down liquid until it thickens and coats the vegetables is the same.

Simple Sauces
and Dressings

Recipes

Independent Sauces

Compound Butters

Dressings and Mayonnaise

Dessert Sauces

Not all sauces need be ambitious. Some are simple, straightforward, and speedy, combining just a few choice ingredients. Some of the most popular sauces today are cooked quickly to retain the freshness of ingredients, and many require no cooking at all.

Sauces should always enhance and uplift, not overwhelm food. Delicate salad greens weighted down by a heavy dressing or overpowered in flavor are ruined, and meats and vegetables drowned in thick sauces lose their inherent appeal quickly.

There are many sauces and dressings included in this book within recipes, but the ones in this chapter serve unique purposes. Some of the sauces in this chapter are similar to the flavors of dishes that require lengthy cooking, placing them within the reach of hurried cooks. Making these sauces transforms leftovers, giving them a fresh look and taste, and it allows you to grill or broil food and still enjoy accompanying moisture and intriguing flavor.

Compound Butters

Compound butters, packed with a variety of flavors, may be the easiest, most versatile sauces for the quick cook. They are simply a blend of softened butter and flavorful ingredients such as garlic, capers, anchovies, peppercorns, or any of your favorite herbs and spices. Spread compound butters on bread or tortillas, pita halves, or wontons and bake until the butter is melted and the base is crisp. Top grilled or sautéed meats, fish, and poultry or cooked vegetables or pasta with a tablespoon or two of compound butters for an effortless sauce.

Under ideal circumstances, let unsalted butter come close to room temperature before making compound butter. If you don't have time to soften the butter at room temperature, microwave it briefly or chop it into small pieces and then process or whip. The constant cutting or beating will make the butter smooth. Any of these recipes can be made by hand or whipped with a hand mixer, but the food processor makes it a snap.

The butters can be chilled or frozen, so they make an ideal way to store an abundance of fresh herbs. Use just as much of the butter as you need at once, rewrap and store the rest. Since its uses vary widely, season with salt and pepper after it's been incorporated into a dish.

Dressings and Mayonnaise

Keeping a stash of fragrant salad dressings ready to use from the refrigerator is a culinary security blanket. Making dressing on the spot doesn't require much time, but for those meals when you lack the mental energy or when even seconds count, it's assuring to be guaranteed delicious choices straight from the refrigerator.

The biggest advantage to making dressings yourself is that you control the quality of ingredients. Aside from avoiding the preservatives used in commercial preparations, you can insist on extra virgin olive oil, the most aromatic vinegars, and the freshest herbs and spices.

Commercially prepared dressings and mayonnaises fall far short of the quality of homemade, but, thankfully, the food processor makes producing marvelously aromatic dressings at home a snap. All of the ingredients are contained in one bowl, and the process is practically labor-free. I make dressings in quantity, some to store for myself and others to give away as gifts from the kitchen that are a welcome alternative to traditional heavy sweets.

The processor makes it possible to create mayonnaise with whole eggs, instead of egg yolks alone, and a tiny hole in the bottom of its feed tube allows oil to drip ever so slowly into the workbowl to create emulsified sauces effortlessly. Blenders also emulsify dressings and mayonnaises, but without the convenience of a drip control.

Remove vinaigrettes from the refrigerator as soon as you begin to make a salad. This time will allow it to come almost.to room temperature, so that it will be fluid and full-flavored, before using. Microwave, if the dressing is still congealed and you're pressed for time.

Dessert Sauces

Simple dessert sauces, although they take only minutes to prepare, can also be stored in the refrigerator and heated to make practically instant desserts accompanied by ice cream or purchased cakes.

Most fruits, jams, and jellies make simple bases for sweet sauces, and their selection has improved greatly in the last decade. Add wine or liqueur for a more complex flavor, add cream or swirl in unsalted butter for richness.

Serve any of these sauces warm or at room temperature over fresh fruit, ice cream, frozen yogurt, prepared cakes, or a combination of them.

Indian Curry Sauce

Curry powder is an English adulteration of carefully chosen, blended, roasted, and ground spices that Indian cooks vary for each particular dish. What it lacks in authenticity, however, it compensates for in convenience. Brands vary in flavor and heat, so try a sampling to suit your taste. Turmeric gives curry its bright yellow color, and a hodgepodge of spices gives it heat and flavor. Curries that border on incendiary are sheer bliss to some and grounds for divorce to others.

This sauce gives leftovers a facelift, rarely resembling some roast that you've eaten four times in the last three days. It makes a grand cover-up for cooked seafood, poultry, and especially leg of lamb. Vary this basic sauce by adding onion, fresh ginger, or diced apples, if you like. Serve your completed curry with plain white rice, chutney, and an assortment of nuts, raisins, dried coconut, and fresh fruits, such as diced apple, banana, and mango. It also enlivens cooked noodles with bits and pieces of leftover meats and vegetables.

4 tablespoons unsalted butter
4 tablespoons all-purpose flour
2 tablespoons curry powder, or to taste
2 cups chicken or beef stock
salt and freshly ground pepper, to taste

In a heavy medium saucepan, melt the butter over medium heat. Whisk in the flour and curry and cook, stirring occasionally, 1-2 minutes. Pour in the stock, bring to a simmer, and whisk occasionally until thickened, about 3-4 minutes. Adjust the seasoning, if needed, with salt and pepper, and toss with about 4 cups of diced cooked poultry, meat, seafood, or vegetables. Serve immediately.

Yield: Enough sauce to coat 4 cups of cooked food

Despite all the spices that commercial curry powder contains, it is not complete. It still needs salt, and a brief sautéing heightens its flavor. To alter curry powder to suit your own taste, add ground ginger, nutmeg, mace, allspice, or cinnamon.

Double the amount of curry you make and freeze a few portions. It comes in handy at a moment's notice and freezes with no obvious loss of flavor or texture.

Substitute sour cream for the yogurt, if you'd rather, for a richer, slightly less tangy sauce. Since both yogurt and sour cream can curdle when heated, they should be added off the heat or, at the very least, not allowed to simmer. Either one performs beautifully without cooking.

Satay Sauce

Satay, a common Indonesian dish, combines skewered meat, fish, or poultry, that is grilled or broiled and served with a sharp, piquant peanut sauce. It's a favorite snack food and can also be served as an appetizer or entrée. Traditionally, satays require long marinating, but this sauce packs enough flavor that you can experience the essence of satay by grilling or broiling your favorite meat and serving this sauce alongside. If you only have chunky peanut butter on hand, use it to make a coarser sauce. Also, you can use this versatile recipe as a dip, especially for fruit, such as sliced raw apples, or over cooked and drained Asian noodles.

4 cloves garlic
1 2-inch slice fresh ginger (about 1/4 cup minced)
1/2 cup creamy peanut butter
4 teaspoons reduced-sodium soy sauce
4 teaspoons fresh or bottled lemon juice
1/2 cup plain low-fat or nonfat yogurt
salt and freshly ground pepper, to taste

Drop the garlic and ginger through the feed tube of a food processor with the motor running. Add the peanut butter, soy sauce, and lemon juice, and purée until smooth, scraping down the sides of the bowl as needed. Add the yogurt and process to blend. Adjust the seasoning with salt and pepper, if needed. If not serving immediately, keep covered and chilled up to one week.

Yield: About 1 cup

Sauerbraten Sauce

Short of dashing to a German restaurant, there's no way for a quick cook to satisfy a sudden craving for the distinctive taste of sauerbraten. The problem with this piquant German braised beef is that you have to start marinating it in wine vinegar, onion, peppercorns, bay leaf, garlic, salt, and sometimes, juniper berries five to seven days before serving it. The beef must cook for 3 hours or until tender. Most cooks reduce the marinade and whisk in sour cream before serving it with the cooking juices, and some add crushed ginger snaps as a thickener.

If you love sauerbraten, but you're not willing to work on it for a week, this pan sauce is a convenient, albeit unorthodox, alternative. Pan-fry steak, hamburger, or even leftover roast beef in a small amount of butter and remove the meat to a warm plate. Pour off any fat and make the sauce in the same pan. Instant sauerbraten flavor, minus the pickling process.

This recipe allows for lots of sauce to accompany traditional spaetzle or potato pancakes.

Often when a recipe calls for a small onion, or a part of one, it's easier to use a large shallot to avoid dealing with leftover raw onion. Regardless of the inconvenience of leftover parts of vegetables, an onion that has been cut and refrigerated loses most of its aroma.

> **3 tablespoons unsalted butter**
> **1 1/2-inch thick slice of medium-size white onion (or 1 large shallot)**
> **3 tablespoons all-purpose flour**
> **2 cups beef stock or broth**
> **1 tablespoon red wine vinegar**
> **2 teaspoons sugar**
> **1/2 teaspoon freshly ground black pepper**
> **2 tablespoons sour cream**
> **salt and extra freshly ground black pepper, to taste**

In a heavy small saucepan, melt the butter over medium-low heat. Meanwhile, mince the onion and cook it with the butter, stirring until softened, about 3 minutes. Add the flour and whisk 1-2 minutes. Pour in the stock, whisking until thickened.

When the sauce is smooth, blend in the vinegar, sugar, and pepper. Cook, stirring occasionally, 3-4 minutes. Whisk in the sour cream, heat through, and adjust the seasoning with salt and additional pepper, if needed. Serve immediately.

Yield: 4 servings

Flour needs to simmer a minute to rid it of a pasty taste. In making sauces or gravies, blend the flour with melted butter or drippings and allow it to bubble a minute without burning before adding liquid, such as stock. If a vegetable or seasoning has been sautéed in the butter first, it will continue to cook with the flour.

Stroganoff Sauce

In this quick rendition of Stroganoff, mushrooms, onions, and Worcestershire blend into a savory sauce enriched with sour cream that's traditionally served with beef. Aside from grilled steak, hamburger, or chicken, stroganoff is delicious over noodles, spaetzle, or rice. It keeps well, so I often chill it to reheat a few days later. Be careful not to let it boil, however, since the sour cream will separate. This recipe is written for maximum efficiency. If you're a novice cook or you're cooking other things simultaneously, prepare the onion and mushrooms before starting the sauce.

> **4 tablespoons unsalted butter**
> **1 small onion**
> **4 ounces mushrooms (or 1 1/2 cups sliced)**
> **3 tablespoons all-purpose flour**
> **2 cups beef stock or broth**
> **1 1/2 teaspoons Worcestershire sauce**
> **3 tablespoons sour cream**
> **salt and freshly ground pepper, to taste**

In a heavy medium saucepan, melt the butter over medium-low heat. Meanwhile, mince the onion and cook it with the butter while preparing the mushrooms. Slice the mushrooms and stir them into the butter. Cook about 4 minutes. Add the flour and stir 1 minute.

Pour in the stock and Worcestershire, stirring until thickened. Simmer about 5 minutes, blend in the sour cream, and adjust the seasoning with salt and pepper, if needed. Do not allow to boil. Serve immediately.

Yield: 4 servings

Dijon-Honey Sauce

This simple mustard sauce, given a bit of sweetness from orange juice and honey, is ideal over cooked fish or roast or sautéed poultry. It reduces without much attention, freeing you to do other chores. Add a spoonful of orange marmalade, if you like, for a sweeter, more intense orange flavor. Or sprinkle with freshly grated orange zest (see page 104). Try it with minced fresh ginger, minced garlic, or fresh or dried tarragon.

> **2 cups orange juice**
> **2 cups chicken stock or broth**
> **2 tablespoons Dijon mustard**
> **2 tablespoons mild honey**
> **2 teaspoons Worcestershire sauce**
> **salt and freshly ground pepper, to taste**

Blend the orange juice, stock, mustard, honey, and Worcestershire in a heavy medium saucepan. Bring to a boil and simmer vigorously until reduced by about two-thirds, or to the desired thickness, about 20 minutes. Adjust the seasoning, if needed, with salt and pepper, and serve immediately.

Yield: About 1 cup

When reducing a sauce, the wider the pan, the faster it will evaporate and reduce. Use this principle if you're in a hurry, and conversely, if you're preoccupied with other chores, reduce a sauce slowly in a smaller pan.

Be sure to allow the butter to
cool briefly before adding the
lemon juice, or the sauce will
burn as soon as the juice is
added.

Brown Butter Sauce

This simple French sauce, called *beurre noisette* due to its hazelnut color, cooks
so quickly that it can be made in the same pan that vegetables or fish were cooked
in while they are kept warm. If cooking in the pan used for vegetables, let them
drain while making the sauce. If using it for fish, remove the cooked fish to a
warm plate, tent with foil, if you like, and make the browned butter in the same
pan. However, it can be cooked separately. For variety and even more of a nutty
flavor, add pine nuts, slivered almonds, or skinned hazelnuts to the hot butter.

> 1/2 cup unsalted butter
> 2 tablespoons fresh or bottled lemon juice
> 2 tablespoons chopped fresh parsley (optional)
> salt and freshly ground pepper, to taste

Heat the butter in a heavy small saucepan over medium-low heat. Swirl the butter occasionally, and when it turns golden and gives off a nutty aroma, remove it
from the heat. Let it cool about 30 seconds. Stir in the lemon juice and parsley, if
using. Adjust the seasoning with salt and pepper, if necessary, and serve immediately.

Yield: 4 servings

Spicy Apricot Glaze

Hot and sweet, this fruity glaze dresses up roast chicken, shrimp, and ham, and can be used as a dipping sauce for hors d'oeuvre, such as Cumin-Scented Wontons (page 55). For variety, add minced fresh ginger or garlic and adjust the amount of red pepper to vary its heat. The glaze makes an unusual gift from the kitchen—no one but you needs to know how quickly it was made.

> **3/8 cup apricot jam (or orange marmalade)**
> **2 tablespoons Dijon mustard**
> **2 tablespoons low-sodium soy sauce**
> **1 teaspoon crushed red pepper**
> **salt and freshly ground pepper, to taste**

In a heavy small saucepan, blend the jam, mustard, soy sauce, and crushed pepper over medium heat. Stir until the mixture is smooth and bubbling. Adjust the seasoning, if needed, with salt and pepper.

Yield: About 5/8 cup

Sauces that contain a lot of sugar can burn easily during long roasting or very hot temperatures. If you are roasting a chicken for an hour in a moderate oven or an outdoor grill, brush on the glaze during the last 15 minutes of cooking. To broil shrimp or ham, keep a close eye on the sauce. If it begins to smoke, move the rack farther away from the heat and continue to broil.

Arugula Butter

For those of us who can't find arugula as often as we'd like, this gorgeous, bright green butter preserves its robust flavor. It makes an unusual, grassy, peppery accompaniment to chicken and fish. Substitute equal amounts of watercress, if you prefer. This butter takes advantage of the flavorful stems of arugula, which are usually removed before serving raw. Since the stems are minced in the butter, their texture is unimportant. Serve the leaves in a salad, if you like, and reserve the stems to make the butter.

> **6-8 ounces arugula leaves and stems**
> **(about 8 cups, lightly packed)**
> **8 ounces unsalted butter, softened**
> **2 tablespoons fresh or bottled lemon juice**

Trim off the root end of the arugula and place the leaves and stems in a food processor. Mince, scraping down the sides of the bowl, as needed. Add the butter and lemon juice and process until thoroughly blended. If not using immediately, wrap in foil or wax paper in a log shape and chill or freeze.

Yield: About 1 1/2 cups

Thai Chili Butter

Butter transports the savory depth of fish sauce and flecks of fiery chilies in this compound butter, but if you prefer less heat, substitute a milder chili. Melt a tablespoon or two over grilled or broiled fish, or use it to sauté shrimp for instant heat and flavor.

4 fresh red or green Thai chilies
8 ounces unsalted butter, softened
1 tablespoon fish sauce

Trim and discard the stems from the chilies. Mince the seeds and flesh of the chilies fine and blend thoroughly with the butter and fish sauce. If not using immediately, wrap in foil or wax paper in a log shape and chill or freeze.

Yield: 1 cup

In choosing chilies, keep in mind that generally the smaller the chili, the hotter it is, and green chilies are more incendiary than red, since the red ones have had more time to ripen and sweeten.

The log shape is traditional for compound butters, since it makes it easy to slice off a tablespoon or two at a time, even when frozen. Rewrap the remaining butter and freeze it for another use.

Escargot Butter

This butter is named for its best known use—melted over hot escargots. It's also delicious on pasta, clams, mussels, and oysters or spread in abundance over sliced French or Italian bread to make garlic toast. This recipe will give more color to ordinary garlic bread, due to the parsley, and lots of pungent flavor.

4 cloves garlic
1 large shallot
1/2 cup lightly packed fresh parsley leaves
8 ounces unsalted butter, softened

Drop the garlic, shallot, and parsley through the feed tube of a food processor with the motor running. Thoroughly blend in the butter. If not using immediately, wrap in foil or wax paper in a log shape and chill or freeze.

Yield: 1 cup

Green Peppercorn Butter

Fresh-flavored, pungent green peppercorns make ideal spicy accompaniments to beef and fish steaks, especially fresh tuna or salmon. The soft texture of green peppercorns makes them easy eating compared to hard, dried peppercorns. Try this butter on cooked pasta and hamburgers, as well.

1 clove garlic
8 ounces unsalted butter, softened
1 tablespoon fresh or bottled lemon juice
2 tablespoons green peppercorns

Drop the garlic through the feed tube of a food processor with the motor running. Thoroughly blend in the butter and lemon juice. Add the peppercorns and process just to blend. If not using immediately, wrap in foil or wax paper in a log shape and chill or freeze.

Yield: 1 cup

When using a food processor or blender to make a smooth sauce dotted with a whole ingredient, such as capers or green peppercorns, blend or purée all of the ingredients except the whole ones first. Add the whole ingredients and pulse the machine just to blend, or stir in the whole ingredients by hand.

When draining the oil from cans of anchovies, save the oil to use in a salad dressing or for cooking. Save sun-dried tomato oil for the same purposes.

Anchovy Butter

Robust anchovy butter makes a flavor-packed accompaniment to roasted potatoes, brussels sprouts, pasta, or on cold sliced meats. Since the anchovies are salty, you may want to cut down on the salt, if any, used to cook the vegetables, pasta, or meat.

8 anchovy fillets
8 ounces unsalted butter
2 teaspoons fresh or bottled lemon juice

Rinse and drain the anchovies. Pat them dry with paper towels and mince in the bowl of a food processor. Thoroughly blend in the butter and lemon juice. If not using immediately, wrap in foil or wax paper in a log shape and chill or freeze.

Yield: 1 cup

Berry Vinaigrette

Sharp and fruity, this dressing complements practically any salad containing berries or other fruit. You don't really need a food processor, but it's faster and allows you to double or triple the recipe effortlessly. If making the dressing by hand, mince the garlic, whisk in the remaining ingredients except the oil, and drizzle in the oil while whisking vigorously. Use half olive oil and half walnut or hazelnut oil for an intriguing nutty aroma.

In a pinch, versatile vinaigrettes make delicious pan sauces or toppings for grilled foods. This one in particular complements cooked chicken or fish beautifully. Sauté or pan-fry the meat, remove it from the pan, and splash in a few tablespoons of vinaigrette. It will bubble up quickly. Scrape any browned bits from the bottom of the pan to blend into the sauce, and it should be ready to serve in about 15 seconds.

> 1 clove garlic
> 1 teaspoon salt (or more, to taste)
> 1/2 teaspoon pepper (or more, to taste)
> 1/3 cup blueberry or raspberry vinegar
> 1/4 cup fresh or bottled lemon juice
> 1 tablespoon Dijon mustard
> 2 teaspoons honey
> 2/3 cup olive oil

Drop the garlic, salt, and pepper through the feed tube of a food processor with the machine running. Add the vinegar, lemon juice, mustard, and honey, and blend. Drizzle in the oil in a stream through the feed tube with the machine running to emulsify the dressing. Cover and chill, if you are not using it immediately.

Yield: About 1 1/4 cups

Caper Vinaigrette

This vinaigrette has such a sophisticated taste that I reserve it for serving over plain greens, so that no other ingredients mask its flavor. In a hurried moment, I've even splashed it in a hot pan after sautéing chicken breasts or fish for a mindless pan sauce.

1 clove garlic
1/2 teaspoon salt
1/4 teaspoon pepper
1 teaspoon Dijon mustard
1 egg
3 tablespoons balsamic vinegar
2 tablespoons fresh or bottled lemon juice
5/8 cup olive oil
2 tablespoons drained capers

Drop the garlic, salt, and pepper through the feed tube of a food processor with the motor running. Add the mustard, egg, vinegar, and lemon juice, and process until blended.

With the machine running, drizzle in the oil through the tiny hole in the pusher of the feed tube. When all the oil is used and the dressing is emulsified, blend in the capers. Store covered in the refrigerator.

Yield: 1 1/4 cups

If making a large quantity of a dressing that contains heavy ingredients which may sink to the bottom of the batch, be sure to include all of the ingredients equally in each portion. Shake the dressing or pulse in a processor to blend well just before dividing. If heavy ingredients, such as capers or green peppercorns, sink, retrieve them with a spoon and divide them evenly among containers.

Garbanzo Vinaigrette

This healthy, nutty-flavored dressing makes an especially tasty accompaniment to salads containing fruit and poultry. Add more sesame oil for stronger nutty aroma, or add a bit of mild honey for a slightly sweet dressing.

1 8-ounce can chickpeas (garbanzo beans)
1 large clove garlic
2 tablespoons rice vinegar
1 tablespoon low-sodium soy sauce
2 tablespoons vegetable oil
1 teaspoon sesame oil
salt and freshly ground pepper, to taste

Drain the beans. Drop the garlic through the feed tube of a food processor with the motor running. Add the vinegar, soy sauce, vegetable oil, and sesame oil with 3-4 tablespoons of water, and purée until smooth. Adjust the seasoning, if needed, with salt and pepper. Cover and chill, if you are not using it immediately.

Yield: About 1 cup

Double, triple, or quadruple salad dresssings, according to your food processor's capacity. It's as easy to make a stash as it is a little, and you'll have a supply for a month.

Cayenne powers Cajun spice blends, so if your heat tolerance is low, it's easy to tame the flames. Reserve the cayenne and blend it in, bit by bit, to taste.

Cajun Mayonnaise

This flavor-packed mayonnaise is a staple at my house as a salad dressing, a spread for sandwiches and hamburgers, and a dip. Try it on egg salad, with smoked mussels on crackers, with crudités or, as one guest put it, with a spoon. It keeps for months, if tightly covered, and makes an unusual gift.

1 clove garlic
1/2 teaspoon black pepper
1/2 teaspoon ground cumin
1/2 teaspoon ground red pepper (cayenne)
3/4 teaspoon salt
1 teaspoon dry mustard
2 eggs
2 tablespoons cider vinegar
1 1/2 cups vegetable oil

Place the garlic, pepper, cumin, red pepper, salt, and mustard in the food processor. Mince the mixture, scraping down the sides of the bowl as needed. Add the eggs and vinegar and process to blend.

With the motor running, pour the oil into the feed tube of the processor, allowing the oil to drip slowly into the bowl. Repeat until all the oil is used and the sauce is emulsified. Cover and chill the mayonnaise until ready to use.

Yield: About 2 cups

Processor Aïoli

Often called the "butter of Provence," anyone who loves garlic will find a hundred uses for this creamy, pungent mayonnaise. Use it as a salad dressing, with steamed or smoked fish and shellfish, as a dip for crudités, or as a spread for garlic bread, sandwiches, and burgers. To vary the flavor, blend in fresh herbs, olives or olivada, or minced, roasted, sweet and hot red peppers.

> **8 garlic cloves**
> **2 eggs**
> **1/4 cup fresh or bottled lemon juice**
> **1 1/2 cups olive oil, preferably extra-virgin**
> **salt and freshly ground pepper, to taste**

Drop the garlic through the feed tube of a food processor with the motor running. Add the eggs and lemon juice and blend. Drizzle in the oil, drop by drop, until the sauce starts to thicken. Pour in the remaining oil in a thin stream. Season with salt and pepper. Cover and chill until ready to use.

Yield: About 2 cups

To make an emulsified sauce as quickly as possible, instead of using the feed tube to drip oil into the workbowl, drizzle it in very slowly until the sauce begins to thicken. Increase the stream of oil to a thin stream until all the oil is used.

Lemon Cream Sauce

This simple sauce delivers tangy creaminess and can be served cool or at room temperature. Try it on Souffléd Omelet (page 266) or over ice cream or frozen yogurt. Lemon curd, a bright yellow mixture of lemon juice, butter, sugar, and egg yolks, is paste-like in consistency. It's available in specialty shops and most major supermarkets alongside the jams and jellies, since it can also be used as a breakfast spread. The work of cooking, straining, and chilling it has been done for you, so it's convenience-in-a-jar.

1/2 cup lemon curd
1/2 cup cream

Whisk the lemon curd and cream in a small bowl or 2-cup glass measure until smooth. Cover and chill, if not using immediately. To serve warm, blend the ingredients in a small saucepan over medium-low heat or microwave gently, stirring occasionally until heated through. Serve immediately.

Yield: 1 cup

Raspberry Dessert Sauce

The tartness of raspberries makes a delightful foil for most things sweet, but especially rich chocolate. Consider serving a duo of simple sauces, such as a pool of Silky Chocolate Sauce (page 233), paired with this raspberry sauce, separated by a fresh pear half, vanilla ice cream, or a slice of purchased cheesecake. If raspberries are in season, puree them and add sugar to taste, depending upon their natural sweetness. Strain and store as below.

> **1 10-ounce package frozen raspberries in heavy syrup,**
>   **defrosted**
> **2 tablespoons framboise, Chambord, or orange-flavored liqueur**
>   **(optional)**

Purée the raspberries in a food processor and place in a strainer, food mill, or conical sieve over a medium bowl. Strain out the seeds, pressing against them with the back of a spoon, the blade of a food mill, or the wooden pestle of a sieve. Whisk in the liqueur, if using. Serve immediately, or cover and chill up to a week. Freeze, if storing longer.

Yield: About 1 cup

For speed and ease, it's best to learn to appreciate the crunch of raspberry seeds. If you're persnickety about smoothness in sauces, prepare for an extra step in cooking. Food mills and conical sieves are designed to rid fruit of seeds, cores, and skins. I prefer the mill to the sieve, since it has interchangeable disks, depending upon the size of the culprits to be eliminated, and its blade is well designed to move the food over its disks efficiently. A plain strainer and large spoon will do the job, also, but with more effort from the cook.

To save on cleanup time, make simple sauces directly in serving bowls, or in the case of a warm sauce, a decorative stove-proof pot. With a paper towel, wipe the inside rim of the bowl to give it a clean appearance. I like to use an ibrik, the small copper pot with a long handle used to make Turkish coffee. It's decorative enough to bring to the table, and it has a spout that's easy to pour from.

Easy Orange Sauce

With the various marmalades on the market today, especially in specialty shops, this sauce could taste different every time it's made. All marmalades, however, will lend body and sweetness with a bitter edge to a sauce. For those who like intensely sweet, fruity flavors with meat, use this sauce as a glaze for roast chicken, pork, or ham.

1/2 cup orange marmalade
1/4 cup orange juice
1 tablespoon orange-flavored liqueur (optional)

Blend the marmalade with the orange juice, and orange liqueur, if using, in a heavy small saucepan over medium-low heat. Cook, stirring, until bubbling. Serve immediately.

Yield: 3/4 cup

Silky Chocolate Sauce

This dark, rich sauce must be served warm or room temperature, since it will solidify when cool, but if you don't want to use it immediately, store the sauce and reheat it gently. Bittersweet chocolate delivers deep, intense chocolate flavor, but semisweet, and even milk chocolate, will do. Add orange-flavored liqueur, amaretto, crème de menthe, or your favorite flavor of extract for variety in taste. Add the grated rind of one orange or lemon, a quarter-cup of chopped nuts, or slivers of candied ginger, if desired. Double, triple, or quadruple the recipe, if needed.

> **4 ounces semisweet or bittersweet chocolate**
>   **(about 3/4 cup grated)**
> **1/2 cup cream**
> **1 tablespoon liqueur or 1/2 teaspoon extract (optional)**

Chop the chocolate into small pieces and blend it with the cream in a heavy small saucepan over medium heat. Stir until the mixture melts and is smooth. Stir in a liqueur or extract, if you like, heat through, and serve immediately.

   If not using right away, cover and chill the sauce up to 2 weeks. Reheat gently when ready to serve.

Yield: About 3/4 cup

Melting chocolate can be ticklish, since it scorches easily. Adding cream to the chocolate before melting it insulates the chocolate, so you can use fast, direct heat to cook the sauce. Even microwaving chocolate to melt it is made safer by the addition of cream.

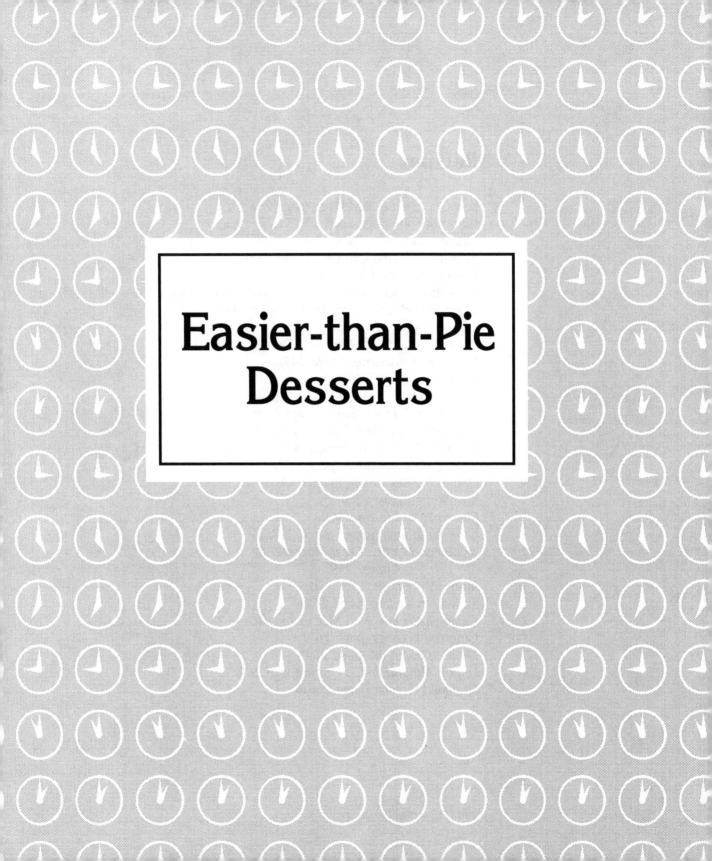

Easier-than-Pie Desserts

Recipes

If you're like my husband perusing a restaurant menu, you're already reading the dessert chapter, having skipped the last 236 pages. Desserts are frivolous, fattening, indulgent, and practically everyone's favorite course.

They typically require multiple stages of cooking, and therefore extensive amounts of time to prepare. The recipes in this chapter require only a few minutes of preparation and need to be chilled or frozen only the length of time it takes to eat dinner. However, many can be made ahead, if you like. Frozen concoctions are few here, since they require time to set up, but sorbets and ice creams can be frozen in a labor-free electronic ice-cream maker while you're eating dinner. Many taste best straight out of the ice cream or gelato machine.

Most easy-to-prepare desserts are based on fruit. They come in naturally beautiful, sweet, nutritious packages, so simple treatments are in order to retain their beauty and taste.

Fruits and wines or liqueurs make natural, easy pairings, as do fruits and cheeses. In my heyday of complicated culinary undertakings, it was a tremendous frustration for a perfectly ripe wheel of Brie and fresh fruit to outshine a seven-layer torte that took a labor-intensive day to assemble.

Presentation is especially important and easy with desserts. Often it's as simple as serving wine-drenched berries in a stemmed wine glass or a quick mousse in especially attractive bowls. A sprig of fresh mint, a stick of cinnamon, or a dusting of grated chocolate or chopped nuts can raise a simple dessert from the ordinary to the exciting.

Fresh spearmint and its cousin, orange mint, make lovely, simple garnishes for many desserts. Use a single whole leaf at the top of a pear, peach, plum, or apple half, if you like, to resemble the fruit's natural leaf. Store mint with its stems in water at room temperature or chilled. It will root in the water in about two weeks.

Pears Poached in Red Wine

This beautiful, low-fat dessert fills the house with the tantalizing aroma of vanilla and cinnamon while cooking. If you have the time to let it chill, the pear absorbs the wine's deep red color. Fanned out and topped with a sprig of mint, it looks exquisite.

2 cups dry red wine
2/3 cup sugar
2 cinnamon sticks
1 vanilla bean, split lengthwise, or 2 tablespoons vanilla extract
1 whole clove
2 firm ripe pears
4 sprigs fresh mint (optional)

Blend the wine, sugar, cinnamon, vanilla, and clove in a heavy saucepan large enough to hold the pear halves in a single layer and bring the mixture to a boil. Meanwhile, peel, halve, and core the pears. Add them to the wine and simmer, turning occasionally, until just tender when pierced with a sharp knife, about 15 minutes.

Remove the pears to a shallow bowl. Continue to simmer the wine mixture until reduced by about half. Pour over the pears and serve immediately or refrigerate until chilled, at least 4 hours. When ready to serve, discard the vanilla bean, if using, and the clove. Make several lengthwise slits in each pear half, without cutting through the stem end (see page 109).

Place on individual serving plates core side down, press lightly to fan out the slices, and serve the pears with the syrup. Garnish with fresh mint, if desired.

Yield: 4 servings

Chestnut Fool

This dessert is firmer if chilled for an hour before serving, but if you can't make it before cooking dinner, it still delivers velvety texture and nutty flavor. If possible, chill the canned purée ahead of time, so that dessert will be cool immediately upon making. Fools can be made from any fruit purée, berries being particularly attractive since their colors are brilliant and the cream balances their acidity. The Chestnut Fool is out of the ordinary, and there's no simpler way to relish the subtle flavor of chestnuts.

> **1 cup canned unsweetened chestnut purée**
> **1/2 cup sugar**
> **2 tablespoons brandy or orange-flavored liqueur**
> **1 1/2 cups cream, cold**

In a food processor or blender, mix the chestnuts with the sugar. With the machine running, drizzle in the brandy or liqueur. When smooth, remove to a medium-size bowl.

Whip the cream to soft peaks. Fold 1/2-3/4 of the whipped cream into the purée and spoon into small stemmed glasses. If not serving immediately, cover and chill the desserts. Continue to whip the remaining half of the cream to stiff peaks. If not serving right away, cover and chill the cream.

When ready to serve, mound the reserved whipped cream by tablespoons onto the fool and serve immediately.

Yield: 4 servings

Heavy cream will whip to double its volume. If you measure the amount of cream called for in a cup measure 2-3 times the size called for, you can whip the cream directly in the measuring cup, thereby saving on cleanup time. Cream will whip faster if the bowl and beaters are chilled. For speed, stash them in the freezer for 5 minutes before whipping.

To claim that chestnut purée is a convenience product is an understatement. To prepare it from scratch, the nuts must be pierced with a sharp knife, simmered for 30 minutes, drained, and cooled. Then the shell and inner skin must be peeled, a time-consuming chore, and the nuts must be puréed.

Orange-Cranberry Cream

Cream provides the perfect foil for flecks of tart cranberries and orange in this flavor-packed dessert. It takes only about 5 minutes to prepare with the help of a food processor and stationary mixer. The cream makes a festive fall or holiday dessert, but if you have cranberries in the freezer, you can make it all year. It's surprisingly refreshing in summer. There's no need to defrost cranberries, since the processor cuts through them frozen. If you would like, reserve 1/2 cup of the whipped cream to decorate the desserts.

> **1 small orange**
> **1 12-ounce bag cranberries**
> **1 1/2 cups sugar**
> **2 cups cream**

Quarter the orange and remove the seeds. Purée the orange with the cranberries and sugar in a food processor or blender.

In a medium bowl, whip the cream to stiff peaks. Fold the sweetened fruit into the cream, and spoon into glass bowls or stemmed wine glasses. Serve immediately, or cover and chill up to 4 hours.

Yield: 4 large servings

When cranberries are in season, stash a half-dozen bags in the freezer to use throughout the year. They'll store beautifully in the plastic bags they come in, so there's no reason to repackage them for freezing. Cranberries are easy to separate, unlike other fruits or vegetables, when frozen, so you can remove a precise amount from the bag and then replace the partially filled bag in the freezer.

Fastest-Ever Lemon Mousse

A mousse with a mere two ingredients never tasted so creamy and tart, especially one made in only five minutes. If you'd like an extra dollop of whipped cream on top of the mousse, whip 1 1/4 cups of cream, instead of just 1 cup, in the first step. Remove and reserve 1/2 cup of the whipped cream (it will have doubled when whipped) before blending in the lemon curd. Once the mousse is made, top each serving with 2 tablespoons whipped cream.

1 11 1/4-ounce jar lemon curd
1 cup cream
4 sprigs of fresh mint (optional garnish)
4 thin slices of lemon (optional garnish)

In a medium bowl, whip the lemon curd until smooth. In a separate bowl, whip the cream to soft peaks.

Blend the cream into the curd until it's barely smooth. Spoon into stemmed wine glasses or small glass bowls. Cover and chill, if not using immediately.

If desired, garnish with fresh mint sprigs or cut each lemon slice from the perimeter to its center and place it, twisted into a curl, onto the mousse.

Yield: 4 servings

Lemon curd delivers tart, refreshing, lemony flavor and provides substantial body, eliminating the need to make a complicated base for a mousse. You can make lemon curd at home with egg yolks, sugar, butter, and the juice and zest of lemon, but buying it prepared makes this lemon mousse one of the fastest on record.

If you want to serve the mousse from a large bowl, make it in the serving bowl itself, and wipe the inside top of the bowl to give it a clean appearance.

Fresh Berry Gratin

Often a fruit gratin is made with a sabayon or a crème anglaise, both time-consuming undertakings. Here, sour cream provides a richly flavored substitute that requires practically no preparation. Ideally, use fruit that is cold, since even after broiling, the fruit should provide temperature contrast to the warm caramelized topping. In a kitchen with time to kill, the dishes would be placed in a larger pan filled with ice, to ensure that the fruit will be cold. For variety, whisk a bit of cinnamon, nutmeg, brandy, or liqueur into the cream, and make the gratin with any ripe fruit—mangoes, kiwis, and peaches are favorites. If the fruit is especially tart, add 1/4 cup sugar to the sour cream.

4 cups fresh blueberries and/or raspberries
1 cup sour cream
3/4 cup brown sugar

Preheat the broiler and place a rack 4-5" under it. Place the berries in an even layer in 4 individual gratin dishes or in a 9" pie plate.

Whisk the sour cream until it is soft and fluffy, and spread it evenly over the berries. Cover and chill, if not using immediately. Place the sugar in a large strainer and shake it over the dishes, sprinkling the fruit evenly with the sugar. Broil until the sugar melts and bubbles, about 4 minutes. Serve immediately.

Yield: 4 large servings

Amaretto Chocolate Cream with Strawberries

Amaretto, an Italian almond-flavored liqueur now also made in the United States, lends this simple, rich cream a complex, nutty aroma. Substitute your favorite liqueur for the amaretto, if you prefer. Crème de Menthe and Grand Marnier, in particular, pair beautifully with chocolate. If you prefer, stir in a teaspoon of orange, almond, or mint extract, instead of the liqueur.

12 ounces dark or semisweet chocolate, coarsely chopped
3/8 cup cream
1/4 cup amaretto
24 perfect strawberries, stems intact
sprigs of fresh mint (optional garnish)

Melt the chocolate and cream in a heavy saucepan over low heat or melt gently in the microwave, stirring occasionally until the mixture is smooth and warm. Whisk in the amaretto and pour into 4 stemmed wide-mouthed glasses or glass bowls.

Place each glass or bowl on a plate and surround with 6 strawberries. Garnish the cream with a sprig of fresh mint, if desired. Serve immediately after pouring.

Yield: 4 servings

Giant Driscoll strawberries with long stems attached are ideal for dipping, when available. If strawberries are not in season, substitute cigarette-shaped cookies, biscotti, prepared ladyfingers, or bananas sliced into 1-inch chunks.

Sugar-Seared Cinnamon Apples

These apple halves heat through in 8-10 minutes, filling the house with the scent of cinnamon, and they retain an appealing texture without becoming mushy. Set them up a day ahead, if you like, core side down in the spice mixture, and cover the cut rounded sides tightly with plastic. The apples can be grilled as well, which caramelizes the sugar, but broiling them allows you to utilize all of the spices. Do not use a stove-top grill, since its shape causes the butter to run off the apples quickly. If you want baked apples for breakfast, but can't wait an hour, use this recipe to duplicate baked flavor and superior texture.

2 tablespoons unsalted butter
2 tablespoons sugar
1 teaspoon ground cinnamon
1/8 teaspoon freshly grated or ground nutmeg
2 red delicious apples
vanilla ice cream (optional)

Preheat a broiler and arrange a rack 6-8 inches away from the heat.

Melt the butter on a medium platter either under the broiler or in the microwave. Blend the sugar, cinnamon, and nutmeg with the butter. Cut the apples in half, core them, and remove a small slice from the rounded side of each half, so they'll sit flat. Place core side down in the butter mixture.

Arrange them core side up on a baking sheet and broil, basting occasionally with the extra butter mixture, until bubbling and heated through, about 8-10 minutes. After the first 5 minutes, watch them carefully so they do not burn.

Serve warm with ice cream, if desired.

Yield: 4 servings

Ginger-Flavored Fruit

This combination of fruit offers stunning variety in color, texture, and flavor; however, you can use whatever's on hand. If you don't have candied ginger, often called sugar ginger, substitute 3-4 teaspoons ground ginger, depending upon the amount of heat you like. Whisk in a bit of the ground ginger at a time, taste, and stop when it suits your palate. Buy prepared fruit, if pressed for time. If serving in one large bowl, blend the sauce directly in the bowl, then toss with the fruit and serve.

> 1 cup plain low-fat or nonfat yogurt or sour cream
> 1/4 cup minced candied ginger
> 2 tablespoons mild honey
> 1/2 medium or 1 very small honeydew melon,
>   cut in bite-size pieces
> 1 1/2 cups ripe strawberries, trimmed, quartered
> 2 kiwis, peeled, sliced (see page 255)
> 4 sprigs fresh mint (optional)

Blend the yogurt, ginger, and honey in a medium bowl. If not using immediately, cover and chill.

Toss the fruit with the sauce, spoon into individual glass bowls or wine glasses, and garnish with fresh mint, if available.

Yield: 4 large servings

When buying melons, check for a fragrant aroma at the stem end. It should give way slightly to pressure, but its aroma is the best test of flavor-to-come. Honeydews are the trickiest as far as detecting fragrance goes. Look for creamy white rind with no traces of green. If a melon is especially firm, plan on letting it sit at room temperature a couple of days before cutting. Avoid melons with bruises or soft spots. To cut them quickly into bite-size pieces, cut them in half and remove the seeds. Cut each half into 2" slices lengthwise. With a sharp knife, remove the rind. Holding each 2" slice, cut into 3 slices lengthwise. Turn 90 degrees and cut across into 3/4" or smaller pieces.

Bananas Baked with Rum and Orange

Bananas are a blessing to fruit-lovers, since they're available all year round and they ripen well off the tree. If you let bananas ripen until their skins develop little brown spots, the fruit will taste sweeter. When they're as ripe as you like, refrigerate them. The skins will turn brown, but the bananas will taste fine.

Rum varies from pale and light-bodied to dark and rich. Dark rum makes an ideal ingredient for cooking, since other ingredients will dilute its flavor. It's made from fermented by-products of sugar production, including molasses, and the best quality comes from Jamaica. The best amber, medium-bodied rum, made from sugarcane juice, hails from Haiti and Martinique. The best light rum is from Puerto Rico.

This is a twist on the New Orleans classic, Bananas Foster, that's made easy by baking it in the oven. You can make it in a traditional chafing dish, however, if you like. Heat the bananas through with the brown sugar sauce, warm the rum, and add it last to the pan. Ignite the rum, and ladle it over the bananas until the flames die. The fuller flavor of dark rum is best for cooking, especially flaming, although the original recipe calls for using either light or dark rum. If pressed for time, serve the sauce over the bananas without baking them These are large portions. If serving after a substantial meal or over ice cream, make half the amounts called for.

> 1/2 cup orange juice
> 1/4 cup lightly packed brown sugar
> 4 tablespoons unsalted butter
> 4 ripe, firm bananas
> 2 tablespoons dark rum (or bourbon)
> 1/2 teaspoon ground cinnamon
> vanilla ice cream (optional)
> 4 3-inch cinnamon sticks (optional)

Preheat the oven to 350 degrees. Stir the orange juice, sugar, and butter in a heavy small saucepan over medium heat until the butter melts and the sugar dissolves. Let simmer without stirring until thickened, about 8 minutes.

Meanwhile, peel the bananas and cut them into 1/2" diagonal slices (see page 199). Place them in a single layer in a baking dish.

Remove the sauce from the heat and blend in the rum and cinnamon. Pour over the bananas and turn them once to coat with the sauce. Bake 10 minutes, or until the bananas are heated through. Serve warm with or without ice cream, with or without a cinnamon stick.

Yield: 4 servings

Drunken Strawberries

This pairing of red wine and strawberries requires no cooking, just time. Start it before making dinner, and it will be ready in time for dessert. This is a convenient dish for a busy hostess, since it can be completely set up an hour or two ahead of time and it requires no refrigerator space.

It's traditional in the Bordeaux region of France to use an older wine that has started its decline, but it's also delightful with light-bodied wines that are drunk young. If you can find berries that are at their peak of sweetness, eliminate the sugar in this recipe. Pour the wine over the berries, crush them lightly to release some of their juice, and you have instant dessert. Some people include a grinding or two of black peppercorns over the strawberries. If you prefer, follow the same instructions for ripe peaches with Sauternes.

Do not wash strawberries until just before using, since the dampness encourages mold, and then only if necessary. Store them in a single layer at room temperature, if using within a day of purchase, or in the refrigerator two-three days, if not using soon.

    1 quart ripe fresh strawberries
    1/2 cup sugar
    2 cups dry red wine

Trim the strawberries and clean them, if sandy. Slice them into quarters, place in a medium bowl, and sprinkle with the sugar. Let rest 30 minutes. Pour the wine over the berries and stir gently to dissolve the sugar.

Spoon the berries into glass bowls or wine glasses and divide the wine among them. Serve within 2 hours.

Yield: 4 servings

Zabaglione

The ideal impromptu dessert, zabaglione uses ingredients and equipment that most of us always have on hand. Ordinary wines can be used, but since the character of the wine in this recipe changes little in its brief cooking, it pays to use a high-quality one. Marsala, a fortified sweet or dry wine from Sicily, is traditional. However, unorthodox versions such as half white wine, half orange-flavored liqueur, are memorable. Zabaglione is often served as a sauce over fruit, but I prefer it straight, perhaps accompanied by a crisp cookie.

4 egg yolks
1/4 cup sugar
1/2 cup Marsala

Pour 2 inches of water in a medium pot and place it over high heat. Whisk the egg yolks and sugar in a metal round-bottomed bowl until pale and creamy. Pour in the Marsala and whisk.

When the water simmers, place the bowl over the water and whisk constantly (using a pot holder to hold the side of the bowl), until the mixture foams and forms soft mounds, 10-15 minutes.

Spoon into wine glasses and serve immediately.

Yield: 4 servings

You can make zabaglione in the top of a double boiler, but a completely rounded metal bowl works better, since a wire whisk can reach every bit of egg yolk to keep it from scrambling. For those who consider ten minutes of whisking major exercise, use a hand-held, preferably cordless, mixer. Special rounded zabaglione bowls are available, usually made of copper, with long wooden handles to grasp while whisking.

Hot and Sour Gingered Rhubarb

This fast dessert is sour from rhubarb's characteristic tartness and mildly hot from candied ginger. It's sweetened lightly and blended with whipped cream to make it smooth and rich. A little goes a long way on flavor. If you prefer, fold the cream into the rhubarb, leaving streaks of its pretty pink color, resembling marble. Be sure to show it off in parfait glasses or small stemmed wine glasses.

> **12 ounces fresh or frozen rhubarb, diced**
> **3/4 cup granulated or brown sugar**
> **3 tablespoons minced candied ginger**
> **1 1/2 cups cream**

In a heavy medium saucepan, combine the rhubarb, sugar, ginger, and 2 tablespoons water. Cook over medium-low heat, stirring occasionally, until the rhubarb is tender, about 5 minutes.

Purée the mixture in a blender or small food processor. Cool completely either in the freezer or whisk in a large metal bowl directly over ice until cool (see sidebar).

Whip the cream to soft peaks and fold into the rhubarb. Pour into parfait glasses or small stemmed wine glasses and sprinkle with extra candied ginger, if desired. Serve immediately or cover and chill.

Yield: 4 small servings

A hot mixture can be cooled quickly by placing it in the freezer and stirring the outer, colder part into the center occasionally to keep any part of it from freezing solid. Remove the mixture when it's cool to the touch. Or place a warm mixture in a metal bowl directly over a larger bowl of ice. Stir occasionally, keeping the small bowl in direct contact with the ice to cool it quickly.

Pears with Caramel Sauce

Hot, buttery pears and smooth, nutty caramel provide a striking combination in color and taste. Here crushed amaretti add welcome crunch and almond flavor to the dessert, or, if you prefer, candied ginger adds intriguing, if unorthodox, heat. Delicious as it is, don't hesitate to gild the lily by serving it over ice cream or frozen yogurt. Chill any leftover caramel for a later use, and substitute bananas for the pears, if you prefer.

This recipe combines cooking the pears and making the sauce in the same pan. Not only is it one-dish cooking, but the whole process shouldn't take longer than about 12 minutes.

1/2 cup sugar
2 ripe pears, peeled, halved, and cored
1/2 cup cream
2 tablespoons unsalted butter
1/2 cup crushed amaretti or minced candied ginger (optional)
4 sprigs fresh mint (optional)

In a heavy medium saucepan, heat the sugar with 1/2 cup water over medium-high heat, stirring until the sugar dissolves. Add the pear halves and cook, turning once, until heated through, about 5 minutes. Remove the pears to a warm plate.

Cook the syrup without stirring until it starts to turn a medium-golden caramel color, about 4 minutes. Stir, or swirl the pan so the syrup darkens evenly. When evenly golden-brown, take off the heat and stir in the cream very carefully, since the mixture will splatter. If any juice has accumulated around the pears, pour it into the sauce. Stir or whisk until smooth, swirl in the butter, and stir until melted.

Place the pears core side down on serving plates, and, if time allows, slice into fan-shapes (see page 109). Pour the caramel sauce over them and, if using, top with the amaretti or ginger. Place a sprig of mint at each stem end, if using, and serve hot or at room temperature.

Yield: 4 servings

Raspberry Chocolate Fondue

Although this fondue is as rich as it is delicious, it's a way of giving your guests or family a choice—they can delicately dip a strawberry or two or devour lots of chocolate. For a perfectly smooth fondue, strain the raspberry seeds before adding the berries to the chocolate, but the crunchy texture of the seeds adds an interesting texture.

Frozen raspberries in syrup provide the convenience of sugar and fruit, so making this two-ingredient fondue is especially simple. Double, triple, or quadruple the recipe, if you like. It keeps for weeks chilled and makes a delicious warm sauce over ice cream. Add 1/4 cup orange-flavored liqueur, for variety.

1 10-ounce package frozen raspberries in heavy syrup
4 ounces semisweet or bittersweet chocolate
strawberries, stems intact
bananas, cut into bite-size pieces
angel food or pound cake, cut into bite-size pieces
biscotti or cigarette-shaped cookies

Place the raspberries in a heavy medium saucepan over medium-high heat, cover, and bring to a simmer, breaking up the frozen mass as it heats. Meanwhile, chop the chocolate into 1-inch chunks and place it in a food processor fitted with the steel blade. Mince until it's fine in texture.

When the raspberries are melted and bubbling, pour them through the feed tube into the chocolate with the motor running. Purée until smooth.

While warm, pour into small glass bowls or stemmed wide-mouthed wine glasses. Serve immediately with whole strawberries, bananas, cake, biscotti, or cookies to dip into the fondue.

Yield: 4 servings

Chocolate can be grated on a dry cutting board with a large knife or in the food processor. When using a food processor, be sure to break the chocolate into small chunks and if it's a warm day, chill the blade and chocolate prior to grating. Chocolate chips make grating unnecessary, but they lack the superior flavor and variety of good chocolate.

Macadamia-Crusted Pineapple

Think of this dessert as a fat-free, fast crème brûlée. Moist, sweet pineapple replaces the cooked cream mixture, and the sugar and nut topping mimics the brûlée's crunchy crust. Substitute canned pineapple, if you must, but fresh is far superior and available year-round.

1/2 cup macadamia nuts
4 1/2-inch thick slices fresh pineapple
1/4 cup lightly packed brown sugar, free of lumps

Preheat the broiler and place a rack about 4" from the heat. Coarsely chop the macadamia nuts and reserve.

Place the pineapple in a single layer in a shallow baking dish lined with foil. Sprinkle evenly with the brown sugar and broil until the sugar is completely melted and golden. While the sugar is still fluid, scatter the macadamia nuts over the brown sugar and serve immediately.

Yield: 4 servings

Strawberries Romanoff

Strawberries Romanoff, an orange-scented strawberries and cream dessert, traditionally requires half an hour for the berries to steep in orange liqueur. This creamy version can be made in five minutes, using ice cream as a convenient base. Let the ice cream soften in the refrigerator while eating dinner, if you like, or make it quickly by breaking it up to soften it at room temperature. Use the recipe for raspberries, eliminating the time required to prepare the fruit, if you prefer.

> 1 pint best-quality vanilla ice cream
> 1 1/4 pints fresh ripe strawberries
> 1/4 cup orange-flavored liqueur

Place the ice cream in a medium bowl in the refrigerator to soften 20-30 minutes or, if preparing sooner, leave it at room temperature while preparing the berries.

Reserve 4 perfect strawberries with their stems intact. Trim and slice the remaining berries. Break up the ice cream with a large spoon or whisk and blend in the liqueur and sliced berries. Pour into stemmed wine glasses or glass bowls, top with a whole strawberry, and serve immediately.

Yield: 4 servings

Using prepared ice cream as a sauce base makes many desserts simple. To soften it as quickly as possible, place the ice cream on a cutting board, chop it into small pieces, and scrape it into a bowl. Let it warm 2-3 minutes before using.

Grapes in Sour Cream

Sweetened sour cream is most versatile, providing a pleasing tartness to balance other flavors. For variety, whisk in ground ginger or cinnamon, a few drops of vanilla extract, different flavored liqueurs, or chopped candied ginger. Use red or green grapes in this recipe, if you like, or a combination of both. The cream combines beautifully with most fruits, and it keeps well if chilled and tightly covered.

> 1 cup sour cream or plain low-fat or nonfat yogurt
> 2 tablespoons granulated or powdered sugar, brown sugar, or honey
> 2 tablespoons orange-flavored liqueur (optional)
> 1 pound seedless grapes, stemmed

Whisk the sour cream in a small bowl with the sugar and liqueur (optional). Divide the grapes among 4 glass bowls or wine glasses. Top with the sour cream mixture and serve immediately or cover and chill until ready to serve.

Yield: 4 servings

Grapes grown in this country are at their best between late summer and November, but grocers keep imports available all year round. Look for firm fruit with pliable stems. Varieties with grapes that are very tightly packed tend to get moldy quickly. To avoid this problem, remove the grapes from the stems when you get them home. Wash grapes just before serving them, since any remaining dampness will encourage mold.

Kiwi Sorbet

This pale green, citrusy sorbet is studded with the light crunchiness of kiwi's many delicate black seeds. Its most amazing characteristic is its creaminess—it's truly smooth enough to pass for ice cream. Midori, a honeydew melon-flavored liqueur, adds color, flavor, and ensures a smooth freeze. Freezing sorbets and ice cream for four is very fast, since the ice-cream maker has only about a quart of food to chill.

1/2 cup sugar
1 cup light corn syrup
9 ripe kiwis
1 tablespoon fresh or bottled lemon juice
4-6 tablespoons Midori (optional)

Combine the sugar, corn syrup, and 3/4 cup water in a heavy medium saucepan. Place over medium heat and stir until the mixture dissolves and looks clear. Remove it from the heat and reserve.

Cut the kiwis in half. Holding each half over the workbowl of a food processor to catch any juice, scoop the pulp into the processor with a medium size spoon. Purée with the lemon juice. Pour the sugar syrup and Midori, if using, into the processor and blend.

Freeze in an ice-cream maker according to the manufacturer's instructions. Serve immediately, or freeze up to 2 months.

Yield: 4 large servings

To make quick work of peeling kiwis, slice each in half and scoop out the pulp with a tablespoon-size spoon instead of peeling the exterior. The kiwi pulp comes out almost perfectly shaped. If using for salads, scoop out the pulp and then slice or dice as needed.

To help preserve ice cream, sorbet, frozen yogurt, or toffutti, place plastic wrap directly over the ice cream and then close the carton. Since there is air in a partially used carton, just closing the lid doesn't protect it. The plastic will also help keep ice crystals from forming.

Mango Sorbet

Mango flavor is often diluted in ice creams and desserts. Since it's a favorite of mine, I've made sure the seductive mango aroma is powerful in this sorbet. If freezing the sorbet to use later, allow it to soften at room temperature 30 minutes before serving.

1/3 cup sugar
1/3 cup light corn syrup
2 large ripe mangoes
1/2 cup orange juice

Combine the sugar, corn syrup, and 3/4 cup water in a heavy small saucepan. Place over medium heat and stir until the mixture dissolves and clears. Remove it from the heat and reserve.

Peel the mangoes. Holding the fruit over the workbowl of a food processor to catch any juice, slice the pulp into the processor. Purée with the orange juice. Pour the sugar syrup into the processor and blend.

Freeze in an ice-cream maker according to the manufacturer's instructions. Serve immediately, or freeze up to 2 months.

Yield: 4 servings

Ripe mangoes will yield to slight pressure in the palm of your hand and give off a slightly floral fragrance. Their skin will show more yellow, orange, and reddish streaks through the green than their underripe company. You can encourage mangoes to ripen quickly by leaving them in a paper bag at room temperature. The best buys on mangoes are usually available in spring and summer.

Gewürztraminer Sorbet

Gewürztraminer, an Alsatian white wine now offered by American vintners, always fools my palate. Its bouquet is fruity and spicy, so my tongue prepares to taste a sweet wine. Instead, Gewürztraminer is off-dry. Its aroma is critical in concocting this unusual snow-white sorbet, and this particular white wine delivers it better than any other. Since this sorbet is fairly soft, even frozen, it's especially important to place serving or storing containers in the freezer while the sorbet is brewing, and it's best eaten within 24 hours.

3/4 cup sugar
1 750-milliliter bottle Gewürztraminer
2 teaspoons fresh or bottled lemon juice

Blend the sugar and about 1 cup of the wine in a heavy small saucepan. Stir over medium heat to dissolve the sugar. When the mixture looks clear, remove it from the heat, and blend it with the remaining wine and the lemon juice.

Freeze in an ice-cream maker according to the manufacturer's instructions. Serve immediately, or freeze up to 1 week.

Yield: 4 servings

Place a freezer-proof container in the freezer while making ice cream or frozen yogurt, so that it doesn't start to melt as soon as you spoon it into the container. If serving immediately in individual dishes, freeze the dishes if they can handle low temperatures. At the very least, place them in the refrigerator.

Be sure to use a dark-roast coffee to maximize its flavor, since the coffee is diluted with other ingredients in cooking. To brew coffee double-strength, pour 3/4 cup boiling water over 3 tablespoons finely ground dark-roast coffee. Let steep five minutes and strain off the grounds. If there's a bit of sediment left in the coffee, so much the better.

Ricotta and Coffee Cream

This traditional Italian combination of coffee and ricotta is a thick, but pourable, creamy dessert. Dark-roasted coffee lends it a roasty, robust aroma and ricotta gives it a rich, slightly grainy texture. Add the grated rind of 1 orange or 1/4 cup chopped toasted hazelnuts or almonds to the cream, if desired, or top it with 1/2 cup crushed amaretti. Spooning it into individual serving glasses speeds its cooling, but, if time allows, chill it in a large serving bowl.

> **1 pound part-skim ricotta cheese**
> **1/2 cup sugar**
> **1/2 cup brewed double-strength dark-roast coffee**
>   **or espresso, cooled**
> **2 tablespoons dark rum or orange-flavored liqueur (optional)**
> **24 chocolate-covered espresso beans (optional)**

Place the ricotta, sugar, coffee, and rum or liqueur, if using, in a food processor. Purée and pour into 4 glass bowls or stemmed wine glasses. Freeze 15 minutes or cover and chill up to 2 days. Just before serving, dot with the espresso beans, if you like.

Yield: 4 servings

Key Lime Fool

This creamy dessert screams with the zestiness of key lime, slightly tempered by sweetened condensed milk. Unfortunately, there isn't a good substitute for key limes. You can make this recipe with fresh or bottled lemon or lime juice, and the dessert will be acceptable, but not the standout that it is made with fresh. Sweetened condensed milk is a tremendous convenience, providing sweetness and body. Pour the mousse into wine glasses and top with thin twists of lime—no one will suspect you didn't spend hours over it. The whipped topping need not be completely defrosted to use—10 or 15 minutes at room temperature will do.

5-6 key limes (to make about 5/8 cup juice)
1 14-ounce can sweetened condensed milk
1 8-ounce container frozen whipped dessert topping,
   defrosted, if possible
4 thin slices fresh lime (optional)

Slice the limes in half and squeeze the juice into a medium bowl. Pour in the milk and beat until smooth. Spoon in the dessert topping and beat until completely blended.

Pour into 4 glass bowls or wine glasses, top with a twist of lime, if desired, and serve immediately. If not using right away, chill, or better yet, freeze the desserts until serving time.

Yield: 4 servings

If you have time, convert these ingredients into a pie by pouring them into a prepared 9-inch graham cracker crust and freezing for a few hours before slicing. This will extend the fool to serve six or even eight people. To give the pie a festive look, arrange 6-8 twists of lime around the perimeter.

Mont Blanc

Flavored, shredded chestnut purée is transformed into an amusing French dessert called *Mont Blanc*, since it resembles a snow-capped mountain peak in the Alps. Luckily, nature is imperfect, so the cook with an unsteady hand can build this dessert without fear. Replace the vanilla with rum or brandy, if you like, but regardless, small portions are in order, due to the richness of chestnut and chocolate.

If you don't have a ricer or food mill, purée the chestnuts and mound onto serving plates. Scrape the surface with the tines of a fork to give it a rugged look. Make the dessert hours ahead of time without the topping and chill it, if you like. Top with the whipped cream just before serving.

3 ounces semisweet chocolate (about 2/3 cup grated or chips)
1 8 3/4-ounce can chestnut purée
6 tablespoons sugar, divided
1 teaspoon vanilla extract
3/4 cup cream

Melt the chocolate in a medium bowl and let it cool slightly. Force the chestnut purée through a food mill or ricer over the chocolate. Blend it with 4 tablespoons sugar and the vanilla extract. Force the mixture through the food mill or ricer onto a large serving plate, forming a large mound.

Whip the cream with the remaining sugar and spoon over the top 1/3 of the mound, forming a "cap of snow." Serve immediately or chill up to an hour.

Yield: 4 servings

Strawberry Gelato

Italian gelato, or ice cream, contains less air than its American counterpart, so it's denser in texture and more intense in flavor. I consider this recipe a sterling example of greatness in food coaxed from a few choice ingredients with ease.

You may want to adjust the amount of sugar, depending upon the ripeness of the berries. This recipe works equally well with fresh raspberries. If you want a perfectly smooth raspberry gelato, however, you'll need to strain out the seeds before freezing.

1 pound fresh ripe strawberries, trimmed
1 cup sugar
1/2 cup cream

Purée the strawberries with the sugar in a food processor. Pour in the cream and process just to blend. Freeze in an ice-cream maker according to the manufacturer's instructions, and serve immediately. If not using right away, pack into an airtight container and freeze. Let sit at room temperature until slightly softened, about 30 minutes.

Yield: 4 large servings

Start ice creams and sorbets before sitting down to dinner, so they'll be waiting for you when you're ready for dessert. Some gelato machines will automatically stop churning, but maintain a cold temperature, when the correct texture of ice cream is achieved. This feature gives the cook leeway as far as serving or storing the gelato for future use goes.

When cooking caramel, quick cooking is a necessity. Keep a close watch on its color (see page 126), since it will turn from golden and fluid to dark brown within minutes. Once the caramel turns dark brown, it will be inedible without other ingredients to soften its texture. Watching its color closely eliminates the need to use a candy thermometer.

Caramelized Brie with Macadamias

This elegant, simple dessert has an intriguing cover—a golden cage of nutty caramel that lends sweetness and warmth to the cheese. Macadamias dot the caramel, which should be cracked before serving.

1 4 1/2-ounce wheel of ripe Brie
1/4 cup sugar
8 whole macadamia nuts
fresh fruit, such as apple or pear wedges

Arrange the Brie on a serving dish. Blend the sugar with 2 tablespoons water in a heavy small saucepan. Stir over medium heat until the sugar dissolves. Without stirring, swirl the pan occasionally until the mixture turns golden brown, about 5 minutes.

Immediately pour over the Brie, allowing a bit of caramel to run over the sides. Quickly arrange the nuts on the Brie and let rest 5 minutes, so the caramel hardens, but serve within 30 minutes, so it does not soften again. To serve, crack the topping with a knife and serve with fresh fruit.

Yield: 4 servings

Gingered Lychees

This hot and sweet dish is typical of simple Chinese desserts. It's made easy with the availability of canned fruits. The rough brown exterior of lychees belies their hidden, tantalizingly smooth texture and their delicately sweet flavor. Unfortunately, eating the fruit fresh requires tedious peeling of their tough outer skin and removing their tenacious pits. Also, fresh lychees are available for a very short stint in summer, so canned ones offer year-round availability as well as the convenience of ready-to-eat fruit. Use all lychees or all oranges in this recipe, if you like, but combined, they offer a colorful combination in color, texture, and flavor. Preserved ginger, exported from Hong Kong, China, and Australia, is also known as "Ginger in Syrup" or "Stem Ginger."

1 11-ounce can lychees
1 11-ounce can mandarin oranges
6 knobs preserved ginger (about 1/4 cup, minced)
1/4 cup sliced almonds, preferably toasted (optional)

Drain the lychees and oranges. Mince the ginger and toss it with the fruit in a medium bowl. Divide between 4 glass bowls or stemmed wine glasses. If not using right away, cover and chill. Sprinkle with the sliced almonds and serve immediately.

Yield: 4 small servings

If using room temperature canned ingredients for a salad or dessert that you want chilled, freeze the can for up to 30 minutes while you prepare other ingredients. Beyond the 30 minutes, remove the can to the refrigerator to avoid freezing the ingredients.

Grapefruits are available all year, but they taste best and cost least in winter and early spring. They should keep in the refrigerator a week. Serrated, curved grapefruit knives are available to cut between the fruit and membrane, but for the quick-cook, grapefruit spoons are in order. Each diner can segment his or her own fruit as they eat.

Minted Grapefruit

Grapefruit and crème de menthe make an unusual combination of flavors, to say the least. The sweetness of the liqueur balances nicely with tart citrus, and the mint adds refreshing aroma. Maraschino cherries aren't my favorite food, but particularly around Christmas, they make a festive garnish.

If you can make the minted grapefruit 8-24 hours ahead of time, place the citrus sections in a shallow glass dish and pour the liqueur halfway up the sides of the fruit. Turn a few hours later, and the fruit will take on the bright green color of the crème de menthe.

> **2 large white grapefruit**
> **1/2 cup green crème de menthe (or less, to taste)**
> **4 sprigs of fresh mint (optional garnish)**
> **4 maraschino cherries (optional garnish)**

With a sharp knife, remove the peel and white pith from the fruit. Section the grapefruit by running the knife between the membranes, nudging the sections out whole.

Divide the grapefruit between 4 glass bowls or wide-mouthed wine glasses. Pour the crème de menthe evenly over the fruit, and cover and chill, if not using immediately. Garnish, if desired, with fresh mint and maraschino cherries.

Yield: 4 servings

Lemon-Almond Peach Gratin

Lemon, almond, and peach flavors blend in this warm summer dessert, and using prepared lemon curd makes it simple. Substitute nectarines, if you prefer, or 8 ripe apricots. The warm fruit is especially enticing over ice cream in summer. Since the fruit is broiled under intense heat, it's important to make peaches sit steady (see page 57), otherwise parts of the topping will burn while others remain uncooked.

> **4 large ripe peaches, halved and pitted**
> **1/2 cup lemon curd**
> **2 tablespoons amaretto (or almond extract, to taste)**
> **2 tablespoons sugar**
> **vanilla ice cream (optional)**

Preheat the broiler, line a baking sheet with foil, and spray it with nonstick vegetable spray. Place the peach halves skin side down on the baking sheet and slice off a bit of the underside, if necessary, to steady them. In a small bowl, blend the lemon curd and amaretto. Spoon the mixture over the peaches and sprinkle evenly with the sugar.

Broil the peaches until the sugar melts and turns golden, about 5 minutes. Remove the peaches to serving dishes and scrape the sauce off the foil to accompany the fruit. Serve immediately with ice cream or without.

Yield: 4 servings

It's often more nutritious and always easier to leave fruit skin intact. For those who're persnickety about fruit skins, cut each peach into quarters by running a sharp knife into the flesh toward the pit and following it around the fruit. Repeat, leaving the peach and pit whole. If the peach is ripe, you can easily peel away each quarter of skin in one piece. If the peaches are not quite ripe, it's easiest to plunge whole peaches into boiling water for a minute, plunge them into ice water, and then remove the skins.

When beating egg yolks and whites separately, recipes invariably instruct you to beat the yolks first, then the whites. Although the whites can deflate if beaten too early, they can rest without any damage while beating the yolks for a few minutes. Since the yolks contain oil that will cause the whites to deflate, beating the whites first saves the cook from washing the beaters in between. The yolks are not so sensitive to extraneous ingredients. Egg whites are particularly resilient when beaten with a bit of sugar, which strengthens their cell walls.

Souffléed Omelet

This stove-top soufflé, like Zabaglione (page 248), makes an ideal impromptu dessert, since its ingredients are staples in most kitchens. It's lightly sweet and as ethereal as a baked soufflé, but it requires about 2 minutes of cooking time compared to at least 20 for an oven soufflé. If you have time, let the eggs come to room temperature before starting. Substitute 2 tablespoons orange-flavored liqueur or 1/4 teaspoon almond extract for the vanilla, if you prefer. If you're squeamish about soft eggs, preheat the broiler before starting the omelet and, after the underside is cooked, place the pan under the broiler until the top side of the omelet is golden. Fill the omelet with fresh fruit or sprinkle with powdered sugar rather than drizzling with a sauce, if you prefer.

> 3 large eggs
> 1/4 cup sugar, divided
> 1/2 teaspoon vanilla extract
> 2 tablespoons unsalted butter
> Easy Orange Sauce (page 232), Lemon Cream Sauce (page 230),
>   or Raspberry Dessert Sauce (page 231) (optional)
> powdered sugar (optional)

Separate the eggs, placing the yolks in a medium bowl and the whites in a small one. Beat the whites until frothy and slightly thickened. Sprinkle with 2 tablespoons sugar and continue to beat until opaque and barely stiff.

Without washing the beaters, whisk the yolks with the remaining sugar and the vanilla until the mixture is thick and smooth. Heat the butter in a well-seasoned or nonstick 10- or 12-inch skillet over medium-high heat. Meanwhile, fold the whites into the yolks.

Swirl the butter around the pan and pour in the egg mixture. Cook 1-2 minutes, or until the omelet is slightly puffed and golden on the underside. Slide it halfway out of the pan over a serving dish and, with a spatula, fold that half over the half in the pan. Top or nap with a sauce, if desired, or sprinkle with powdered sugar, and serve immediately.

Yield: 4 servings

Fast Dessert Ideas

- Slice ripe peeled peaches, toss with sugar to taste and a splash of Sauternes. Let sit up to two hours.

- Trim strawberries, sprinkle with sugar and a few drops of balsamic or raspberry vinegar.

- For margarita-flavored strawberries, toss 2 cups trimmed berries with a blend of 3/8 cup tequila and 3/8 cup orange-flavored liqueur, and serve with a twist of fresh lime.

- For a fast Pear Belle Hélène, slice wedges of ripe pear over vanilla ice cream and top with Silky Chocolate Sauce (page 233).

- For a fast Peach Melba, slice wedges of ripe peach over vanilla ice cream and top with fresh raspberries and Raspberry Dessert Sauce (page 231).

- Slice mangoes or ripe peaches and strawberries, toss with a sweet white wine, and chill while eating dinner.

- Slice equal parts of seedless green, red, and black grapes in half, toss with lemon juice and sugar to taste, and chill up to 3 hours before serving.

- Dice honeydew and toss with Midori or toss diced, seeded watermelon with port and marinate at least 30 minutes.

- Toss fresh raspberries, blueberries, and/or strawberries with sugar to taste and Chambord or port. Chill up to one hour.

- For berries in a Kir Royale, trim and quarter 1 quart strawberries, divide among glasses, sprinkle each with 1 teaspoon sugar, and pour 1/4 cup champagne and 1 teaspoon crème de cassis over each.

- Serve pineapple slices or chunks drizzled with kirsch or rum; drizzle fresh quartered figs with campari.

- Cut a mango or papaya in half, remove the seed(s), and fill with ice cream or frozen yogurt. Sprinkle with crushed amaretti, if desired.

- Top vanilla ice cream with amaretto and a sprinkling of chopped amaretti cookies.

- Buy prepared coeur à la crème, a heart-shaped blend of cream cheese, sugar, and cream, and serve it with fresh berries and Easy Orange Sauce (page 232) or Raspberry Dessert Sauce (page 231).

- Serve room temperature Cambozola or Stilton and wedges of pear, and if desired, a glass of port.

- Serve room temperature l'Explorateur with seedless grapes of varying colors.

Index

Carol Foster is the author of *Cooking with Coffee* (Fireside 1992) as well as dozens of articles for industry and specialty food magazines. She is a Certified Culinary Professional and has a variety of food industry experience, including managing regional gourmet groups, catering, judging recipe contests, and teaching cooking throughout the Northwest. She lives in Anacortes, Washington.

The Crossing Press
publishes a full selection of cookbooks.
To receive our current catalog,
please call, toll-free, 800/777-1048.

Please specify the
"Cookbook" catalog.